The Shapes of Prose

A Rhetorical Reader for College Writing

Charles M. Cobb

Pierce College

Holt, Rinehart and Winston, Inc.
NEW YORK CHICAGO SAN FRANCISCO
ATLANTA DALLAS

Library of Congress Cataloging in Publication Data

Cobb, Charles M comp.
The shapes of prose.
1. English language—Rhetoric. 2. College readers.
I. Title.
PE1417.C633 808'.04275 74-14979
ISBN 0-03-011326-1

Printed in the United States of America
5678 090 987654321

rhetorical contents

Using Logical Patterns

Using Cause and Effect

For Further Study

thematic contents

Man and Animal

Man Being Educated

Man and the Future

Man in Nature

Man and His Nature

Man Seeks Reality

Man and Society

Man in Variation

Man and Words

preface

Why another rhetoric-reader? There *is* a need for one with selections that can be used for Freshman Composition in both the "fundamental" and the "English One" courses. *The Shapes of Prose* fills that need. But there is a better reason for its development. It is designed to be a rhetoric-reader *writer*! The basic arrangement is rhetorical: Narration, Description, Exposition, Argumentation. Each of these four major modes is divided into three subsections. Each of these, in turn, by using three essays, emphasizes one method of development. As any student of rhetoric knows, the modes, in practice, continually overlap; a narrative contains description; exposition may be argumentative; argumentation may be very descriptive. Some of these selections could be used easily and correctly in another section. The same generalization can be made for the thematic table of contents. Instructors may wish to point out to students that the separation into discrete classes is for ease of presentation and study.

Each main section contains an introduction to its particular rhetorical mode, indicating what to look for in individual essays and leading the student to writing skills within that mode. Each major section ends with suggestions for writing that apply the methods displayed by the authors. Following each selection are questions; in Diction, they are designed to develop vocabulary and (hopefully) a mastery of word skills: special uses, the double task of language, contexts, and similar concepts. The questions in Rhetoric and Style are designed to bring about careful reading and an understanding of the mechanics of the writer's craft. There are also questions on Application and Evaluation, which lead to practice in writing, in evaluating, and in thinking. All of these questions range from fairly simple to highly complex. Some suggestions and questions will seem elementary for the more able student, but the plan has been to allow each instructor enough scope to pick questions suited to his class or to certain students within a class.

The Glossary is an integral part of the text. The references to the Glossary, in **boldface type** in the text, lead the student to instruction in writing and better reading. The Glossary is actually a mini-course in writing when used with the other apparatus.

The general plan has been to lead the student from narration, probably the easiest type of writing, through description and exposition to argument and persuasion, surely the most sophisticated. Each section is self-contained, though, so the instructor can fashion the course any way he chooses. The selections themselves have been picked to include topics of interest or value to college students. There are some of the standard essays by Bacon, Swift, Plato, and Orwell; some new selections by writers of proven excellence—Steinbeck, Hall, Saint-Exupéry, and Forster; and some interesting new writers—Deloria, Anderson, Torrey, and van Lawick-Goodall. There are some selections—especially those by Nader, Steinem, Deloria, and Mitford—that discuss the topical matters, while others are more concerned with universals.

The *Instructor's Manual* contains answers for the questions on Diction and Rhetoric and Style, as well as an outline of each selection and a quick quiz to test comprehension. It has, as well, vocabulary, outline, questions, and information about the eight essays "for further study." The entire apparatus, including questions and *Instructor's Manual*, has been designed to help the student read with understanding and write, if not with ease, at least with competence.

C.M.C.

introduction

Rhetoric

Man is the only creature that can communicate with writing. Of the more than four thousand known languages and dialects, only five percent have a written form. Writing trebles the effectiveness of language; it enables man to communicate across time and space. Not only can one know the wisdom of Bertrand Russell writing in London across three thousand miles of ocean; he also can feel the grief of David as he mourned Jonathan over three thousand years ago. Writing allows a person to organize his thoughts, to hold them steady, as it were, on paper while he arranges and rearranges them. Nor is the writer limited to the improvement of his own ideas, for he can build upon the concepts of others, as Shakespeare outshone Marlowe or as Einstein surpassed Leibnitz. The skill of writing bridges time, negates distance, and binds mankind together.

Happily, this paramount skill is one that can be learned by analysis and application. The best way to start is to analyze the writing of able writers. The skill of careful analysis clearly demands the skill of careful reading. The writing/reading skill can be called *discourse* and is usually divided, like Gaul, into three parts: grammar, usage, and rhetoric. Grammar is the analysis of what *is.* Usage is the application of what is *accepted.* Rhetoric is the employment of what is *effective.* This book of readings and lessons is arranged primarily to help the reader become an effective user of language; it is *rhetorically* arranged. Such an arrangement aids the student to analyze material readily and, hopefully, to apply what he learns to his own writing.

Rhetoric is not a new study. It was over two hundred years old when Aristotle wrote his famous *Rhetoric* in the third century B.C. The Romans and the Byzantines modified it and bequeathed it to medieval Europe. It was part of the *Trivium*—rhetoric, logic, grammar—that every Renaissance schoolboy studied. Its skills have been studied and used by every public speaker from Nicodemus to Nixon. Clearly this study has been much thought about and written about, so it is not surprising that rhetoricians classified discourse into four main sections. *Narration* is probably the oldest; man was most likely a storyteller before he was a debater. *Description,* the next, is so often intertwined with narration that it can be difficult to separate.

Works of pure description, like Poe's "Domain of Arnheim" are rare. The third, *Exposition,* is probably the broadest, for it subsumes all explanation, enlightenment, and analysis. The last section, *Argument,* includes *persuasion* as well, although a purist would make a clean division between the two. These four *modes of rhetoric* are in practice much mixed and mingled. As will be seen in the readings, an author may use narrative to prove a point or may spice his argument with a touch of description. They join in practice but are separated for study.

How to Begin

The best way to approach any new textbook is to survey it, to grasp the intent as well as to see the content. Here are some guides.

1. Note the title. Does it offer a clue to the content or purpose?
2. Check the table of contents. Usually, the textbook author has designed the table of contents to be an outline of the book. It can be a great study guide. Note that this book has two tables of contents.
3. Skim down the list of authors in a casebook or anthology. Are there any familiar names, any strangers?
4. Look at a sample selection. Pick one you would like to read. Observe the *headnote*; it was placed there to help you. Read it!
5. Observe the kind of material at the end of the selection. Its purpose is to help bring you understanding. Read it!
6. Check for indices and appendices. Is there a glossary? Use them!
7. Remember, you are permitted to read any selection in the book, not solely those that have been assigned.

How to Read

Mortimer Adler, in *How To Read a Book,* claims that "most of us are not expert readers" and that we all find some writers "too difficult or a great deal of trouble" to read and understand. One of the purposes of this book, obviously, is to help you become a highly competent, perhaps expert, reader. As a start, apply the following pattern to readings in this book.

First, read the selection casually and generally as you would read an article in a magazine or newspaper. Get the main idea and general shape.

Second, pick up a pencil. Always read with a pencil in your hand. If you own the book, you may mark it; if not, get a pad on which to make notes. (Do not mark the books of others as it often generates hostility.)

Third, read the selection again, carefully marking words that are not clear, sentences that seem vague, ideas that appear fuzzy. Many readers comment in the margins, underline the "good parts," argue with the writer.

Next, use a good dictionary to clarify the meaning of words and sentences. By now you should have a clear understanding of the author's meaning. You might try to write his main idea.

This approach is valid with any book on any subject. Naturally, few people would read a spy story, a western, or a violent romance with the amount of care and the depth indicated. These devices are designed for more weighty matter. With this text, or with one that has similar design, be sure to check the material at the end of each section. The questions under Diction should help you to understand the way the author used words and will guide you to difficult vocabulary. The Rhetoric section will show you how the author put his essay together. There will be questions that can lead you to similar techniques. The Applications section should contain ideas to make you think, to enable you to evaluate, questions you may wish to write about or to discuss. They are all designed to help you understand what you have read and to see the value of the selections.

Finally, reflect and ponder the worth of the selection. Was it worth saying? To whom was it worth saying?

Diction

1. The author uses words such as *treble* and *discourse*. Does he use them in accepted fashion? Check your dictionary.
2. The following words should be understood; what do they mean?
    a. validate
    b. Renaissance
    c. subsumes
    d. paramount
    e. analysis

Rhetoric

1. The author uses ten names of people in the Introduction. Why?
2. Can you **infer** who Marlowe and Leibnitz are from their associations with Shakespeare and Einstein?
3. The author pairs the names "from Nicodemus to Nixon" as public speakers. Who was Nicodemus?
4. What is the **allusion** to Gaul? Why is it used?
5. Notice the first paragraph. Does it have a topic sentence? What functions do the first and last sentences do for the paragraph?

Applications

1. Why do you suppose that so few languages have a written form?
2. Would such "languages" as music or mathematics qualify as writing?
3. Make a list of the advantages writing has over speech. Your instructor may ask you to develop this list into a paragraph.
4. Make a list of the advantages speech has over writing.
5. Are there any methods of "storing thought" other than the written word? Do they have any advantages?

narration

Man was first a singer of tales. Long before he argued or debated, described or explained, he told what happened. The earliest literary works of man are **narratives** in song and verse: *The Gilgamesh Epic, The Iliad, The Aeneid, Beowulf, El Poema del Mío Cíd, La Chanson de Roland,* and uncounted tales told around fires by minstrels. These story-poems told of folk heroes, related mighty deeds, and served as a history of the people. The narrative urge seems to be universal in man; it is found in primitive recountings of the hunt as well as in sophisticated dramatic narratives and **symbolic** novels.

Narration, one of the four main classes of **discourse**, has many subclasses and can serve purposes other than the elemental *relation of a sequence of events*. However, we are not concerned here with those fictional narratives that have been classified as novels, short stories, dramas, or narrative poems; they are complex studies and beyond our present scope. We are concerned somewhat with *pure narrative*, the telling of a story for its own sake, and somewhat more with *expository* narrative, the use of a tale to explain a process, set tone or mood. But as college writers we will find *illustrative* narration, the use of a story to illustrate an idea, make a point, serve as an example, our greatest concern.

Rarely does narrative appear in a pure form. It may include any of the other modes—or be included in one of them. Benjamin Franklin wrote a narrative *Autobiography*, but it is filled with **description**, **argument**, and **exposition**. When we study rhetoric, we isolate the narrative so that we can study it, so that we can see how it can be used effectively. When we write, we combine it with other elements. A narrative paragraph or essay, then, is only predominantly narrative.

One of the primary uses of narration is as an **example**. An author uses an example to illustrate a point he is making. Instead of *enumerating* as might a scientist reporting experimental results, the author presents one or two examples as typical instances. The first two tales in this section show how man can respond to the elements. The third uses two brief narratives to illustrate a pressing and growing problem.

Effective narrative writing tells more than a story; it presents an emotional content called **mood**. Authors convey mood primarily by word choice using the **connotative** force of language. The brief tale "The Scorpion" could be rewritten using pedestrian verbs; that alone would rob it of much of the mood it develops. The choice of setting and plot also can be used to emphasize mood. The next two stories, "The Kool-Aid Wino" and "The Hunt" make effective use of locale to help set or create a mood.

One of the most common uses of narration is to substantiate an argument. Most of us use the narrative argument so often that we do not recognize it as such. Someone asks us, "Oh yeah? What makes you think so?" and we respond with a brief narrative to prove our stand. The final three tales in this section do just that. "The Greening of India" offers a rationalization for a position; "Angels on a Pin" uses a single instance to validate a **generalization**; and "The Toolmaker?" shows clearly the impact of concise narration as proof.

How does one tell the difference between narration used for example and to support an argument? Largely by the intent of the author. The argument always tries to prove a specific point; the illustrator usually makes a general statement. There is a spot where the two overlap, but this blending is true with many classifications.

As you read these narratives, you should be aware of some of the writing devices peculiar to the narrative form of rhetoric. Primarily, narrative is the relation of a series of events. It is the easiest type of writing to do; this ease accounts for the innumerable compositions on "What I did last summer," written by generations of students. This simple relation of events in *order of time* develops easily, but it can be dull for both reader and writer. Most of us have an acquaintance who tells a story ponderously and at length, flooding us in a sea of unwanted **detail**. Unless the story itself is exciting and the details interesting, most narratives are best untold. Here are six of the methods used to relieve the tedium.

1. The topic is limited to one aspect of the event. Ronald Fair emphasizes one event in "The Hunt." He does not dwell at length about ghetto life.
2. The author deliberately builds to a climax. He arranges his events so that the **conclusion** is the emotional high point. Note how both Goodall and Fleming use this technique. It would be possible to start with an emotional high point and dwindle down to details, but the tale would lack suspense.
3. Chronology is shifted by use of the **flashback**. The action starts, and then the author tells what happened before the start of the story. Goodall uses flashback most noticeably, although there are touches of it in all of the narratives.
4. The details are carefully selected. As the topic is limited, so are the events selected. Notice how much Steinbeck leaves out of "Hurricane."
5. **Transitional phrases** can be used to tie a story together, to give it coherence. They might be called "road signs." Narrative road signs give the reader direction. (These same signals are used in other modes also.)

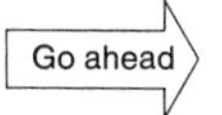

First, second, third . . . , then, next, subsequently, immediately, later, soon.

A month (year) previously, before that, only six weeks ago, prior to this.

Aside from this, by the way, in passing, while on the subject.

Finally, at last, at the end, consequently, in conclusion, with the result that.

6. Limit the author's or narrator's **point of view**. Fleming knows the thoughts of even the insects in his narration; de Saint Exupéry tells his own thoughts; Connery just relates observations.

John Steinbeck (1902–1968) This well-known American novelist had his initial training as a correspondent for the *New York Herald Tribune*. His first really successful novel was *Grapes of Wrath* (1939), which has been called an American classic. Perhaps best known for his portrayal of the happy, carefree people of the Salinas Valley in California in novels such as *Tortilla Flat* and *Cannery Row*, he also won critical acclaim, including the Pulitzer Prize and the coveted Nobel Prize for literature for more serious themes. This selection details the start of a journey he made in 1960 "to rediscover his native land." The book is called *Travels with Charley*, Charley being Steinbeck's gentleman French Poodle. This brief sampling of Steinbeck's style shows a skilled writer developing a narrative quickly, yet forcefully. "Rocinante" is the name Steinbeck has given the camper he plans to use in his travels.

Hurricane

Labor Day approached, the day of truth when millions of kids would be back in school and tens of millions of parents would be off the highways. I was prepared to set out as soon after that as possible. And about that time hurricane Donna was reported tromping her way out of the Caribbean in our direction. On Long Island's tip, we have had enough of that to be highly respectful. With a hurricane approaching we prepare to stand a siege. Our little bay is fairly well protected, but not that well. As Donna crept toward us I filled the kerosene lamps, activated the hand pump to the well, and tied down everything movable. I have a twenty-two-foot cabin boat, the *Fayre Eleyne*. I battened her down and took her to the middle of the bay, put down a huge old-fashioned hook anchor and half-inch chain, and moored her with a long swing. With that rig she could ride a hundred-and-fifty-mile wind unless her bow pulled out. [1]

Donna sneaked on. We brought out a battery radio for reports, since the power would go off if Donna struck. But there was one added worry—Rocinante, sitting among the trees. In a waking nightmare I saw a tree crash down on the truck and crush her like a bug. I placed her away from a possible direct fall, but that didn't mean that the whole top of a tree might not fly fifty feet through the air and smash her. [2]

By early morning we knew by radio that we were going to get it, and by ten o'clock we heard that the eye would pass over us and that it would reach us at 1:07—some exact time like that. Our bay was quiet, without a ripple, but the water was still dark and the *Fayre Eleyne* rode daintily against her mooring. [3]

Our bay is better protected than most, so that many small craft came cruising in for mooring. And I saw with fear that many of their owners didn't know how to moor. Finally two boats, pretty things, came in, one towing the other. A light anchor went down and they were left, the bow of one tethered to the stern of the other and both within the swing of the *Fayre Eleyne*. I took a megaphone to the end of my pier and tried to protest against this foolishness, but the owners either did not hear or did not know or did not care. [4]

The wind struck on the moment we were told it would, and ripped the water like a black sheet. It hammered like a fist. The whole top of an oak tree crashed down, grazing the cottage where we watched. The next gust stove one of the big windows in. I forced it back and drove wedges in top and bottom with a hand ax. Electric power and telephones went out with the first blast, as we knew they must. And eight-foot tides were predicted. We watched the wind rip at earth and sea like a surging pack of terriers. The trees plunged and bent like grasses, and the whipped water raised a cream of foam. A boat broke loose and tobogganed up on the shore, and then another. Houses built in the benign spring and early summer took waves in their second-story windows. Our cottage is on a little hill thirty feet above sea level. But the rising tide washed over my high pier. As the wind changed direction I moved Rocinante to keep her always to leeward of our big oaks. The *Fayre Eleyne* rode gallantly, swinging like a weather vane away from the changing wind. [5]

The boats which had been tethered one to the other had fouled up by now, the tow line under propeller and rudder and the two hulls bashing and scraping together. Another craft had dragged anchor and gone ashore on a mud bank. [6]

Charley dog has no nerves. Gunfire or thunder, explosions or high winds leave him utterly unconcerned. In the midst of the howling storm, he found a warm place under a table and went to sleep. [7]

The wind stopped as suddenly as it had begun, and although the waves continued out of rhythm they were not wind-tattered, and the tide rose higher and higher. All the piers around our little bay had disappeared under water, and only their piles or hand rails showed. The silence was like a rushing sound. The radio told us we were in the eye of Donna, the still and frightening calm in the middle of the revolving storm. I don't know how long the calm lasted. It seemed a long time of waiting. And then the other side struck us, the wind from the opposite direction. The *Fayre Eleyne* swung sweetly around and put her bow into the wind. But the two lashed boats dragged anchor, swarmed down on *Fayre Eleyne,* and bracketed her. She was dragged fighting and protesting downwind and forced against a neighboring pier, and we could hear her hull crying against the oaken piles. The wind registered over ninety-five miles now. [8]

I found myself running, fighting the wind around the head of the bay toward the pier where the boats were breaking up. I think my wife, for whom the *Fayre Eleyne* is named, ran after me, shouting orders for me to stop. The floor of the pier was four feet under water, but piles stuck up and offered hand-holds. I worked my way out little by little up to my breast pockets, the shore-driven wind slapping water in my mouth. My boat cried and whined against the piles, and plunged like a frightened calf. Then I jumped and fumbled my way aboard her. For the first time in my life I had a knife when I needed it. The bracketing wayward boats were pushing *Eleyne* against the pier. I cut anchor line and tow line and kicked them free, and they blew ashore on the mudbank. But *Eleyne*'s anchor chain was intact, and that great old mud hook was still down, a hundred pounds of iron with spear-shaped flukes wide as a shovel. [9]

Eleyne's engine is not always obedient, but this day it started at a touch. I hung on, standing on the deck, reaching inboard for wheel and throttle and clutch with my left hand. And that boat tried to help—I suppose she was that scared. I edged her out and worked up the anchor chain with my right hand. Under ordinary conditions I can barely pull that anchor with both hands in a calm. But everything went right this time. I edged over the hook and it tipped up and freed its spades. Then I lifted it clear of the bottom and nosed into the wind and gave it throttle and we headed into that goddamn wind and gained on it. It was as though we pushed our way through thick porridge. A hundred yards offshore I let the hook go and it plunged down and grabbed bottom, and the *Fayre Eleyne* straightened and raised her bow and seemed to sigh with relief. [10]

Well, there I was, a hundred yards offshore with Donna baying over me like a pack of white-whiskered hounds. No skiff could possibly weather it for a minute. I saw a piece of branch go skidding by and simply jumped in after it. There was no danger. If I could keep my head up I had to blow ashore, but I admit the half-Wellington rubber boots I wore got pretty heavy. It couldn't have been more than three minutes before I grounded and that other Fayre Eleyne and a neighbor pulled me out. It was only then that I began to shake all over, but looking out and seeing our little boat riding well and safely was nice. I must have strained something pulling that anchor with one hand, because I needed a little help home; a tumbler of whisky on the kitchen table was some help too. I've tried since to raise that anchor with one hand and I can't do it. [11]

The wind died quickly and left us to wreckage—power lines down, and no telephone for a week. But Rocinante was not damaged at all. [12]

[1465 words, 12 paragraphs]

Diction

1. The author uses several nautical words and phrases in the early part of this narrative. Locate them and find out what they mean.
2. Sometimes the author's word choice or use of phrases is casual or slangy: "we knew that we were going to get it" [3], and, "Our little bay is fairly well protected, but not that well." (How well?) [3]. How does such language add to or detract from the essay?
3. Why would the author name his camper "Rocinante"?
4. Note some of the unusual verbs the author uses when he writes of the hurricane. What are a few?
5. Many of the words Steinbeck uses have more than one mean-

ing, and he uses them in a special sense. Using a good dictionary, find the meanings of the following words (notice the ones marked with asterisk; they are used in an unusual context): benign [5], flukes* [9], fouled* [6], hurricane [1], megaphone, [4], moor* [4], piles* [9], siege [1], skiff [11], stove* [10].

Rhetoric and Style

1. Steinbeck uses nearly a dozen **similes** in this brief selection. See how many you can find, and note if any of them are stale or trite.
2. Notice the use of **pathetic fallacy**, especially in paragraph [8]. Does it seem appropriate?
3. What is the author's **attitude** tward Donna, and toward all hurricanes? How do you know? (Clue: what he says and how.)
4. How does Steinbeck show the power and the violence of the storm?
5. How is this narrative developed? Does the author use any of the special devices mentioned in the introduction to this section?
6. With all of reality to draw from, a writer must select his **details** carefully; what are some possible details Steinbeck did not use?

Applications and Evaluation

1. Have you ever performed an act normally beyond your abilities when you were under stress? Describe it. Have you known someone else to do so?
2. Is it easier to describe a clear, calm day or a stormy day? Try to **describe** one or the other.
3. Was it fair for the other boatmen to anchor their craft so close to Steinbeck's boat?
4. Was it fair for Steinbeck to cut their lines and let those boats run aground? How much respect do we owe someone else's property?
5. The author, fifty-eight years old, risks his life to save a boat that is worth between four and six thousand dollars. Would you? Do you think you would if you were fifty-eight?
6. After you have developed a **paragraph** or brief **essay** from one of the five Applications above, deliberately revise it by putting in several similes as did Steinbeck. Use fresh ones.

Antoine de Saint Exupéry (1900–1944) A philosophical French flyer, Antoine de Saint Exupéry disappeared on a reconnaissance flight over the Mediterranean Sea in 1944. A commercial pilot during the early days of aviation, his lyrical account of his experiences appears in *Wisdom of the Sands, A Sense of Life, Flight to Arras,* and *Wind, Sand and Stars,* from which this selection is taken. He also wrote a children's book, *The Little Prince,* that has become a classic because of its symbolic overtones. "The Cyclone," although somewhat abridged, shows the metaphorical style and philosophical content that de Saint Exupéry used to enrich a straight narration.

The Cyclone

When Joseph Conrad described a typhoon he said very little about the towering waves, or darkness, or the whistling of the wind in the shrouds. He knew better. Instead, he took his reader down into the hold of the vessel, packed with emigrant coolies, where the rolling and the pitching of the ship had ripped up and scattered their bags and bundles, burst open their boxes, and flung their humble belongings into a crazy heap. Family treasures painfully collected in a lifetime of poverty, pitiful mementoes so alike that nobody but their owners could have told them apart, had lost their identity and lapsed into chaos, into anonymity, into an amorphous magma. It was this human drama that Conrad described when he painted a typhoon. [1]

The cyclone of which I am about to speak was, physically, much the most brutal and overwhelming experience I ever underwent; and yet beyond a certain point I do not know how to convey its violence except by piling one adjective on another, so that in the end I should convey no impression at all—unless perhaps that of an embarrassing taste for exaggeration. [2]

It took me some time to grasp the fundamental reason for this powerlessness, which is simply that I should be trying to describe a catastrophe that never took place. The reason why writers fail when they attempt to evoke horror is that horror is something invented after the fact, when one is re-creating the experience over again in the memory. Horror does not manifest itself in the world of reality. And so in beginning my story of a revolt of the elements which I myself lived through I have no feeling that I shall write something which you will find dramatic. [3]

I had taken off from the field at Trelew and was flying down to Comodoro-Rivadavia, in the Patagonian Argentine. Here the crust of the earth is as dented as an old boiler. The high-pressure regions over the Pacific send the winds past a gap in the Andes into a corridor fifty miles wide through which they rush to the Atlantic in a strangled and accelerated buffeting that scrapes the surface of everything in their path. The sole vegetation visible in this barren landscape is a plantation of oil derricks looking like the after effects of a forest fire. Towering over the round hills on which the winds have left a residue of stony gravel, there rises a chain of prow-shaped, saw-toothed, razor-edged mountains stripped by the elements down to the bare rock. [4]

The sky was blue. Pure blue. Too pure. A hard blue sky that shone over the scraped and barren world while the fleshless vertebrae of the mountain chain flashed in the sunlight. Not a cloud. The blue sky glittered like a new-honed knife. I felt in advance the vague distaste that accompanies the prospect of physical exertion. The purity of the sky upset me. Give me a good black storm in which the enemy is plainly visible. I can measure its extent and prepare myself for its attack. I can get my hands on my adversary. But when you are flying very high in clear weather, the shock of a blue storm is as disturbing as if something collapsed that had been holding up your ship in the air. It is the only time when a pilot feels there is a gulf beneath his ship. [5]

Another thing bothered me. I could see on a level with the mountain peaks not a haze, not a mist, not a sandy fog, but a sort of ash colored streamer in the sky. I did not like the look of that scarf of filings scraped off the surface of the earth and borne out to sea by the wind. I tightened my leather harness as far as it would go and I steered the ship with one hand while with the other I hung on to the longeron that ran alongside my seat. I was flying in remarkably calm air. [6]

Very soon there came a slight tremor. As every pilot knows, there are secret little quiverings that foretell your real storm. No rolling, no pitching. No swing to speak of. The flight continues horizontal and rectilinear. But you have felt a warning drum on the wings of your plane, little intermittent rappings scarcely audible and infinitely brief, little cracklings from time to time as if there were traces of gunpowder in the air. [7]

And then everything round me blew up. [8]

Concerning the next couple of minutes I have nothing to say. All that I can find in my memory is a few rudimentary notions, fragments of thoughts, direct observations. I cannot compose them into a dramatic recital because there was no drama. The best I can do is to line them up in a kind of chronological order. In the first place I was standing still. Having banked right in order to correct a sudden drift, I saw the landscape freeze abruptly where it was and remain jiggling in the same spot. I was making no headway. My wings had ceased to nibble into the outline of the earth. I could see the earth buckle, pivot—but it stayed put. The plane was skidding as if on a toothless cogwheel. [9]

Trapped this way in the first breaking waves of a cyclone about which I learned, twenty minutes later, that at sea level it was blowing at the fantastic rate of one hundred and fifty miles an hour, I certainly had no impression of tragedy. Now, as I write, if I shut my eyes, if I forget the plane and the flight and try to express the plain truth about what was happening to me, I find that I felt weighed down, I felt like a porter carrying a slippery load, grabbing one object in a jerky movement that sent another slithering down, so that, overcome by exasperation, the porter is tempted to let the whole load drop. There is a kind of law of the shortest distance to the image, a psychological law by which the event to which one is subjected is visualized in a symbol that represents the swiftest summing up; I was a man who, carrying a pile of plates, had slipped on a waxed floor and let his scaffolding of porcelain crash. [10]

There was no longer a horizon. I was in the wings of a theatre cluttered up with bits of scenery. Vertical, oblique, horizontal, all of plane geometry was awhirl. A hundred transversal valleys were muddled in a jumble of perspectives. Whenever I seemed about to take my bearings, a new eruption would swing me round in a circle or send me tumbling wing over wing and I would have to try all over again to get clear of all this rubbish. Two ideas came into my mind.

One was a discovery: for the first time I understood the cause of certain accidents in the mountains when no fog was present to explain them. For a single second, in a waltzing landscape like this, the flyer had been unable to distinguish between vertical mountainsides and horizontal planes. The other idea was a fixation: The sea is flat: I shall not hook anything out at sea. [11]

I banked—or should I use that word to indicate a vague and stubborn jockeying through the east-west valleys? Still nothing pathetic to report. I was wrestling with chaos, was wearing myself out in a battle with chaos, struggling to keep in the air a gigantic house of cards that kept collapsing despite all I could do. Scarcely the faintest twinge of fear went through me when one of the walls of my prison rose suddenly like a tidal wave over my head. My heart hardly skipped a beat when I was tripped up by one of the whirling eddies of air that the sharp ridge darted into my ship. If I felt anything unmistakable in the haze of confused feelings and notions that came over me each time one of these powder magazines blew up, it was a feeling of respect. I respected that peak. I respected that sharp-toothed ridge, I respected that dome. I respected that transversal valley opening out into my valley and about to toss me God knew how violently as soon as its torrent of wind flowed into the one on which I was being borne along. [12]

There had been granted me one second of respite. Two seconds. Something was collecting itself into a knot, coiling itself up, growing taut. I sat amazed. I opened my astonished eyes. My whole plane seemed to be shivering, spreading outward, swelling up. Horizontal and stationary it was, yet lifted before I knew it fifteen hundred feet straight into the air in a kind of apotheosis. I who for forty minutes had not been able to climb higher than two hundred off the ground was suddenly able to look down on the enemy. The plane quivered as if in boiling water. I could see the wide waters of the ocean. The valley opened out into this ocean, this salvation— And at that very moment, without any warning whatever, half a mile from the peak of Salamanca, I was suddenly struck straight in the midriff by the gale off that peak and sent hurtling out to sea. [13]

Hanging on with all the power in my engines, face to the coast, face to that wind where each gap in the teeth of the range sent forth a stream of air like a long reptile, I felt as if I were clinging to the tip of a monstrous whip that was cracking over the sea. [14]

Each time I was tossed I became afraid that I might be unable to straighten out. Besides, there was a chance that I should find myself out of fuel and simply drown. I kept expecting the gasoline pumps to stop priming, and indeed the plane was so violently shaken up that in the half-filled tanks as well as the gas lines the gasoline was sloshing round, not coming through, and the engines, instead of their steady roar, were sputtering in a sort of dot-and-dash series of uncertain growls. [15]

It seemed hopeless. In twenty minutes of struggle I had not moved forward a hundred yards. What was more, with flying as hard as it was out here five miles from the coast, I wondered how I could possibly buck the winds along the shore, assuming I was able to fight my way in. I was a perfect target for the enemy there on shore. Fear, however, was out of the question. I was incapable of thinking. I was emptied of everything except the vision of a very simple act. I must straighten out. Straighten out. Straighten out. [16]

I had no thoughts. I had no feelings except the feeling of being emptied out. My strength was draining out of me and so was my impulse to go on fighting. The engines continued their dot-and-dash sputterings, their little crashing noises that were like the intermittent cracklings of a ripping canvas. Whenever they were silent longer than a second I felt as if a heart had stopped beating. There! that's the end. No, they've started up again. [17]

The thermometer on the wing, I happened to see, stood at twenty below zero, but I was bathed in sweat from head to foot. My face was running with perspiration. What a dance! Later I was to discover that my storage batteries had been jerked out of their steel flanges and hurtled through the roof of the plane. I did not know then, either, that the ribs on my wings had come unglued and that certain of my steel cables had been sawed down to the last thread. And I continued to feel strength and will oozing out of me. Any minute now I should be overcome by the indifference born of utter weariness and by the mortal yearning to take my rest. [18]

In an hour and twenty minutes I had succeeded in climbing to nine-hundred feet. A little to the south—that is, on my left—I could see a long trail on the surface of the sea, a sort of a blue stream. I decided to let myself drift as far down as that stream. Here I was, facing west, I was as good as motionless, unable either to advance or retreat. If I could reach that blue pathway, which must be lying in the shelter of something not the cyclone, I might be able to move in slowly to the coast. So, I let myself drift to the left. I had the feeling, meanwhile, that the wind's violence had perhaps slackened. [19]

It took me an hour to cover the five miles to the shore. There in the shelter of a lone cliff I was able to finish my journey south. Thereafter I succeeded in keeping enough altitude to fly inland to the field that was my destination. I was able to stay up at nine hundred feet. It was very stormy, but nothing like the cyclone I had come out of. That was over. [20]

On the ground I saw a platoon of soldiers. They had been sent down to watch for me. I landed near by and we were a whole hour getting the plane into the hangar, I climbed out of the cockpit and walked off. There was nothing to say. I was very sleepy. I kept moving my fingers, but they stayed numb. I could not collect my thoughts to decide whether or not I had been afraid. Had I been afraid? I couldn't say. I had witnessed a strange sight. What strange sight? I couldn't say. The sky was blue and the sea was white. I felt I ought to tell someone about it since I was back from so far away! But I had no grip on what I had been through. "Imagine a white sea . . . very white . . . whiter still." You cannot convey things to people by piling up adjectives, by stammering. [21]

You cannot convey anything because there is nothing to convey. My shoulders were aching. My insides felt as if they had been crushed in by a terrible weight. You cannot make drama out of that, or out of the cone-shaped peak of Salamanca. That peak was charged like a powder magazine; but if I said so people would laugh. I would myself. I respected the peak of Salamanca. That is my story. And it is not a story. [22]

[2600 words, 22 paragraphs]

Diction

1. The author uses the phrase "a house of cards" [12]. What does it mean and how is it appropriate here?
2. List any **clichés** or **trite** expressions used. Does their use or omission add to or detract from the narrative?
3. What can be **inferred** from the author's use of such words as: cockpit [21], longerons [6], ribs on wings becoming unglued [18]?
4. The French phrase *Quelle danse* is translated as "What a dance!" [18] The translation is accurate, but is there a more **idomatic** American English phrase?
5. The author states that "That is my story. And it is not a story" [22]. Why the seeming **paradox**?

6. Check a good dictionary for the meanings of the following words (observe whether they are used in an unusual or secondary manner): amorphous [1], apotheosis [13], chaos [1], chronological [9], cyclone [2], intermittent [7, 17], longeron [6], magma [1], oblique [11], typhoon [1].

Rhetoric and Style

1. This narrative is exceedingly rich in **metaphors** and **similes.** List two or three of the metaphors used to convey the jaggedness of the mountains. Do they seem effective? Commonplace?
2. What consistent **metaphor** is used for the storm? (See **Personification.**) Is it a valid **figure of speech** for a pilot?
3. The first paragraph is a reference to Joseph Conrad, to his written treatment of a typhoon. Why does de Saint Exupéry make such a reference? Who is Conrad?
4. The author makes use of series in his **descriptions.** note some examples.
5. Paragraph [5] starts with five sentence fragments. How is such a deviation from Standard English justifiable?
6. Why is paragraph [8] a single sentence? Would it be as effective if it were attached to paragraph [7]?

Applications and Evaluation

1. Is this essay realistic? Could such an experience happen to someone in today's aircraft?
2. Have you ever been at the mercy of the elements? Perhaps caught in an undertow or a storm? Could you write a narrative either describing your emotion or detailing the event chronologically?
3. The author uses his experience as an **example.** The **generalization** he states is that horror is never experienced but always recollected [3].
   a. Do you agree? Tell why with an example.
   b. Is the same thing true of other emotions? Can you give an example?
4. Try to describe a natural disaster, as nearly as you can from your experiences, by telling what happens to the people (as did Joseph Conrad) instead of "piling one adjective on another."

5. The author writes that "we were a whole hour getting the plane into the hangar" [20]. In a single sentence a normally simple task becomes a massive chore. Try to write a brief narrative showing how a simple task becomes a problem under difficult circumstances.

Richard Restak (1942–   ) is a neurologist at George Washington University. He is listed in the AMA Directory as being on the staff at Mount Sinai Hospital in New York, also. This essay was originally printed in the *Washington Post,* and it shows how two narratives can be used to make vivid and graphic two problems that have been brought about by advances in medical science.

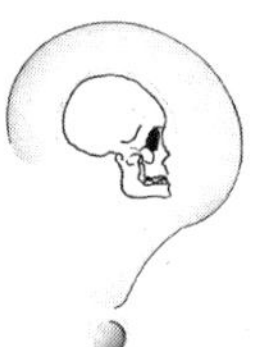

What Is Death?

Martin Carter's daily routine begins with an early morning visit to his son Robert's room in a Pennsylvania hospital. In late 1966 Robert's brain was critically damaged in an auto accident, and though his eyes sometimes open, he has not regained consciousness in six years. [1]

Robert's mother believes she has occasionally seen signs of recognition on the face of her 27-year-old son, and several doctors have observed Robert's hand or feet withdrawing from annoyances such as nail clippers. But never since his accident has Robert shown any sign of conscious activity. [2]

His heart and lungs continue working normally only because of regular intravenous feedings: stop these and the organs soon would cease. Is Robert dead or alive? [3]

This is the anguishing question that Martin Carter (not his real name) has discussed time and again with Robert's doctor, and it is a question that our society—individuals, doctors, legislatures, courts, hospitals—is groping with today. At what moment can a life be said to end? [4]

Robert's doctor explained to Carter, quite correctly, that his son's condition was a "coma vigil," a term describing a patient with irreversible brain destruction who maintains a semblance of conscious activity. Such patients can appear to be awake when their eyes wander blankly about a room; they breathe on their own, and some may even swallow food that is placed in their mouths. [5]

All activities not requiring consciousness may continue, because the lower portion of the brain necessary for such acts is intact. But the cerebral cortex, responsible for conscious, meaningful activity, is reduced to a mush, eliminating any possibility of a return to truly human functions. In Robert's case several medical studies of his brain revealed no cure for his continuous coma. [6]

A little over a year ago, after years of deeply painful talks and tests and talks again, Robert's parents and his doctor agreed: Robert was, for all intents and purposes, dead. They would stop the intravenous feedings. [7]

Martin Carter remembers the 24 hours after the decision to stop feeding as filled with terror. He dreamed that night that his son was not dead at all, but alive. He could not go through with it. He would not. The next morning he told Robert's doctor to resume the feedings immediately. [8]

The doctor did so, and Robert continues to lie in his hospital bed today, his condition unchanged. [9]

Robert is only one of a growing number of "the living dead" in this country and abroad. In any sizable U.S. hospital, there usually are one or two patients whose brains are irreversibly destroyed and who have no chance of recovering consciouness. [10]

Ironically, their number is increasing because of medical advances, chiefly heart-lung machines which, along with intravenous feedings, can maintain such persons' heartbeats, breathing and pulses indefinitely, even though there is no hope they will ever return to anything remotely resembling normal "life." [11]

With their increase have emerged perhaps the most agonizing questions of 20th century medicine: Can such patients be declared dead? Should the machines be unplugged? Who is to make such a decision? On what basis? What is death? [12]

In a sense, patients are dead when doctors state they are dead. Despite the overwhelming importance of this judgment, the subject usually is not covered in medical school or in postgraduate medical education. [13]

Presumably, this is because it was taken for granted over the ages that people were dead when they stopped breathing, or when there was no longer a heartbeat or pulse. Indeed, "Black's Law Dictionary" still defines death as the "total stoppage of circulation of the blood and cessation of the animal and vital functions consequent thereon, such as respiration and pulse." [14]

But modern medicine has rendered this definition obsolete. [15]

Clearly, the functioning of the heart and lungs alone cannot determnie the presence or absence of life when they are entirely the work of a machine. The advent of this and other technology has created the need for a new definition, and in fact we are moving—gradually and with the utmost caution—toward this definition, one that equates death with irreversible destruction of the brain. [16]

So far two states—Kansas in 1970 and Maryland this year—have adopted laws allowing the machines to be turned off and death to be declared if the brain is found to be hopelessly destroyed. And a Virginia jury, in judging a lawsuit involving a heart transplant, also accepted the destruction of the heart donor's brain as evidence that death had occurred. [17]

The Virginia story began on May 25, 1968, when William E. Tucker, a 47-year-old black from Charlottesville, arrived at the Medical College of Virginia to ask about his brother Bruce. Tucker learned that the previous afternoon Bruce had fallen over and struck his head hard on a radiator. After being rushed to the college by ambulance, Bruce underwent surgery for a brain hemorrhage. [18]

Forty-five minutes after the operation, the surgeon wrote in the chart: "The prognosis for recovery is nil and death imminent." One hour later Bruce was examined by a neurologist, who ran a brain wave test that failed to demonstrate evidence of cerebral activity. He concluded that Bruce's brain was dead. At that time Tucker's pulse, blood pressure and temperature were normal, being artificially maintained by a respirator. [19]

It was decided to use Bruce Tucker's heart for a transplant and plans were made for the removal of his heart. The official pronouncement of death occurred three hours later, three minutes before the first incision on Joseph Kleit, the recipient of Bruce's still-beating heart. The respirator was turned off at the time of pronouncement. [20]

One year later, William Tucker, in a suit against the doctors at the Medical College of Virginia, charged that Bruce had been murdered when the respirator was shut off. [21]

At the conclusion of the trial Judge A. Christian Compton listed two measures of death from which the jury could choose: absence of circulation and other vital functions such as respiration and pulse; or complete and irreversible loss of brain function. The jury, for the first time in history, chose the brain death definition, thus exonerating the doctors. [22]

Obviously, the Tucker case was a close call for the doctors involved, and there almost certainly will be similar cases, unless laws like those in Kansas and Maryland are widely adopted. Both those laws declare that people are dead if they have no "spontaneous brain function" and if "reasonable attempts" fail to restore or maintain "spontaneous circulatory or respiratory function." [23]

It would be a serious mistake to view the turning off of heart-lung machines in brain death cases as euthanasia, or mercy killing. It is true that these patients are a pitiful sight, and that relatives go through long periods of intense emotional strain before feeling a numb desire for it all to be over. It is also true that the cost of maintaining the living dead is enormous—approaching about $30,000 a year per patient—and insurance usually covers only a fraction of the amount. [24]

But this is not the basis of these laws. The essential point is that such patients are already dead. [25]

Although the Kansas and Maryland laws state that doctors' judgments should be based on "ordinary standards of medical practice," the fact is that there are no "ordinary" medical standards in this area. [26]

In 1968 a Harvard group sought to establish clinical standards—those a bedside physician could use without the aid of extra equipment—for diagnosing death. It suggested three criteria: (1) that the patient be unreceptive and unresponsive; (2) that there be no movement or breathing; and (3) that there be no reflexes. [27]

But these standards have turned out to be unsatisfactory. Patients suffering from drug overdoses, for example, have been totally unresponsive for several days while machines artificially maintained them, and they have survived. [28]

Clearly, medicine could never use such clinical standards alone. To do so would be to raise the age-old fear of declaring as dead a person who is actually alive. [29]

Medicine, then, had to turn to methods other than clinical ones to determine brain death. The first place to look was the brain wave test, or electroencephalogram (EEG). [30]

But what about the fallibility of the EEG? Such tests measure the activity of only a small number of the billions of basic cells in the brain. Conclusions are drawn on the basis of statistical probability, not absolute certainty. [31]

The history of the EEG has been one of increasing refinement of the technique. But the EEG still has not reached the state of being an infallible diagnostic tool. [32]

Physicians thus have also begun relying heavily on another diagnostic aid, cerebral angiography. This involves the injection under pressure of a dye into the blood vessels filling the brain, allowing the vessels to be seen by X ray. Experience at the Karolinska Hospital in Sweden has confirmed a 100% correlation between brain death and failure to see the blood vessels after injection. [33]

However, this is a terribly impractical diagnostic test, since it requires the attendance of a neurosurgeon or neurologist. Both specialists are in short supply here and abroad. [34]

Finally, physicians at Columbia Presbyterian Hospital in New York are attempting to measure cerebral blood flow itself. Demonstration of an absolute lack of oxygenation would simplify matters greatly, since all physicians agree that a total lack of oxygen leads rapidly to cerebral death. However, partial oxygenation and an inability to demonstrate exactly whether vital brain centers are oxygenated limit the utility of this concept. [35]

To some medical men, the final definition of death is too important a question to be left to physicians. This is the view of Dr. W. Spann of the Institute of Legal Medicine: [36]

"It is not a question of the scientific boundary between life and death, but what is involved is a value judgment as to what is considered *human* life in its real sense. This kind of judgment is not a matter for doctors, it is a matter for society." [37]

It is to be hoped that the decision will be soon in coming. For the Carters and Tuckers, and others like them, as well as for the thousands of potential transplant donors and recipients around the world, the brain death issue is not something we can put off for very long. [38]

[1420 words, 38 paragraphs]

Diction

1. The author, a medical doctor, uses a great many medical and technical words in this essay (euthanasia, electroencephalogram, cerebral angiography). How does he keep the reader from being confused?
2. Are there any examples of **slang** or **jargon** in this essay?
3. The vocabulary of this essay is very complex. Some phrases—infallible diagnostic tool [32], semblance of conscious activity [5], potential transplant donors [38]—may make it hard to read.

Do such phrases hinder understanding? If they do, why are they used?

4. In the main, does the author use **abstract** or **concrete** words?
5. The author uses a basic method to achieve emphasis; he modifies key words with emphatic adjectives. Locate some instances of this method.
6. Using a good dictionary, find the meanings of some of the many difficult words in this essay—for example: advent [16], cerebral [34], coma [5], criteria [27], death [12], fallibility [31], obsolete [15], potential [38], prognosis [19], spontaneous [23].

Rhetoric and Style

1. Why are so many paragraphs—thirty-eight—in such a short narrative?
2. How does the author tie these many paragraphs together? Notice, for example, [8] to [9] to [10] to [11] to [12]. Does he use the same device elsewhere?
3. Can you find the paragraph where the doctor abandons his **objectivity** and tells his personal opinion of death and the law?
4. The author notes that William Tucker was a 47-year-old black. He does not tell the race or color of any of the other patients or people he mentions. Why? Why mention Tucker's?
5. Can you find any **metaphors** or **similes** in these narratives?
6. This essay consists of two narratives and several other shorter **anecdotes**. How are they all tied together?

Applications and Evaluation

1. Should the final decision of what is death be made by doctors, judges, society? Perhaps a combination?
2. Try to write an extended definition of death. Of life.
3. Science fiction writers have postulated cybernetic organisms, "cyborgs," or men who have machines attached to them, like pacemakers, or machines that use human parts—brains or hearts —as part of their mechanism. Would such creatures be alive? Is a machine alive when it is running?
4. Dr. Restak uses two narratives to exemplify two of the problems caused by advancing medical science. Think of a problem

that advances in science have caused (people living longer all over the world, rapid transportation everywhere, elimination of various life forms, for example), and use a narrative as an example. Clarify the problem first, perhaps through discussion.

5. A recent medical proposal was to develop "Organ Banks" to store parts for people. Is such a suggestion moral? Practical? Consider that plasma already is stored for future use.

Ian Fleming (1908–1964) An author well-known to adventure-story fans, Ian Fleming is the creator of James Bond, the daring agent 007. After an apprenticeship as a working journalist and editor, Fleming wrote his first James Bond novel, *Casino Royale,* in 1953 and followed it with a dozen more novels and two books of shorter tales. He also wrote *Chitty-Chitty Bang-Bang,* a children's book, and *Thrilling Cities,* a travel book of surprising descriptive power. The following brief narrative is the opening of *Diamonds Are Forever* and shows how a writer can use narration to set a mood. In this case Fleming prepares the reader for the grim violence of the novel.

The Scorpion

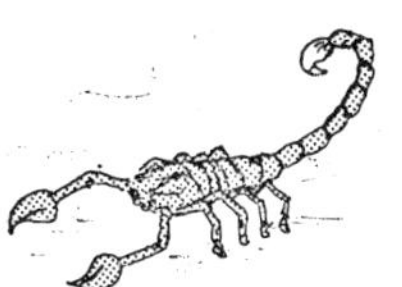

With its fighting claws held forward like a wrestler's arms the big *pandenus* scorpion emerged with a dry rustle from the finger-sized hole under the rock. [1]

There was a small flat patch of hard flat earth outside the hole, and the scorpion stood in the centre of this on the tips of its four pairs of legs, its nerves and muscles braced for a quick retreat and its senses questing for the minute vibrations which would decide its next move. [2]

The moonlight glittered down through the great thornbush, threw sapphire highlights off the hard black polish of the six-inch body and glinted palely on the moist, white sting which protruded from the last segment of the tail, now curved over parallel with the scorpion's flat back. [3]

Slowly the sting slid home into its sheath and the nerves in the poison sac at its base relaxed. The scorpion had decided. Greed had won over fear. [4]

Twelve inches away, at the bottom of a sharp slope of sand, the small beetle was concerned only with trudging on towards better pastures than he had found under the thornbush, and the swift rush of the scorpion down the slope gave him no time to open his wings. The beetle's legs waved in protest as the sharp claw snapped around his body, and then the sting lanced into him from over the scorpion's head and immediately he was dead. [5]

After it had killed the beetle, the scorpion stood motionless for nearly five minutes. During this time it identified the nature of its prey and again tested the ground and air for hostile vibrations. Reassured, its fighting claws withdrew from the half-severed beetle and its two small feeding pincers reached out and into the beetle's flesh. Then for an hour, and with extreme fastidiousness, the scorpion ate its victim. [6]

The great thornbush under which the scorpion had killed the beetle was a landmark in the wide expanse of rolling veldt some forty miles south of Kissidougou in the southwestern corner of French Guinea. On all horizons there were hills and jungle, but here, over twenty square miles, there was flat rocky ground which was almost desert; and amongst the tropical scrub only this one thornbush, perhaps because there was water deep beneath its roots, had grown to the height of a house and could be seen many miles away. [7]

The bush grew more or less at the junction of three African states. It was in French Guinea, but only about ten miles north of the northernmost tip of Liberia and five miles east of the frontier of Sierra Leone. Across this frontier are the great diamond mines around Sefadu. These are the property of Sierra International, which is part of the powerful mining empire of Afric International which in turn is a rich capital asset of the British Commonwealth. [8]

An hour earlier, in its hole among the roots of the great thornbush, the scorpion had been alerted by two sets of vibrations. First there had been the tiny scraping of the beetle's movements, and these belonged to the vibrations which the scorpion immediately recognized and diagnosed. Then there had been a series of incomprehensible thuds around the bush followed by a final heavy quake which had caved in part of the scorpion's hole. These were followed by a soft rhythmic trembling of the ground which was so regular that it soon became background vibration of no urgency. After a pause the tiny scraping of the beetle had continued, and it was greed for the beetle that, after a day of sheltering from its deadliest enemy, the sun, finally got the upper hand against the scorpion's memory of the other noises and impelled it out of its lair into the filtering moonlight. [9]

And now, as it slowly sucked the morsels of beetle flesh off its feeding pincers, the signal for the scorpion's own death sounded far away on the eastern horizon, audible to a human, but made up of vibrations which were far outside the range of the scorpion's sensory system. [10]

A few feet away, a heavy, blunt hand, with bitten fingernails, slowly raised a jagged piece of rock. [11]

There was no noise, but the scorpion felt a tiny movement in the air above it. At once its fighting claws were up and groping and its sting erect in the rigid tail, its near-sighted eyes staring up for a glimpse of the enemy. [12]

The heavy stone came down. [13]

"Black bastard." [14]

The man watched as the broken insect whipped in its death agony. [15]

[770 words, 15 paragraphs]

Diction

1. Why is "centre" [2] "misspelled"?
2. This is a highly **descriptive** passage; note the various ways the author describes the moonlight.
3. As another aid to the descriptive power of this place, the author uses sprightly verbs. Note the verbs in paragraph [5] that tell of the scorpion's actions.
4. What is the general effect of the use of *thornbush* (as big as a house!), *veldt, Sefadu, Liberia?*
5. Check the meaning of the following words in your dictionary: audible [10], fastidiousness [6], junction [8], lair [9], questing [2], sapphire [3].

Rhetoric and Style

1. In addition to vivid verbs and adjectives, does the author use any **figures of speech** in this narartive?
2. The author makes use of sense impressions other than the usual ones of sight. Find, perhaps list, the words that affect sense other than vision.

3. This little tale has an ominous, forbidding **tone**; what seems to be the main emotions here?
4. How does the author express the character of the human in the tale without a single bit of description? What is his main trait as far as can be detected?
5. There seem to be unanswered questions because this is but the opening for a novel. What were the vibrations that alarmed the scorpion? What were the vibrations that signaled its death? (Guess.) Why was all that material about diamonds inserted?

Applications and Evaluation

1. What is the general **attitude** toward scorpions? Spiders? Beetles? What are some of the names given to teams and cars in an attempt to show supposed animal characteristics. (*Stingray*, *Spyder*, for example)? From a list of names that seem desirable for vehicles and a list that seem undesirable, develop a paragraph or essay showing man's atttiudes toward beasts and insects.
2. Is it valid to equate men and animals? For example, does a scorpion seeking dinner feel greed as a man does? Was the trudging beetle really seeking "greener pastures"? (See **Personification**.)
3. Write a descriptive or narrative passage in which the sense appeal to most is not sight. For a start, recall an actual meal, noisy place, stinking spot.
4. Fleming does not tell about the man's character but has him perform an action that leads the reader to assume what kind of person he is. In a brief narrative show a person in action and let that person's actions tell what kind of person he is. It would be best to concentrate on just one element: greed, sweetness, kindness, lust.
5. As an alternative, you might wish to write a brief episode from nature (like the insect world) patterned after—or mocking—something that men do. Perhaps you could introduce a person as Fleming did.

Richard Brautigan (1935–) Richard Brautigan was born and raised in the Pacific Northwest, a fact that may be observed in the content and tone of some of his writing. He is the author of several books, some he calls "novels," but they do not fit the standard pattern. They all have intriguing titles like *A Confederate General from Big Sur, The Pill Versus the Springhill Mine Disaster, Please Plant This Book,* and *Trout Fishing in America* from which the following brief narrative is a selection. It treats a mood and serves as a modern parable about rituals and the nature of reality.

The Kool-Aid Wino

When I was a child I had a friend who became a Kool-Aid wino as the result of a rupture. He was a member of a very large and poor German family. All the older children in the family had to work in the fields during the summer, picking beans for two-and-one-half cents a pound to keep the family going. Everyone worked except my friend who couldn't because he was ruptured. There was no money for an operation. There wasn't even enough money to buy him a truss. So he stayed home and became a Kool-Aid wino. [1]

One morning in August I went over to his house. He was still in bed. He looked up at me from underneath a tattered revolution of old blankets. He had never slept under a sheet in his life. [2]

"Did you bring the nickel you promised?" he asked. [3]

"Yeah," I said. "It's here in my pocket." [4]

"Good." [5]

He hopped out of bed and he was already dressed. He had told me once that he never took off his clothes when he went to bed. [6]

"Why bother?" he had said. "You're only going to get up, anyway. Be prepared for it. You're not fooling anyone by taking your clothes off when you go to bed." [7]

He went into the kitchen, stepping around the littlest children, whose wet diapers were in various stages of anarchy. He made his breakfast: a slice of homemade bread covered with Karo syrup and peanut butter. [8]

"Let's go," he said. [9]

We left the house with him still eating the sandwich. The store was three blocks away, on the other side of a field covered with heavy yellow grass. There are many pheasants in the field. Fat with summer they barely flew away when we came up to them. [10]

"Hello," said the grocer. He was bald with a red birthmark on his head. The birthmark looked just like an old car parked on his head. He automatically reached for a package of grape Kool-Aid and put it on the counter. [11]

"Five cents." [12]

"He's got it," my friend said. [13]

I reached into my pocket and gave the nickel to the grocer. He nodded and the old red car wobbled back and forth on the road as if the driver were having an epileptic seizure. [14]

We left. [15]

My friend led the way across the field. One of the pheasants didn't even bother to fly. He ran across the field in front of us like a feathered pig. [16]

When we got back to my friend's house the ceremony began. To him the making of Kool-Aid was a romance and a ceremony. It had to be performed in an exact manner and with dignity. [17]

First he got a gallon jar and we went around to the side of the house where the water spigot thrust itself out of the ground like the finger of a saint, surrounded by a mud puddle. [18]

He opened the Kool-Aid and dumped it into the jar. Putting the jar under the spigot, he turned the water on. The water spit, splashed and guzzled out of the spigot. [19]

He was careful to see that the jar did not overflow and the precious Kool-Aid spill out onto the ground. When the jar was full he turned the water off with a sudden but delicate motion like a famous brain surgeon removing a disordered portion of the imagination. Then he screwed the lid tightly onto the top of the jar and gave it a good shake. [20]

The first part of the ceremony was over. [21]

Like the inspired priest of an exotic cult, he had performed the first part of the ceremony well. [22]

His mother came around the side of the house and said in a voice filled with sand and string, "When are you going to do the dishes? . . . Huh?" [23]

"Soon," he said. [24]

"Well, you better," she said. [25]

When she left, it was as if she had never been there at all. The second part of the ceremony began with him carrying the jar very carefully to an abandoned chicken house in the back. "The dishes can wait," he said to me. Bertrand Russell could not have stated it better. [26]

He opened the chicken house door and we went in. The place was littered with half-rotten comic books. They were like fruit under a tree. In the corner was an old mattress and beside the mattress were four quart jars. He took the gallon jar over to them, and filled them carefully not spilling a drop. He screwed their caps on tightly and was now ready for a day's drinking. [27]

You're supposed to make only two quarts of Kool-Aid from a package, but he always made a gallon, so his Kool-Aid was a mere shadow of its desired potency. And you're supposed to add a cup of sugar to every package of Kool-Aid, but he never put any sugar in his Kool-Aid because there wasn't any sugar to put in it. [28]

He created his own Kool-Aid reality and was able to illuminate himself by it. [29]

[750 words, 29 paragraphs]

Diction

1. What are the **connotations** of calling the main character a "Kool-Aid wino" instead of something like *addict* or *Kool-Aid lover*?

2. "The water spigot thrust out of the ground" [18]. What word do you use for *spigot*? Do you know any others?
3. The author mentions that Bertrand Russell "could not have stated it better." Who is Bertrand Russell, and why is he referred to in such fashion?
4. The five-cent piece is referred to as a "nickle." What is its official name? Are the other names for money **slang** or standard? What are some **colloquial** names for money?
5. Understanding the precise meaning of the following words will help you to understand the narrative (use a dictionary): anarchy [8], cult [22], epileptic seizure [14], exotic [22], potency [28], rupture [1], truss [1].

Rhetoric and Style

1. Why are there so many paragraphs—twenty-nine—in such a short selection?
2. The author uses many **metaphors** and **similes** in his story. Are they effective aids to narration?
3. What is the effect on you of the field "fat with pheasants"? Have you ever seen such a field? Have you ever seen fruit littered under a tree or an actual pig? Should a writer use images that all of his readers would not know?
4. What can the reader **infer** from the fact that the grocer automatically reached for a package of grape Kool-Aid?
5. What seems to be the narrative function of the mother's interruption of the ceremony?

Application and Evaluation

1. Write a brief narrative of some ordinary function that has taken on almost ceremonious style. Observe, for example, the opening of a pack of cigarettes and the lighting, the filling and lighting of a pipe, hair-fixing, or dressing or undressing.
2. Can you think of an area where ritual seems to satisfy a real emotional or physical need? Using specific examples, tell about it.
3. The logic of sleeping in one's clothes because one just has to get dressed again is quite valid. Why do we bother to get undressed anyway?

4. Write a brief narrative about someone who is "hooked" on a relatively simple substance like coffee, cough drops, or seltzer.
5. Reread the last paragraph of the story and see if you can rephrase it as a "moral."

Ronald L. Fair (1932–   ) Mr. Fair began writing as a youngster of twelve or fourteen out of the anger and frustration of the Chicago ghetto. He wrote his first two novels while employed as a court reporter and stenographer. He has subsequently taught at Columbia College in Chicago, Northwestern University, and Wesleyan University. The following narrative appeared in *The American Scholar* and in an anthology, *19 Necromancers from Now.* It is remarkable for the matter-of-fact acceptance of an environment that would be shocking and frightening to a middle-class white.

We Who Came After

This is a narrative of what it was like for those of us born in the Thirties. Our parents had come from Mississippi, Louisiana, Tennessee, Georgia, Alabama and so many other southern states where the whites were so perverse in their treatment of the blacks, but mostly they came from Mississippi. They came to the big cities armed only with glorious fantasies about a new and better world, hoping to find the self-respect that had been cut out of them. They came north, and we were the children born in the place they had escaped to—Chicago. [1]

You know, we were so young that we didn't know we were supposed to be poor. We were so young and excited with the life we knew that we had not yet learned we were the ones that were supposed to be deprived. We were even so young that sometimes we forgot we were supposed to be hungry, because we were just too busy living. [2]

I can remember one spring, after the snow had finally seeped into the earth, and the mud in the vacant lots had become dirt again, how we would move over those lots cautiously, like the old rag man, our eyes sparkling with enthusiasm, our minds pulsating with the thrill of finds we surely knew would be there because there had been a whole winter of snow covering up the treasures that grownups had discarded—unknowingly to our advantage. Things that we needed because they were treasures and were of value to us. [3]

There would be razor blades, some broken in half, some whole, all rusty; a new metal. [4]

"Careful, Sam Don't cut yourself, man. If you do, man, your whole hand'll rot off." [5]

A bottle! God a bottle like we had never seen. [6]

"I bet some ole rich white lady came along here and threw it away." [7]

"Naw." [8]

"I bet she did. Bet it was full of some rich perfume or somethin. Lets see if we can find the top?" [9]

"Here's a top." [10]

"Naw, too big." [11]

"I bet she kept the top." [12]

"Ain't no rich lady been by here." [13]

"She was." [14]

"She wasn't." [15]

"Well I don't care. I know what I'm gonna do with it anyway so it don't matter. I'm gonna take it home to mama. She'll like it. She ain't never had no bottle like this before." [16]

"Hey," somebody would say, "let's go kill rats." [17]

A unanimous roar of approval would go up and we would begin searching for sticks and bricks. Once sufficiently armed, we would leave our land of treasures and move down the alley toward one of the very best games we knew. [18]

Each of us had relatives who had either been bitten by rats or frightened out of their wits by then. There was the story of the friend who used to live in the neighborhood but whose parents moved out when his baby sister had her right ear eaten away by one of them. There was also the story we whispered among ourselves about one of the group whose grandmother was said to have cooked her very best stew from rats she trapped in her pantry. [19]

Almost from infancy we had been fighting them; in our sleep, fighting the noise they made in the walls as they chewed their way through the plaster to get at what few provisions we had; in our alleys, our Black Boulevards, fighting to get them out of the garbage and into their holes so we could play a game of stickball with no fear of being bitten while standing on second or third base. Outside of the white insurance men who made their rounds daily collecting quarters and half dollars for the burial policies our parents paid for over and over, making the insurance companies richer and ending with our parents in their old age having almost enough money to pay the price of a pine-box funeral, outside of those strange little white peddlers who came into the neighborhood every week and trapped our mothers with flashy dresses, petticoats, slips and shoes supposedly half-priced ("No-money-down, lady." but the records were kept by the salesmen in their payment books, and the payments never ended.) outside of the white men from the telephone company who came far too often to take away somebody's phone, outside of the *strangers* who moved among us with all the authority and arrogance of giants, we hated the rats most. [20]

We didn't always win against them, but we kept fighting because we knew if we didn't continue killing them they would soon make the alleys unsafe even for us. Once a new boy moved into the neighborhood with a BB gun, and with the large supply of ammunition he had, we killed two hundred rats in one day. We made bows and used umbrella staves for arrows and got so good with them that we only missed about two thirds of the time. [21]

But the best way to kill them was with bricks and clubs. We'd walk quietly down the alley, our little platoon advancing on the army of rats, plowing, in the sumertime, through mounds of junk piled against the fences (always there because the garbage trucks came around so seldom), until we reached a mound that gave off sounds of their activity. We would surround it, leaving only the fence as their escape route, look at each other, nervous, excited, our blood blasting away inside our temples, then one of us would poke a stick into the pile of garbage, and, with our anxiety mounting, we would wait for them to react. [22]

The rats had already sensed our presence and had grown silent, waiting for the danger to pass. The stick would go in again, and then, quickly, they would frantically dig their way farther into the garbage. They would not come out. Another stick, and finally a gray thing, its teeth sparkling like daggers in the early morning sun, would spring from the pile and charge one of us with all the rage and hostility of the killer it was. A brick would miss him, but a club would catch him in mid-air just as he was about to dig his teeth into someone's leg. His insides would explode out of him and blood would shoot into the air like a spurt from a fountain. Another one was out. A brick would stun him and then the clubs would beat him to death. Two others began climbing the fence and we left the fence stained with their blood. And then as it often happened, the biggest and oldest of them dashed between us and quickly disappeared into another pile of garbage. Including his tail, he was at least two feet long and as fat as any cat in the neighborhood, and even though we chased him, and spread the pile he had hidden in all over the alley, he was able to escape by squeezing through a small hole in the fence. It seemed to us we had been trying to kill that one rat for years, but there were so many that were two feet long that we could never be sure. [23]

We were often victorious, but once in a while the rats would get the better of us; a child would be bitten by one of them. Sometimes we would club the rat away from his leg. Sometimes we would run home crying, afraid of them all over again and thankful that it was someone else who had felt the needle-like teeth, and sometimes we would carry our crying friend home to his mother, hoping that he would not have to go through the torture of the shots. [24]

Then, after our parents finally let us out again, we would group around a light pole on the street or a fire hydant, propping our feet on it pretending to be grown-up waiting for the news from the hospital about our wounded comrade. [25]

[1991 words, 25 paragraphs]

Diction

1. Some phrases used in this narrative may not be familiar to readers born since the thirties. Can you find out what "old rag man," "pine box," and "stickball" mean?
2. Mr. Fair writes of "treasures" that were found in vaacnt lots. How does he make this **abstraction** more **concrete**?
3. Does the author make use of **slang** or **jargon** in this narrative?
4. Does the dialogue seem realistic or false or invented?
5. One of the books mentioned in the headnote is *19 Necromancers From Now.* What is a necromancer? Are necromancers sequential?
6. Some of the following words may not be common enough to be understood precisely (check the meanings in a good dictionary): arrogance [20], deprived [2], pantry [19], perverse [1], platoon [22], pulsating [3], route (check also spelling and pronunciation of "rout" [22], staves [21], stun [23], unanimous [18].

Rhetoric and Style

1. In paragraph [20] the author uses but two sentences. The second one is **periodic** and is over 140 words long. Why so complex, and what is its meaning?
2. Are there any unusual or notable **figures of speech** used? Check especially for **simile** and **metaphor**.
3. Observe, and list, at least two examples of **understatement** (see **Figures of speech**), a very difficult type of writing to use well.
4. Explain the **irony** of paragraph [2]; explain the irony of the entire narrative!
5. What is the **tone** imparted by the phrase "in our alleys, our Black Boulevards" [20]?
6. What is the **mood** of the entire narrative, and how is it shown?

Applications and Evaluation

1. Have you ever lived in a community where rats were a problem? Have you ever had any kind of wildlife, or vermin, cause an annoyance? Would such an annoyance be rare or common in most of the world? In the United States?
2. The youngsters in this story go off cheerfully to war with the rats, their platoon against the rat army. Is the author making a social comment? Could you outline a brief story comparing children's games to grownups' "games"?
3. The ghetto children make a game of what could be a grim duty, staying even with the rats for survival. Can you think of any other duty that could be made into a game? How about a game or sport that becomes deadly and earnest?
4. Are people deprived and poverty-striken before someone tells them that they are? Does being told benefit them?
5. The children find "treasures" in the dirt. Prepare an essay or a narrative considering: "One man's discards may be another's treasure."

Donald S. Connery (1926–) Donald Connery was born in New York and educated at Harvard University. He worked as a correspondent for Time-Life News Service for over twelve years. He has written two books about the people of other lands, *The Irish* and *The Swedes,* as well as *One American Town.* The following selection will be part of a new book about India. It is an outstanding example of how narrative can be used to argue that India is on her way to producing enough food. It also ties in with the previous section showing how narrative can set mood, witness here the first eight paragraphs.

The Greening of India

Krishna

One recent balmy evening in Bombay I met several Indian friends for dinner at Gaylord's on Vir Nariman Road, just a few blocks down from my hotel on Marine Drive. Vir Nariman is the nearest thing in India to a Parisian boulevard, and Gaylord's, like other restaurants nearby, gives you a choice of sitting indoors with air conditioning or outdoors in its sidewalk café. Unfortunately, we chose the sidewalk. [1]

At first, it was pleasant sitting in the open. We could hear both the sounds of Indian street life and the Latin rhythms of the Gaylord band. People at adjoining tables were eating heartily. All were Indian and apparently well able to afford a meal at one of the more expensive restaurants in India's fastest growing metropolis. I looked over the French-Chinese menu and ordered a lobster cocktail, a *poulet cordon bleu,* a garlic roll, and coffee. [2]

The food was served and it was delicious. But as we ate and talked I began to have an uncomfortable feeling that people were staring at us. I then noticed a crowd standing on the other side of the well-manicured hedge that separated us from the passersby on the broad sidewalk. Although they were in the shadows while we were bathed in soft light, I could make out their gaunt faces, the naked torsos of men and children, and ragged women clutching babies. They were not hostile. They simply stood silently, respectfully, asking nothing, just staring. It was as if the mere sight of our dinner provided some kind of nourishment. Their eyes would follow the food from plate to mouth. [3]

I remember feeling sick at heart: ashamed for being a well-fed rich man stuffing himself in front of the emaciated poor. At the same time I was just a bit embarrassed for reacting so strongly. Surely I ought to be used to these things by now. I had once lived in this tragic country. This is the way it is in India. This is the way it has been for centuries. [4]

One of my companions noticed my discomfort and remarked casually, "These aren't the usual sidewalk people. They must be from the villages. The drought, you know. There isn't any water or food in the villages so they are swarming into Bombay. Thousands of them. You see them everywhere." [5]

"Shouldn't we . . .?" I started to say. [6]

"No, we shouldn't!" he said firmly. "Do you want to start a riot? Feed one and you'll have to feed the whole street. Give them money and you'll never get rid of them. It's impossible. Just keep eating. Take no notice." [7]

It was a disturbing way to encounter the drought and near famine that had fallen like a shroud over more than half the Indian countryside. I had been too busy with my visits to what Jawaharlal Nehru once called "the new temples of India"—the factories, universities, steel mills, hydroelectric dams, atomic-energy stations—to find the time to inquire into the current conditions of village India. Now, with those staring faces before me, I began to take a fresh look at Indian agriculture and the nation's life-and-death struggle to make food production catch up with the relentless rise of population. [8]

What was obvious ever since the summer of 1972 was that India, in its twenty-fifth year of independence, had been struck a cruel blow in the form of a late monsoon that failed to drench the land with anything like the amount of water needed. Water was so short in large areas of rural India that millions of tons of crops were lost and cattle collapsed in the fields or were sold off for a few rupees. Whole villages were abandoned. Hungry multitudes trudged to the pavements and shantytowns of the already overcrowded towns and cities. The authorities rushed in food and sent water in scrubbed-out oil trucks to parched communities. Huge work-relief projects, paying a few cents for a day's labor, were started to provide employment for hordes of people who could no longer work their farms. The water shortage caused a crisis in hydroelectric-power supplies thus crippling whole industries. [9]

By early 1973 a *New York Times* headline reported that "Worst Drought in Decade Perils India's Food Supply." Relief might come with the next monsoon, beginning in June, but if it too failed to satisfy India's great thirst, then the suffering would continue. Perhaps there would be famine. [10]

There is something terribly familiar about the spectacle of India stricken with drought and facing famine. The very name India convey's an image of half-naked, half-starved masses enduring poverty on a scale unknown anywhere else on earth. But the spectacle is bewildering as well, for in recent years there has been a steady flow of good news from India about a Green Revolution that was supposed to be the solution to the country's chronic shortage of food. [11]

Reports from India told of amazing annual increases in grain output as the result of "miracle seeds," artificial fertilizers, pesticides, the spread of irrigation and electricity ,and a popular awakening to the benefits of scientific agriculture. Wheat production had doubled in five seasons. A major breakthrough in rice production was beginning. Fertilizer plants were going up, tube wells were going down, tractors were replacing bullocks, and farmers were earning money as never before. [12]

Remarkably enough, the Indians were able not only to feed nearly 10 million refugees from the civil war in East Pakistan in 1971 but to rush a million tons of food to newborn Bangladesh early in 1972. Shipments of American wheat under the U.S. Food for Peace program had saved countless Indians from starvation for fifteen years, but now a proud India could say that foreign grains were no longer required. Such a degree of self-reliance, coming on top of their swift defeat and dismemberment of Pakistan during the Bangladesh crisis, gave Indians a self-confidence never before seen. [13]

The euphoria lasted only half a year. It began to evaporate as last summer's monsoon sprinkled rather than drenched the thirsty land. Once again, India had to turn to the rich nations for grain. Once again, India's future looked bleak. [14]

What happened to the Green Revolution? Is it more a mirage than a miracle? With the population of 560 million increasing by a million every four weeks, by 25 percent every ten years, is there any hope that India will produce food faster than babies? [15]

The last thing that a supposedly seasoned observer of the Indian scene wants to do is sound optimistic. David Holden, a veteran British foreign correspondent, wrote a few years back that "There are times, in any appraisal of modern India, when despair seems almost the only appropriate reaction." [16]

My own restrained optimism about India's chances for conquering its food deficit rests largely on the new evidence of the Indian peasant's willingness to modernize his methods, but it begins with the conviction that Indian agriculture is still so backward compared with other nations that it has nowhere to go but up. [17]

The typical Indian village is far less isolated than it used to be, and one village in five, instead of one in a hundred, now has electricity, but overall farming practices are positively biblical. The farmer barely scratches at the soil with a wooden plow pulled by a pair of bullocks. He uses cow dung for fuel instead of saving it for fertilizer. He is likely to be at the mercy of the landlord and the moneylender as well as natural forces. More than two-thirds of India's cultivable land depends on the monsoon for irrigation. [18]

Dr. M. S. Swaminathan, director-general of the Indian Council of Agricultural Research, said that the Indian peasant may indeed be illiterate and fatalistic, "but it is forgotten that people everywhere respond to economic stimuli. A farmer may be hesitant to change if there is a real risk involved and the gain is small, but if you can show him that he will earn three hundred rupees instead of one hundred rupees, then he is definitely interested. That is why the new hybrid varieties have had a catalytic role in transforming the outlook of the farming community. The greatest battle we have to win is changing the outlook of the farmers. They have ascribed everything to the will of God, believing that things are beyond the control of man. But now with the large quantum jump that has taken place in yield and income wherever we are using the new seeds with proper fertilizer and irrigation, there is a striking effect. The farmer sees a kind of miracle and he definitely reacts." [19]

The full impact of the Green Revolution is so far limited to a few fortunate areas, but as I traveled through the country I kept on discovering centers of rapid growth, particularly in the surroundings of the new agricultural universities. Fourteen of these aggressively modern institutions, inspired by the U.S. Land Grant Colleges and developed with American assitance, have sprung up in the last dozen years. [20]

One day in Ludhiana I drove into the countryside to visit Baddwal village, population 3000, a place I had selected at random. It had all the classic touches of rural India, from the pancakes of cow dung drying on the walls to the women who hid their faces and scurried indoors at the sight of a male stranger. But the evidence of better times was overwhelming. The lanes had been paved and cramped mud dwellings were being replaced by more spacious brick houses. The village now boasted a bank as well as a post office, and a high school as well as a grade school. It was electrified, of course, like almost all villages of Punjab and the neighboring state of Haryana. Ten families owned tractors. I was told that the average farmer's income was three times higher than it was a decade ago. [21]

"Everyone eats well these days," said Dalip Singh, a bearded elder statesman of the village. "Everyone has more money, even the Harijans—the Untouchables. They dress as we do and their children go to college just like the others." Other village spokesmen said that there was a White Revolution coming on the heels of the Green Revolution. Milk and poultry, so badly needed by the nation, offered great opportunities for rural entrepreneurs with get-up-and-go. [22]

What was most impressive was the certainty that the future would be better and that it could be made better. No one was ready to simply accept things as they are. I had to keep reminding myself that all of this was something extraordinary in India, not typical, and that the Punjabis are a particularly energetic people. I knew, too, that rewards of the Green Revolution were not being distributed evenly —better-off farmers benefited more than poorer farmers and the landless, whose ranks were fast increasing—and that there were any number of obstacles in the way of a nationwide agricutural renaissance. [23]

And yet, for all that, it seemed to me that the nation's long-delayed rural awakening had to begin somewhere, and that these enclaves of alert people and lush harvests might be the start of the greening of India. A great human story was unfolding, even in a year of terrible drought. "The farmers are being shaken out of their inertia and old beliefs," Dr. Swaminathan had said. "They want to take part in the new technology, and they will insist that they be able to take part. It is a very positive spirit, and you can see it all over the country." India may never become an affluent society nor a land without poverty, certainly not until its runaway population growth is halted, but its chances are brighter than ever of becoming a nation that no longer fears a great hunger. [24]

[2020 words, 24 paragraphs]

Diction

1. The term "Green Revolution" has been in current use for the last several years; to what does it refer?
2. What is the author's purpose in telling us what he ordered for dinner [2]?
3. This narrative is filled with exotic words, names ,and phrases. Note a few and comment on their **connotations** for you.
4. What is a monsoon? How does it differ from other types of weather such as typhoon, hurricane, cyclone?
5. The author uses two terms, "biblical" [18] and "Renaissance" [23], that are historical rather than agricultural; why?
6. The use of your dictionary to define these words might well make this selection more understandable: bullocks [12], catalytic [19], chronic [11], emaciated [4], enclaves [24], euphoria [14], impact [20], quantum jump [19], shroud [8], stimuli [19].

Rhetoric and Style

1. Although not numerous there are **figures of speech** used to heighten communication in this narrative. Find three and **classify** them.
2. The author also uses a device not normally used in prose writing. Can you identify it?
   Examples: more mirage than miracles [15]
   relentless rise of population [8]
3. Paragraph [12] is only four sentences long. It has a **topic sentence** and merely three **details**. Is it not incomplete? (See **Paragraph development**.)
4. Within this longer selection are two parts that are straight narration; what paragraphs limit these two parts?
5. What seems to be the author's **tone** toward his subject? What internal evidence leads you to that conclusion?
6. What is the **thesis statement** that the author uses the narrative mode as evidence for?

Applications and Evaluation

1. Various Hindu religious groups have gained a following in the United States, among them Hari Krishna groups and some types of transcendental meditation. How do they seem to be regarded by more traditional people? Write a paragraph stating your views.
2. Using a brief narrative to introduce the topic, write a selection indicating that there may be other reasons for lack of food than poor crops (distribution, price controls, hoarding, for example).
3. The article mentions that "even the Harijans, the untouchables, go to college." Limiting your evidence to the United States, write a paragraph or essay with the title "The Untouchables Go to College."
4. The caste system has helped to make India one of the most backward of nations. Do we have a caste system in America? Using a brief narrative as evidence write a paragraph or essay either pro or con.
5. This article appeared in *World*, a "slick" magazine. Of what value was it to you? What possible value could it be to anyone? Be either practical or philosophical in your answer.

Alexander Calandra (1911–   ) Dr. Calandra is a member of the Department of Physics at Washington University, St. Louis, Missouri. He was educated at Brooklyn College, Columbia, and New York University. Very active professionally, he has been the editor of the American Chemical Society's *Reporter* since 1964. This narrative, from the old *Saturday Review*, is credited as being part of his book *The Teaching of Elementary Science and Physics*. The narrative is brief, but it makes the author's point more vividly and more graphically than several pages of argument would.

Angels on a Pin

A Modern Parable

Some time ago I received a call from a colleague who asked if I would be the referee on the grading of an examination question. He was about to give a student a zero for his answer to a physics question, while the student claimed he should receive a perfect score and would if the system were not set up against the student. The instructor and the student agreed to submit this to an impartial arbiter, and I was selected. [1]

I went to my colleague's office and read the examination question: "Show how it is possible to determine the height of a tall building with the aid of a barometer." [2]

The student had answered: "Take a barometer to the top of the building, attach a long rope to it, lower the barometer to the street, and then bring it up, measuring the length of the rope. The length of the rope is the height of the building." [3]

I pointed out that the student really had a strong case for full

"Angels on a Pin" from *The Teaching of Elementary Science and Physics*, by Alexander Calandra (ACCE Reporter) first appeared in *Saturday Review*, December 21, 1968. Reprinted by permission of the author and Saturday Review/World.

credit, since he had answered the question completely and correctly. On the other hand, if full credit were given, it could well contribute to a high grade for the student in his physics course. A high grade is supposed to certify competence in physics, but the answer did not confirm this. I suggested that the student have another try at answering the question. I was not surprised that my colleague agreed, but I was surprised that the student did. [4]

I gave the student six minutes to answer the question with the warning that the answer should show some knowledge of physics. At the end of five minutes, he had not written anything. I asked if he wished to give up, but he said no. He had many answers to this problem; he was just thinking of the best one. I excused myself for interrupting him and asked him to please go on. In the next minute he dashed off his answer which read: [5]

"Take the barometer to the top of the building and lean over the edge of the roof. Drop that barometer, timing its fall with a stopwatch. Then using the formula $S = ½ at^2$, calculate the height of the building." [6]

At this point I asked my colleague if *he* would give up. He conceded, and I gave the student almost full credit. [7]

In leaving my colleague's office, I recalled that the student had said he had many other answers to the problem, so I asked him what they were. "Oh yes," said the student. "There are a great many ways of getting the height of a tall building with a barometer. For example, you could take the barometer out on a sunny day and measure the height of the barometer and the length of its shadow, and the length of the shadow of the building, and by the use of a simple proportion, determine the height of the building." [8]

"Fine," I asked. "And the others?" [9]

"Yes," said the student. "There is a very basic measurement method that you will like. In this method you take the barometer and begin to walk up the stairs. As you climb the stairs, you mark off the length of the barometer along the wall. You then count the number of marks, and this will give you the height of the building in barometer units. A very direct method." [10]

"Of course, if you want a more sophisticated method, you can tie the barometer to the end of a string, swing it as a pendulum, and determine the value of 'g' at the street level and at the top of the building. From the difference of the two values of 'g' the height of the building can be calculated." [11]

Finally, he concluded, there are many other ways of solving the problem. "Probably the best," he said, "is to take the barometer to the basement and knock on the superintendent's door. When the superintendent answers, you speak to him as follows: 'Mr. Superintendent, here I have a fine barometer. If you tell me the height of this building, I will give you this barometer.' " [12]

At this point I asked the student if he really did know the conventional answer to this question. He admitted that he did, said that he was fed up with high school and college instructors trying to teach him how to think, using the "scientific method," and to explore the deep inner logic of the subject in a pedantic way, as is often done in the new mathematics, rather than teaching him the structure of the subject. With this in mind, he decided to revive scholasticism as an academic lark to challenge the Sputnik-panicked classrooms of America. [13]

[790 words, 13 paragraphs]

Diction

1. This selection is subtitled "A Modern Parable." What is a **parable**, and why is this a modern one?
2. The author mentions the "scientific method" in paragraph [12]. What does the phrase **imply**? What does it **denote**?
3. The student says in paragraph [13] that he has been taught to "explore the deep inner logic of the subject." What exactly is **denoted** by the phrase "deep inner logic of the subject"?
4. Another phrase that may not be clear is "the new mathematics." What does that phrase **connote** and **denote**?
5. The following interesting words are worth knowing; look them up in your dictionary: arbiter [1], certify [4], colleague [1], competence [4], formula [6], pedantic [13] polemic (introduction), proportion [8], scholasticism [13], sophistication [11].

Rhetoric and Style

1. There seem to be few or no **metaphors**, **similes**, or other **figures of speech** in this selection, nor are any of the technical devices such as flashback used. Why?
2. The author speaks of an "academic lark" [13], clearly not a learned bird; what does he mean?
3. The use of "sputnik-panicked" to describe classrooms is an historical **allusion**; what does it mean here?

4. What do you think is the **attitude** of the writer toward the student?
5. What is the point of this little narrative?

Applications and Evaluation

1. Think of a situation where the "conventional answer" was neither the best nor the only solution. Describe the situation in a brief narrative.
2. What is the "real" answer to the problem in the narrative? Is it superior to the answers proposed in the story?
3. Often students delight in outwitting their professors, as this lad obviously did. Why? Is this delight basic? Could it be carried over to other examples of confounding the one in authority? A specific example in a paragraph would make interesting reading.
4. Industry and government use several methods of getting away from standard solutions to problems. What do you think of buzz-sessions, think-tanks, and brain-storming?
5. Might the "right" answer to a problem ever be the only solution? Pick a specific area, such as religion, education, marriage, mathematics, or architecture, and defend your position.

Jane van Lawick-Goodall (19 –) became interested in animals when she was a child and was delighted when, as a young lady, she was invited to visit a friend in Africa. In Nairobi she met the late Louis Leakey, who urged her to follow through with her desire and make a study of the wild chimpanzee. With her mother she set up a camp and, although plagued by many hardships including malaria, she soon began to send in reports that astonished the scientific world. Leakey sent a photographer, Baron Hugo van Lawick, to join her to record these events. Eventually the two married and had a son but still continued the work. Their first accounts appeared in *The National Geographic Magazine* and in a lavishly illustrated book, *My Friends the Wild Chimpanzees*. This selection, which shows the power of narrative to present a strong argument by the clear presentation of factual evidence, is taken from her second book, *In the Shadow of Man*.

The Toolmaker?

Since dawn I had climbed up and down the steep mountain slopes and pushed my way through the dense valley forests. Again and again I had stopped to listen, or to gaze through binoculars at the surrounding countryside. Yet I had neither heard nor seen a single chimpanzee, and now it was already five o'clock. In two hours darkness would fall over the rugged terrain of the Gombe Stream Chimpanzee Reserve. I settled down at my favorite vantage point, the Peak, hoping that at least I might see a chimpanzee make his nest for the night before I had to stop work for the day. [1]

I was watching a troop of monkeys in the forested valley below when suddenly I heard the screaming of a young chimpanzee. Quickly I scanned the trees with my binoculars, but the sound had died away before I could locate the exact place, and it took several minutes of searching before I saw four chimpanzees. The slight squabble was over and they were all feeding peacefully on some yellow plumlike fruits. [2]

The distance between us was to great for me to make detailed observations, so I decided to try to get closer. I surveyed the trees close to the group: if I could manage to get to that large fig without frightening the chimpanzees, I thought, I would get an excellent view. It took me about ten minutes to make the journey. As I moved cautiously around the thick gnarled trunk of the fig I realized that the chimpanzees had gone; the branches of the fruit tree were empty. The same old feeling of depression clawed at me. Once again the chimpanzees had seen me and silently fled. Then all at once my heart missed several beats. [3]

Less than twenty yards away from me two male chimpanzees were sitting on the ground staring at me intently. Scarcely breathing, I waited for the sudden panic-stricken flight that normally followed a surprise encounter between myself and the chimpanzees at close quarters. But nothing of the sort happened. The two large chimps simply continued to gaze at me. Very slowly I sat down, and after a few more moments, the two calmly began to groom one another. [4]

As I watched, still scarcely believing it was true, I saw two more chimpanzee heads peering at me over the grass from the other side of a small forest glade: a female and a youngster. They bobbed down as I turned my head toward them, but soon reappeared, one after the other, in the lower branches of a tree about forty yards away. There they sat, almost motionless, watching me. [5]

For over half a year I had been trying to overcome the chimpanzees' inherent fear of me, the fear that made them vanish into the undergrowth whenever I approached. At first they had fled even when I was as far away as five hundred yards and on the other side of a ravine. Now two males were sitting so close that I could almost hear them breathing. [6]

Without any doubt whatsoever, this was the proudest moment I had known. I had been accepted by the two magnificent creatures grooming each other in front of me. I knew them both—David Graybeard, who had always been the least afraid of me, was one and the other was Goliath, not the giant his name implies but of superb physique and the highest-ranking of all the males. Their coats gleamed vivid black in the softening light of the evening. [7]

For more than ten minutes David Graybeard and Goliath sat grooming each other, and then, just before the sun vanished over the horizon behind me, David got up and stood staring at me. And it so happened that my elongated evening shadow fell across him. The moment is etched deep into my memory: the excitement of the first close contact with a wild chimpanzee and the freakish chance that cast my shadow over David even as he seemed to gaze into my eyes. Later it acquired an almost allegorical significance, for of all living creatures today only man, with his superior intellect, overshadows the chimpanzee. Only man casts his shadow of doom over the freedom of the chimpanzee in the forests with his guns and his spreading settlements and cultivation. At that moment, however, I did not think of this. I only marveled in David and Goliath themselves. [8]

The depression and despair that had so often visited me during the preceding months were as nothing compared to the exultation I felt when the group had finally moved away and I was hastening down the darkening mountainside to my tent on the shores of Lake Tanganyika. [9]

As the weeks went by the chimpanzees became less and less afraid. Quite often when I was on one of my food-collecting expeditions I came across chimpanzees unexpectedly, and after a time I found that some of them would tolerate my presence provided they were in fairly thick forest and I sat still and did not try to move closer than sixty to eighty yards. And so, during my second month of watching from the Peak, when I saw a group settle down to feed I sometimes moved closer and was thus able to make more detailed observations. [10]

It was at this time that I began to recognize a number of different individuals. As soon as I was sure of knowing a chimpanzee if I saw it again, I named it. Some scientists feel that animals should be labeled by numbers—that to name them is anthropomorphic—but I have always been interested in the *differences* between individuals, and a name is not only more individual than a number but also far easier to remember. Most names were simply those which, for some reason or other, seemed to suit the individuals to whom I attached them. A few chimps were named because some facial expression or mannerism reminded me of human acquaintances. [11]

Two of the chimpanzees I knew well by sight at that time were David Graybeard and Goliath. Like David and Goliath in the Bible, these two individuals were closely associated in my mind because they were very often together. Goliath, even in those days of his prime, was not a giant, but he had a splendid physique and the springy movements of an athlete. He probably weighed about one hundred pounds. David Graybeard was less afraid of me from the start than were any of the other chimps. I was always pleased when I picked out his handsome face and well-marked silvery beard in a chimpanzee group, for with David to calm the others. I had a better chance of approaching to observe them more closely.

Before the end of my trial period in the field I made two really exciting discoveries—discoveries that made the previous months of frustration well worth while. And for both of them I had David Graybeard to thank.

One day I arrived on the Peak and found a small group of chimps just below me in the upper branches of a thick tree. As I watched I saw that one of them was holding a pink-looking object from which he was from time to time pulling pieces with his teeth. There was a female and a youngster and they were both reaching out toward the male, their hands actually touching his mouth. Presently the female picked up a piece of the pink thing and put it to her mouth: it was at this moment that I realized the chimps were eating meat. [14]

After each bite of meat the male picked off some leaves with his lips and chewed them with the flesh. Often, when he had chewed for several minutes on this leafy wad, he spat out the remains into the waiting hands of the female. Suddenly he dropped a small piece of meat, and like a flash the youngster swung after it to the ground. Even as he reached to pick it up the undergrowth exploded and an adult bushpig charged toward him. Screaming, the juvenile leaped back into the tree. The pig remained in the open, snorting and moving backward and forward. Soon I made out the shapes of three small striped piglets. Obviously the chimps were eating a baby pig. The size was right and later, when I realized that the male was David Graybeard, I moved closer and saw that he was indeed eating piglet. [15]

For three hours I watched the chimps feeding. David occasionally let the female bite pieces from the carcass and once he actually detached a small piece of flesh and placed it in her outstretched hand. When he finally climbed down there was still meat left on the carcass; he carried it away in one hand, followed by the others. [16]

Of course I was not sure, then, that David Graybeard had

caught the pig for himself, but even so, it was tremendously exciting to know that these chimpanzees actually ate meat. Previously scientists had believed that although these apes might occasionally supplement their diet with a few insects or small rodents and the like they were primarily vegetarians and fruit eaters. No one had suspected that they might hunt larger mammals. [17]

It was within two weeks of this observation that I saw something that excited me even more. By then it was October and the short rains had begun. The blackened slopes were softened by feathery new grass shoots and in some places the ground was carpeted by a variety of flowers. The Chimpanzees' Spring, I called it. I had had a frustrating morning, tramping up and down three valleys with never a sign or sound of a chimpanzee. Hauling myself up the steep slope of Mlinda Valley I headed for the Peak, not only weary but soaking wet from crawling through dense undergrowth. Suddenly I stopped, for I saw a slight movement in the long grass about sixty yards away. Quickly focusing my binoculars I saw that it was a single chimpanzee, and just then he turned in my direction. I recognized David Graybeard. [18]

Cautiously I moved around so that I could see what he was doing. He was squatting beside the red earth mound of a termite nest, and as I watched I saw him carefully push a long grass stem down into a hole in the mound. After a moment he withdrew it and picked something from the end with his mouth. I was too far away to make out what he was eating, but it was obvious that he was actually using a grass stem as a tool. [19]

I knew that on two occasions casual observers in West Africa had seen chimpanzees using objects as tools: one had broken open palm-nut kernels by using a rock as a hammer, and a group of chimps had been observed pushing sticks into an underground bees' nest and licking off the honey. Somehow I had never dreamed of seeing anything so exciting myself. [20]

For an hour David feasted at the termite mound and then he wandered slowly away. When I was sure he had gone I went over to examine the mound. I found a few crushed insects strewn about, and a swarm of worker termites sealing the entrances of the nest passages into which David had obviously been poking his stems. I picked up one of his discarded tools and carefully pushed it into a hole myself. Immediately I felt the pull of several termites as they seized the grass, and when I pulled it out there were a number of worker termites and a few soldiers, with big red heads, clinging on with their mandibles. There they remained, sticking out at right angles to the stem with their legs waving in the air. [21]

Before I left I trampled down some of the tall dry grass and constructed a rough hide—just a few palm fronds leaned up against the low branch of a tree and tied together at the top. I planned to wait there the next day. But it was another week before I was able to watch a chimpanzee "fishing" for termites again. Twice chimps arrived, but each time they saw me and moved off immediately. Once a swarm of fertile winged termites—the princes and princesses, as they are called—flew off on their nuptial flight, their huge white wings fluttering frantically as they carried the insects higher and higher. Later I realized that it is at this time of year, during the short rains, when the worker termites extend the passages of the nest to the surface, preparing for these emigrations. Several such swarms emerge between October and January. It is principally during these months that the chimpanzees feed on termites. [22]

On the eighth day of my watch David Graybeard arrived again, together with Goliath, and the pair worked there for two hours. I could see much better: I observed how they scratched open the sealed-over passage entrances with a thumb or forefinger. I watched how they bit the ends off their tools when they became bent, or used the other end, or discarded them in favor of new ones. Goliath once moved at least fifteen yards from the heap to select a firm-looking piece of vine, and both males often picked three or four stems while they were collecting tools, and put the spares beside them on the ground until they wanted them. [23]

Most exciting of all, on several occasions they picked small leafy twigs and prepared them for use by stripping off the leaves. This was the first recorded example of a wild animal not merely *using* an object as a tool, but actually modifying an object and thus showing the crude beginnings of *toolmaking*. [24]

Previously man had been regarded as the only toolmaking animal. Indeed, one of the clauses commonly accepted in the definition of man was that he was a creature who "made tools to a regular and set pattern." The chimpanzees, obviously, had not made tools to any set pattern. Nevertheless, my early observations of their primitive toolmaking abilities convinced a number of scientists that it was necessary to redefine man in a more complex manner than before. Or else, as Louis Leakey put it, we should by definition have to accept the chimpanzees as Man. [25]

I sent telegrams to Louis about both of my new observations—

the meat-eating and the toolmaking—and he was of course wildly enthusiastic. In fact, I believe that the news was helpful to him in his efforts to find further financial support for my work. It was not long afterward when he wrote to tell me that the National Geographic Society in the United States had agreed to grant funds for another year's research. [26]

[2400 words, 26 paragraphs]

Diction

1. Jane van Lawick-Goodall is British; are there any characteristics in her writing that would so indicate?
2. The author sometimes calls the animals "chimpanzees" and sometimes "chimps." Why the distinction?
3. Is there any particularly vivid language in this selection (striking verbs, sparkling adjectives as are used by Steinbeck and Fleming)?
4. The author is an acute observer of details. Note one or two paragraphs where this trait is most obvious.
5. She calls one of the chimps "handsome," actually says he has a "handsome face" [12]. Has she been in the brush too long? Why apply such an adjective to an animal?
6. The following words may be of interest to vocabulary builders; look up their meanings in the dictionary: allegorical [8], anthropomorphic [11], emigrations [22], elongated [8], frustration [13], inherent [6], mandibles [21], modifying [24], nuptial [22], terrain [1].

Rhetoric and Style

1. This narrative does not seem to be as marked with many **figures of speech** as some of the others in this book. Can you find any?
2. What is the **allusion** in paragraph [12], and is it appropriate or not?
3. It is standard scientific method to give numbers to members of a group of animals under observation, yet this author gives them names, some fanciful. Why? (In the full text she names some of the chimpanzees Flo, Mr. McGregor, Flint, Mike, Fifi, Figan, and Rodolf.)
4. The book from which this selection is taken is called *In the*

Shadow of Man. Why? After you have speculated, reread paragraph [8] again and tell why.

5. Reread paragraph [18] and note the lack of precise scientific language. Why, then, is this observation important enough to get a grant of funds from the National Geographic Society? A comparison of paragraphs [22 and 23] with [18] might help.
6. Are there any indications that this narrative is other than a straight relation of sequential events?

Applications and Evaluation

1. If man can no longer be defined as the "toolmaking animal," how can he be defined? Write a brief definition of man that clearly distinguishes him from any other animal.
2. Should we preserve chimpanzees in their wild, natural environment? Why? Should we do the same for *all* beasts?
3. Is narrative the best rhetorical mode for a report of a scientific discovery? Can you think of any other such narratives? Take a section of this narrative (suggested: paragraphs [19, 20, and 21] and rewrite it as a straight report. Does it gain or lose?
4. As late as 1965 the *World Book Encyclopedia* (Vol. 3, p. 374) stated that the diet of chimpanzees is "fruit, leaves, and sometimes . . . insects." Speculate on how much of the present information in encyclopedias is inaccurate.
5. The author observed one band of chimpanzees very thoroughly for over a dozen years. Are her conclusions valid for all chimpanzees everywhere? Is it possible that this is a unique group? How much of our knowledge is based on a limited sample? An interesting essay could be written on the topic: "How We Know What We Know Is True."

Helen Gurley Brown (19 –) attended Texas State College for Women and Woodbury College. She has worked at various jobs in the business world, some of which she details in this selection. More recently she has become the editor-in-chief of *Cosmopolitan* magazine and changed its style and format. Her first book, *Sex and the Single Girl,* was so popular (it was even made into a film) that she has revised it and updated it in *Sex and the New Single Girl,* from which this selection is a chapter.

Sex and the New Single Girl

From Nine to Five

The biographies of large numbers of successful women reveal that they have arrived at their careers by three methods:

(1) Vision; (2) Gravitation; and (3) Accident. [1]

Many successful women heard Joan of Arc voices early in life.

Never deviating from what the voices told them to do, they nurtured, babied, watered, fed and hatched their dream into an adult career. Most of them became architects, doctors, lawyers, astronomers, actresses, writers, bacteriologists, paleontologists, ballerinas—in short, the "I've got a vision" group were attracted to the demanding arts and professions. [2]

Madelyn Martin, co-author of the "I Love Lucy" television show, is a good example. From age ten, when her prize-winning poem "Sunset" was read aloud to the sixth-grade, Madelyn was determined to become a writer. She never faltered in the pursuit of her goal and she reached it. [3]

The gravitators are equally ambitious but not so inner-directed to a specific goal. From pigtail time these determined lasses work hard. They make A's, become student-body wheels, class valedictorians and the instant darlings of management. There is never much question they will arrive. It's just a matter of their gravitating to the work they were meant to do. Thousands of top-flight women business executives arrived through gravitation. [4]

Motion picture and TV producer Joan Harrison is one. A graduate of St. Hughes College of Oxford University, she was brought from London to Hollywood by Alfred Hitchcock to be his secretary. Though an eager beaver, Joan never dreamed she would one day produce the chills that ran up America's back every Tuesday when Alfred Hitchcock Presents was seen by millions of viewers. Joan was a relatively early example of gravitation (mid-fifties). Today thousands more girls have become successful, some even famous, through this same method. [5]

Half the country's male tycoons didn't know as office boys exactly what course *their* careers would take either. They did not so much plot their way to the summit as just arrange to their advantage whatever happened to them! [6]

The third group—accidental successes—are no less impressive than the visionaries and gravitators. These are the girls on whom a career just sort of fell. [7]

Swimsuit wizardess Rose Marie Reid made it somewhat by "accident." As a young girl in love with a lifeguard, Rose Marie spent every possible moment at the beach. She hated the shapeless shifts that passed for swimsuits, wouldn't wear them, designed and made her own suits instead. These svelte, form-fitting sheaths raised eyebrows as well as female spirits and male hopes. One day the owner of a department store asked Rose Marie if she would whip up a few of her designs for him. She was off and running at the success steeplechase. [8]

Like Elizabeth Barrett Browning, who might never have had a chance to be a grande amoureuse if Robert Browning hadn't happened to her, the nonplanning career whizzes never realized *they* had it either until some wise, wonderful or libidinous employer got it out of them. Then they seem to have one thing in common with the planners and gravitators . . . drive. Their drive is latent, but once liberated, it makes them the greatest stretch runners of all time. [9]

We are not so concerned here with career women who planned ahead. Chances are they are already nearing the launching pad. We are more interested in making you accident-prone in the right way and getting you into orbit if you aren't already. [10]

These accidents are not quite so accidental as they seem. Rose Marie Reid did have the initiative to make swimsuits at home—and the imagination to make them beautiful. [11]

The "accidental successes" usually help luck along by creating a favorable atmosphere around themselves. They are charming, pretty, fresh, alert, obedient and possessors of other Girl Scout virtues that attract opportunity. [12]

I believe thousands more girls could be "accident-prone" and have careers if they were to give fate ever so small a boost. And I mean girls who started late and may not have any idea they have talent. [13]

To spur you to action I ask you to project next Memorial Day. Could that be you at the washbasin with the Lux flakes doing your undies one more year because no one asked you to a picnic? Does the possibility lurk that next New Year's Eve will find you sipping eggnogs with your landlady? The bottom has been known to drop out for perfectly charming and popular single women on these grisliest days of the year. Think how much easier to bear if you have a really intriguing job to return to next morning and enough money to buy yourself a Ferrari to race around in and forget. [14]

I hereby set down Mother Brown's Twelve Rules for Squirming, Worming, Inching, and Pinching Your Way to the Top. They apply specifically to girls who work in offices (the only places I've ever worked) and presuppose you have a boss. Hopefully you might adapt some of them to retailing, door-to-door selling or whatever you do for a living. [15]

1. DON'T DEMAND INSTANT GLAMOUR

Just what are you putting up in return for the fascinating stream of callers, the luncheons at 21, your name on the masthead, trips to faraway places and tubs of money which you require in your first assignment after graduation? . . .

Keep your shirt on! Give yourself time to get useful before you get difficult. [16]

2. IN SWITCHING FIELDS PLAN FOR A TEMPORARY LOSS IN SALARY AND PRESTIGE

The important thing is to get *into* the coveted new firm [17]

An aircraft factory bookkeeper who wants a career in fashion may have to start as a department store salesgirl for *no* money, move into the gown shop, then to assistant buyer's job, to buyer, and finally fashion coordinator for several departments. A legal secretary on the same mission may plummet from her $600-a-month salary to $325 to start as secretary to the fashion coordinator. (Secretaries have a wonderful entree into almost any business. Jumping from girl Friday to girl executive is the hurdle. Read rules 3 through 12.) [18]

Most companies get nervous when you come to them with vast experience in one field, but you're twitching to switch! Make it easy for them to take you. When being interviewed for totally unfamiliar work, don't chat too much about your ultimate ambitions. You've obviously talked them over with advisers who think you can make good. Just get *in*. Insist you won't be a malcontent in the menial job that's open. Save up money like mad beforehand, so you can subsidize yourself for a year of two. [19]

3. GIVE YOURSELF FIVE YEARS TO DRY BEHIND THE EARS

Don't commit hari-kari if you're a slow starter. I held seventeen jobs (that's all I can count up now, but I think there were more) before "falling" into the secretarial job that led to copywriting that led to the fun and the money. (Eleven years ago I became Los Angeles' highest-paid advertising woman, though some other people have probably caught up by now.) [20]

Child labor deserves a chance to mature! You need a few years to put boys first, to goof (my specialty was poison ivy. I would "come down" with it on Sunday and be unable to report to work until Wednesday, plastered with Mercurochrome and milk of magnesia to "hide the infected areas") and try on different jobs. A lot of just plain luck is involved in getting into scoring position with *the* boss in *the* company. Of course if you keep spelling better and typing faster in some of your less exalted positions, your chance to score may come sooner. [21]

4. TRY TO WORK FOR A BENEVOLENT MANAGEMENT

Some companies are still so narrow, mean and stuffy, particularly regarding women, that Elizabeth Cady Stanton couldn't have cracked them. A personnel manager I know gives un-pep talks to all girl pob applicants to discourage them from ever trying to hold even minor executive posts. A chat with Old Ironsides and you're ready to will your corneas to the eye bank. [22]

You'll never do all you're capable of doing until somebody fans you and loves you and appreciates you into it! . . . [23]

If you are working for toads, drain all the experience you can from the pond and move to a new one. Don't be a scaredy-cat. Be sure *you* aren't the toad who's holding you back, however. [24]

5. WORK FOR SOMEBODY RUNGS ABOVE YOU

The more brilliant the boss, the more you will have to reach and stretch and use all your faculties to keep up with him or her. Elizabeth Orndufff (one of the early lady business whizzes in Los Angeles), vice president of I. Magnin Stores, credited her success with "always having had the luck to work for brilliant bosses." [25]

You don't usually start with one. If you did, you might not be ready for him. Usually you have to work your way through some toads. Shiny bright junior executives are the worst. They're afraid to send you to the accounting department to cash their expense check for fear you'll pick flowers on the way. Poor things have to have secretaries, but try to work them off during *your* junior years, too. . . . [26]

6. DRESS BETTER THAN YOU CAN AFFORD

Rumpsprung gabardine skirts with nondescript paisley blouses do not *guarantee* failure, but it's a fact bosses love to have chic, sleek cats around to show off to company. [27]

Do put everything on your back (or almost) for a promising job. Time enough to trade down to $12.95 shirtwaists when you're married and laundromatting or living on social security. I know one forty-five-year-old woman who landed a job as wardrobe selector for a network television show on the strength of her beautiful personal wardrobe. [28]

7. BE A WOMAN

We owe the "battle-axes" of another era more than we can ever pay. They had to be hard as nails and drive themselves *in* like nails too to compete with men. Not you, magnolia blossom! The charm that brings him to your side after five will enlist him in your behalf at the six-months' salary review. [29]

Publishing and advertising are both wonderful fields for women because you are paid handsomely *not* to think like a man. However, a company that deals in Geiger counters or paper-milling equipment can reap the benefits of women's business acumen as well as those selling products with purely woman-appeal. [30]

8. DON'T BE A PILL

Was it you who told the switchboard where Iris really was the afternoon she was supposed to be at the dentist's? Was the last time you worked overtime without pay when you put up prom decorations in the high school gym? Do you manage to be frantically busy (writing a letter to your cousin) when a co-worker is stuck with a mimeograph assembly job? So don't be a Girl Scout, but I have never ever seen a genuine 102 percent whiner-skirker-pill get anywhere. [31]

9. LEARN THE FACTS ABOUT RAISES

It is up to a company to pay you as little as it can and still get you to stay (any company that makes a profit, that is). It is not in business to keep you contented like Elsie the Cow! . . . [32]

The only way I know to get a raise is to be so good they can't get anybody like you for the same money, or even slightly more, so they may as well give it to *you*. It may take six months while they check the vaults to be *certain* that extra twenty-five bucks isn't going to bankrupt the company. Stay on their tail! . . . [33]

10. IF YOU'RE AFRAID YOU'RE REALLY A SLUG, START THINGS

Plan a picnic with a friend, write a fan letter to an architect who's completed a great new house, enroll for contract bridge lessons, visit a bakery to see how pastries are made, take your aunt to lunch, make a batch of fudge brownies for the kids in the mailroom. No frontal attack on your job or yourself at this point (we'll *get* to them!). Just start minor creative gambits that will establish you in your own eyes as a woman of action. [34]

11. FINISH THE PROJECTS

If you don't finish them, it doesn't count! These are relatively painless projects, however, and take only low-grade will power. If you've promised your pal at the service station to bring him the picture from *Life* that looks like him, bring it. If you've promised yourself an entire Sunday in bed reading movie magazines and drinking hot chocolate, flake out! Make your personal life a history of started and completed projects if you want to be the kind of person a career can happen to. There *is* a connection. [35]

12. WHEN YOU GET IN SCORING POSITION, DO EVERYTHING YOU CAN

This takes straight high-grade will power. When you get with the right boss in the right company and figure this must be the place, pull out all the stops. *Do* take your shirt off. If there's work you could finish at home and impress the hell out of somebody at 9 A.M. next morning, take it home! If your fat little tummy should have been lopped off two years ago, lop it off. [36]

Read, read, read. People have parlayed an ability to quote statistics at meetings into general managerships. (And I think some of them fitted the statistics to the need; they were never the same twice!) If your boss owns stock, check the market quotations, so you can chart *his* highs and lows. If he's for Beethoven, you're for Beethoven, Brahms and Mahler. Report your evenings at the concert. [37]

If he likes his wife, *you* like his wife. If he hates his wife, you *like* his wife. (This will establish you as a saint.) Learn to run the projector so that when the hired projectionist has his coronary at the switches, you can be rushed in. Empty ash trays. Sharpen pencils. (Or the equivalent, if you aren't an office employee. Remember, you must translate these instructions to your own environment.) At this crucial stage you must do *everything you can.* [38]

When I got the job as secretary to the ad man who later let me write copy, it was the first good job I'd ever had. I was so over my head I had to pump water out of my ears at five-thirty. Ordinary run-of-the-mill fluffs I couldn't seem to avoid—leaving two pages out of his speech to a high school graduation class, sending him to a luncheon at the Beverly Hills Hotel that was really downtown at the Statler. Somebody even stole $100 from petty cash the first week I had charge of it. Not *me,* but it might as well have been for all the raised eyebrows. But sensing that this was the man and here was the place (he really was pretty impressive with his autographed pictures of U.S. Presidents and Cabinet members brocaded along the walls with his best campaigns for Purex Bleach and Breast O' Chicken Tuna), I just did the best I could. He was a madman about punctuality. When he walked into the office every morning twenty minutes before everybody else, I was at my desk ten minutes before *him*—uncombed, unbreakfasted and unconscious but *there.* (During the change-over from Daylight Saving Time at the end of October, the moon was still up when I left home.) No coffee breaks. No typing errors. I did everything over until it was perfect. I figure I used about two reams of paper a week the first year. All this saved me until I had time to become a good secretary. [39]

A friend preparing for an interview with the late David Selznick (who dictated like the runaway choo-choo in *The Great Train Robbery*) shut herself in her apartment for three days while her mother gave her dictation. She also scanned every book or play he had made a picture from, including the 954 pages of *Gone With the Wind.* She got the job; [40]

After you get used to being introduced as the mayor's secretary or the girl with the highest sales book in her department or the only woman who eats in the executive dining room, you'll wear it like mink and wonder what took you so long. [41]

A career is the greatest preparation for marriage. You are better organized, better able to cope with checkbooks, investments, insurance premiums, tradesmen, dinner parties and the mixing of a really dry manhattan. You know how to please men. If a few more rushing brides stopped rushing and worked for a few years, they might not find themselves so thoroughly bored at thirty. [42]

[1818 words, 42 paragraphs]

Henry David Thoreau (1817–1862) Harvard educated Henry Thoreau was a constant rebel against the intrusions of society upon individual freedom. He was equally hostile toward the ever more complex society that was evolving in the United States. Although he published but two books during his lifetime, *A Week on the Concord and the Merrimack Rivers* and *Walden,* his collected works—poetry, journals, speeches—bulk up to twenty volumes. The following narrative is taken from *Walden,* the chronicle of his two years spent living in a hut at Walden Pond near Concord. The title is his own for the second chapter.

Where I Lived, and What I Lived For

I went to the woods because I wished to live deliberately, to front only the essential facts of life, and see if I could not learn what it had to teach, and not, when I came to die, discover that I had not lived. I did not wish to live what was not life, living is so dear; nor did I wish to practise resignation, unless it was quite necessary. I wanted to live deep and suck out all the marrow of life, to live so sturdily and Spartan-like as to put to rout all that was not life, to cut a broad swath and shave close, to drive life into a corner, and reduce it to its lowest terms, and, if it proved to be mean, why then to get the whole and genuine meanness of it, and publish its meanness to the world; or if it were sublime, to know it by experience, and be able to give a true account of it in my next excursion. For most men, it appears to me, are in a strange uncertainty about it, whether it is of the devil or of God, and have *somewhat hastily* concluded that it is the chief end of man here to "glorify God and enjoy him forever." [1]

Still we live meanly, like ants; though the fable tells us that we were long ago changed into men; like pygmies we fight with cranes; it is error upon error, and clout upon clout, and our best virtue has for its occasion a superfluous and evitable wretchedness. Our life is frittered away by detail. An honest man has hardly need to count more than his ten fingers, or in extreme cases he may add his ten toes, and lump the rest. Simplicity, simplicity, simplicity! I say, let your affairs be as two or three, and not a hundred or a thousand; instead of a million count half a dozen, and keep your accounts on your thumb-nail. In the midst of this chopping sea of civilized life, such are the clouds and storms and quicksands and thousand-and-one items to be allowed for, that a man has to live, if he would not founder and go to the bottom and not make his port at all, by dead reckoning, and he must be a great calculator indeed who succeeds. Simplify, simplify. Instead of three meals a day, if it be necessary eat but one; instead of a hundred dishes, five; and reduce other things in proportion. Our life is like a German Confederacy, made up of petty states, with its boundary forever fluctuating, so that even a German cannot tell you how it is bounded at any moment. The nation itself, with all its so-called internal improvements, which, by the way are all external and superficial, is just such an unwieldy and overgrown establishment, cluttered with furniture and tripped up by its own traps, ruined by luxury and heedless expense, by want of calculation and a worthy aim, as the million households in the lands; and the only cure for it, as for them, is in a rigid economy, a stern and more than Spartan simplicity of life and elevation of purpose. It lives too fast. Men think that it is essential that the *Nation* have commerce, and export ice, and talk through a telegraph, and ride thirty miles an hour, without a doubt, whether *they* do or not; but whether we should live like baboons or like men, is a little uncertain. If we do not get out sleepers, and forge rails, and devote days and nights to the work, but go to tinkering upon our *lives* to improve *them,* who will build railroads? And if railroads are not built, how shall we get to heaven in season? But if we stay at home and mind our business, who will want railroads? We do not ride on the railroad; it rides upon us. Did you ever think what those sleepers are that underlie the railroad? Each one is a man, an Irishman, or a Yankee man. The rails are laid on them, and they are covered with sand, and the cars run smoothly over them. They are sound sleepers, I assure you. And every few years a new lot is laid down and run over; so that, if some have the pleasure of riding on a rail, others have the misfortune to be ridden upon. And when they run over a man that is walking in his sleep, a supernumerary sleeper in the wrong position, and wake him up, they suddenly stop the cars, and make a hue and cry about it, as if this were an exception. I am glad to know that it takes a gang of men for every five miles to keep the sleepers down and level in their beds as it is, for this is a sign that they may sometimes get up again. [2]

Why should we live with such hurry and waste of life? We are determined to be starved before we are hungry. Men say that a stitch in time saves nine, and so they take a thousand stitches to-day to save nine to-morrow. As for *work*, we haven't any of any consequence. We have the Saint Vitus' dance, and cannot possibly keep our heads still. If I should only give a few pulls at the parish bell-rope, as for a fire, that is, without setting the bell, there is hardly a man on his farm in the outskirts of Concord, notwithstanding that press of engagements which was his excuse so many times this morning, nor a boy, nor a woman. I might almost say, but would foresake all and follow that sound, not mainly to save property from the flames, but, if we will confess the truth, much more to see it burn, since burn it must, and we, be it known, did not set it on fire,—or to see it put out, and have a hand in it, if that is done as handsomely; yes, even if it were the parish church itself. Hardly a man takes a half-hour's nap after dinner, but when he wakes he holds up his head and asks, "What's the news?" as if the rest of mankind had stood his sentinels. Some give directions to be waked every half-hour, doubtless for no other purpose; and then, to pay for it, they tell what they have dreamed. After a night's sleep the news is as indispensable as the breakfast. "Pray tell me anything new that has happened to a man anywhere on this globe,"—and he reads it over his coffee and rolls, that a man has had his eyes gouged out this morning on the Wachito River; never dreaming while that he lives in the dark unfathomed mammoth cave of this world, and has but the rudiment of an eye himself. [3]

For my part, I could easily do without the post-office. I think that there are very few important communications made through it. To speak critically, I never received more than one or two letters in my life—I wrote this some years ago—that were worth the postage. The penny-post is, commonly, an institution through which you seriously offer a man that penny for his thoughts which is so often safely offered in jest. And I am sure that I never read any memorable news in a newspaper. If we read of one man robbed, or murdered, or killed by accident, or one house burned, or one vessel wrecked, or one steamboat blown up, or one cow run over on the Western Railroad, or one dog killed, or one lot of grasshoppers in the winter,—we never need read of another. One is enough. If you are acquainted with the principle, what do you care for a myriad instances and applications? To a philosopher all *news*, as it is called, is gossip, and they who edit and read it are old women over their tea. Yet not a few are greedy after this gossip. There was such a rush, as I hear, the other day at one of the offices to learn the foreign news by the last arrival, that several large squares of plate glass belonging to the establishment were broken by the pressure,—news which I seriously think a ready wit might write a twelvemonth, or twelve years, beforehand with sufficient accuracy. As for Spain, for instance, if you know how to throw in Don Carlos and the Infanta, and Don Pedro and Seville and Granada, from time to time in the right proportions,—they may have changed the names a little since I saw the papers,—and serve up a bull-fight when other entertainments fail, it will be true to the letter, and give us as good an idea of the exact state or ruin in Spain as the most succinct and lucid reports under this head in the newspapers: and as for England, almost the last significant scrap of news from that quarter was the revolution of 1649; and if you have learned the history of her crops for an average year, you never need attend to that thing again, unless your speculations are of a merely pecuniary character. If one may judge who rarely looks into the newspapers, nothing new does ever happen in foreign parts, a French revolution not excepted. [4]

Shams and delusions are esteemed for soundless truths, while reality is fabulous. If men would steadily observe realities only, and not allow themselves to be deluded, life, to compare it with such things as we know, would be like a fairy tale and the Arabian Nights' Entertainments. If we respected only what is inevitable and has a right to be, music and poetry would resound along the streets. When we are unhurried and wise, we perceive that only great and worthy things have any permanent and absolute existence, that petty fears and petty pleasures are but the shadow of the reality. This is always exhilarating and sublime. By closing the eyes and slumbering, and consenting to be deceived by shows, men establish and confirm their daily life of routine and habit everywhere, which still is built on purely illusory foundations. Children, who play life, discern its true law and relations more clearly than men, who fail to live it worthily, but who think that they are wiser by experience, that is, by failure. [5]

Let us spend one day as deliberately as Nature, and not be thrown off the track by every nutshell and mosquito's wing that falls on the rails. Let us rise early and fast, or breakfast, gently and without perturbation; let company come and let company go, let the bells ring and the children cry,—determined to make a day of it. Why should we knock under and go with the stream? Let us not be upset and overwhelmed in that terrible rapid and whirlpool called a dinner, situated in the meridian shallows. Weather this danger and you are safe, for the rest of the way is down hill. With unrelaxed nerves, with morning vigor, sail by it, looking another way, tied to the mast like Ulysses. If the engine whistles, let it whistle till it is hoarse for its pains. If the bell rings, why should we run? We will consider what kind of music they are like. Let us settle ourselves, and work and wedge our feet downward through the mud and slush of opinion, and prejudice, and tradition, and delusion, and appearance, that alluvion which covers the globe, through Paris and London, through New York and Boston and Concord, through Church and State, through poetry and philosophy and religion, till we come to a hard bottom and rocks in place, which we can call *reality*, and say, This is, and no mistake; and then begin, having a *point d'appui*, below freshet and frost and fire, a place where you might found a wall or a state, or set a lamp-post safely, or perhaps a gauge, not a Nilometer, but a Realometer, that future ages might know how deep a freshet of shams and appearances had gathered from time to time. If you stand right fronting and face to face to a fact, you will see the sun glimmer on both its surfaces, as if it were a cimeter, and feel its sweet edge dividing you through the heart and marrow, and so you will happily conclude your mortal career. Be it life or death, we crave only reality. If we are really dying, let us hear the rattle in our throats and feel cold in the extremities; if we are alive, let us go about our business. [6]

Time is but the stream I go a-fishing in. I drink at it; but while I drink I see the sandy bottom and detect how shallow it is. Its thin current slides away, but eternity remains. I would drink deeper; fish in the sky, whose bottom is pebbly with stars. I cannot count one. I know not the first letter of the alphabet. I have always been regretting that I was not as wise as the day I was born. The intellect is a cleaver; it discerns and rifts its way into the secret of things. I do not wish to be any more busy with my hands than is necessary. My head is hands and feet. I feel all my best faculties concentrated in it. My instinct tells me that my head is an organ for burrowing, as some creatures use their snout and fore paws, and with it I would mine and burrow by way through these hills. I think that the richest vein is somewhere hereabouts; so by the divining-rod and thin rising vapors I judge; and here I will begin to mine. [7]

[2260 words, 7 paragraphs]

Writing Suggestions for Narration

First, review the general material under **Paragraph** in the Glossary. Note how the **narrative pattern** can be applied to paragraph, essay, or—by using chapters instead of paragraphs—to a longer work such as a pamphlet or a book.

The Narrative Pattern

THE PARAGRAPH	THE ESSAY
1. Introductory sentence (main point in flash-back)	1. First paragraph introduces, gives reasons for narrative, may foreshadow.
2. First event	2. Next brief paragraph may set scene, give first event.
3. Second event	3. Sequence of events continued.
4. Subsequent event	4. Next highlight given.
5. And so on, as necessary	5. As many paragraphs used as are needed to finish.
6. Final event	6. Final or climactic event given.
7. Moral or application (an optional element)	7. Moral stated or point made.

Be aware that the short story or fictional narrative pattern is somewhat different, for it sets a scene, introduces characters, presents a problem, and then shows the development and solution, usually at a climax.

Selected Topics for Narration

1. Write a simple chronological, or stey-by-step, narrative showing how you got involved in a cause, a club, an action of some kind.
2. Try the reverse: starting with a statement of the involvement or action—participating in a demonstration, taking a carload of children to an event—and show by **flashback** how you got involved.
3. Use a short narration of a traffic tie-up or an automobile accident to show the need for better highway planning or traffic safety programs.
4. Tell a narrative showing inept performance at a sport—surfing, skiing, riding, cycling, for example—and let the narrative show that preparation is necessary if a sport is to be enjoyed.
5. Try to use a brief narration to show your reaction during a moment of stress, physical or emotional. Let *what* you did relate the emotion; do not pile adjective on adjective.
6. Show a prevalent **mood** by relating a sequence of events at a party.
7. Try for a different **mood** by giving the events at a wedding, a funeral, a sporting event where the team you root for is losing (or winning).
8. Try, through a careful selection of events, to capture the **tone** at a haughty department store or fancy restaurant. Dialogue may be necessary here.
9. Through relation of their actions, show how a group of people respond to an individual. To an outré event.
10. Try to write a simple narration that can also be an **allegory.** The easiest category is education; the next easiest is politics.
11. Use an **anecdotal** narration as support for an argument. Prove why your favorite brand is best, for example.
12. Try to write a **myth** explaining an American folkway such as keeping pets, Sunday picnics, summer vacations, neckties.

description

"Tell me about the trip. What was the Grand Canyon like?" "What was the new man like?" "How does this differ from last year's model?" "Can you describe the man?" We use **description** more often than we realize in everyday communication, both by itself and in combination with the other rhetorical modes of narration, exposition, and argumentation. Although the sage Confucius is reported to have claimed that one picture is worth ten thousand words, there are instances when a hundred well-chosen words are far superior to any picture. To use description effectively, we should study the two main types,

realistic and **impressionistic**, and note some of the ways in which they work.

A photograph is usually realistic; the realistic type of description shows the impression of reality on our senses. We try to tell what an object or an event was like, the color, the texture, the size, the smell, the sound, or taste. We observe as well as we can and relate our observations. These observations may be highly objective:

> One male human, age 20 years and 2 months, 1.8 meters tall, 73 kilograms weight, eyes brown, hair brown, no distinguishing marks.

A painting, especially more modern ones, may be nonrealistic or impressionistic; the impressionistic description filters reality through our social and personal biases. The object outside may be the same, but the selection of details tends to differ as does the emphasis:

> Nice looking young man about five feet eleven, average weight, even white teeth and a friendly smile, neatly combed brown hair, and large intelligent brown eyes.

It is clearly possible to go to extremes and describe what is happening within and not what has happened without:

> I saw this guy and he was a real fox; long, neat hair and real neat eyes, and wearing an outasight shirt, and really foxy.

We must distinguish carefully between realistic and impressionistic description, especially the highly subjective one. Both are valid; one is valid as a report of an external event; the other is equally valid as a report of what is going on inside. Just remember that most descriptions contain some of each. It is in the interpretation of reports and in the description of emotions, impressions, and sensations that description can go beyond the Chinese sage's ten thousand words.

It would be possible to observe enough detail in one minute to describe for one hour. (Doubters, try to tell *all* about the chair you are sitting in. Describe the wood, the grain, the methods of construction, and so on, and so on.) It could take pages. Some technical reports do go into such detail; they do take pages. Most of them are dull and sometimes useless. Usually we present the *dominant impression* and support it with selected details. If we are describing a thing unknown, we often explain by comparing it to a familiar item. Description, then, becomes the cause for **metaphor** and **simile**. "What did it sound like?" "How big was it?" "How ugly was he?" All such questions readily lead to **figurative language.** (They also lead to the often sprightly kind of humor that has kept comedians performing for many years.) It seems to be an automatic tendency for us to place items in a **class** and to compare them with other items in that class.

The readings in this section emphasize description, although they use the other modes of rhetoric. The first two, "New Directions in Sports" and "Flight or Fight?" show how careful observation of data that has been available for years can lead to new insights about man and his world. The third, by Mark Twain, notes—with typical sardonic wit—how inept interpretation of valid data can lead us into error. The next three show us how an accurate description can aid understanding. Note that the Indian view of anthropologists may be highly impressionistic. "The Voices of Time" help us to understand behavior we have known all our lives, and the selection by R. Kirsch helps us to evaluate Skinner's book. The final trio offer examples of **classifying** Hobbits, medieval beasts, and reclassifying some language concepts.

Stuart Miller (1937–   ), the author of this selection, is a professor of comparative literature, having taught at Rutgers and The University of California at Berkeley. He has published many articles and essays and has been a consultant with the United States Office of Education in addition to his work with Esalen.
Esalen Institute (1962–   ) The Esalen Institute was founded to explore behavioral science, philosophy, and religion to find how man can increase his potential as a human being. Located on the coast at Big Sur, California, it has gained wide renown by its work on creativity, perceptual awareness, and encounter groups. Michael Murphy, a co-founder, is president. The name is from an Indian tribe that used to dwell in the vicinity.

New Directions in Sports

It is a cool but sunny morning in West Virginia, and a class of 13-year-olds, girls and boys, stands under the high shadow of a chinning bar that threatens them like a guillotine. The physical education instructor stands beside the group, his clipboard stiff in hand, his whistle a silver gleam on his chest. "Babcock, go up to the bar." Babcock is a fat kid, the necessary blimp in any group of children. "I can't do it," Babcock pleads. "Try!" insists the voice from the T-shirt. [1]

The story is told by George Leonard, author of *The Transformation,* who as a writer about education has witnessed and catalogued various horrors perpetrated in the name of learning. There are many of us who were not fat kids, I suspect, but we remember our own scenes of humiliation because, whether at basketball or football or track, whether in intramural, little league or intercollegiate games, we didn't measure up. We might even have been "good" but not quite "good enough." My own athletic performance was such that, after some years of struggling, I just gave up. The criticisms about contemporary athletics have come up many times: the emphasis on competition, on performance, on technical excellence, on beating the next guy. The result is that we become increasingly, not a nation of sportsmen and women, but a nation of spectators. [2]

Viewed in the narrowest terms of teaching Americans to keep fit, the sports and physical education establishment is a dreadful failure. Examining it more closely and in a more human way, we see at nation of people turned off to their bodies. Even for those who do measure up athletically, the results are doubtful. Studies of successful ahtletes show that past the age of 40 they end up in worse physical shape than their nonathletic counterparts: they put on more weight and they exercise less. And the correlation between high success in athletics and success in life is not impressive. [3]

Until recently, attacks on the established physical culture came from outside the centers of the athletic world: irate college presidents and disgruntled intellectuals. But recently the existing realities of sports have been scourged by an increasing number of successful athletes and sportswriters. The list of critical books is impressive: Jim Bouton's *Ball Four,* Dave Meggyesy's *Out of Their League,* Patsy Neal's *Sport and Identity,* Jack Scott's *The Athletic Revolution,* Harry Edwards' *The Revolt of the Black Athlete,* Bernie Parrish's *They Call It a Game,* David Wolf's *Foul* and Paul Hoch's *Rip Off the Big Game.* [4]

As one of those thoroughly disillusioned with sports, I would not ordinarily have known about these books, let alone read them, if it were not for my colleagues at Esalen Institute. To my deep astonishment, many of them retain an interest in organized sports and athletics along with their commitments to self-actualization and consciousness exploration. In recent months, a number of these colleagues have been reconsidering sports from a variety of viewpoints. But there is, as yet, no simple "Esalen Approach to Sports." The dialogue is very much unfinished and in process, nondogmatic and open. The dialogue also contains ambiguities; some of the most exciting new ideas present difficulties and even dangers. [5]

Such is the case with one area of discussion: using psychological techniques to increase sports performance. Coaches have always informally understood the value of the psychological dimension in winning: the common practice of "psyching up" players before a game is one example. Recently, however, some baseball coaches have systematically used psychological techniques of relaxation with their players. A number of football coaches have developed elaborate psychological profiles that pinpoint the personality of a good player (e.g., blocker: aggression, lack of empathy, etc.), and they use these tests to screen applicants. [6]

Perhaps the most dramatic example of psychologizing sports with the limited aim of increasing performance is the work of Lee Pulos, an assistant professor in the psychiatry department at the University of British Columbia. For a period of years Pulos has used a variety of psychological techniques in combination with hypnosis to try to improve the performance of the Canadian Women's National Volleyball Team. Many of us, however, are uncertain about using such techniques in the mere pursuit of winning. Some years ago, as Pulos tells it, the Canadian Women's Volleyball Team met the American team in Honolulu. When the Canadian women walked on the court, they were startled to find their American opponents handing them voodoo dolls. Perhaps the Americans were simply trying to psyche out their opponents in the informal and time-honored manner. But the incident also indicates a collective resistance to the psychotechnologizing of games, the total rationalization of the human beings involved and the introduction of mind-control techniques into something that is supposed to be play. The American ladies, in equating hypnosis, imaginative training, suggestion, etc., with voodoo, may have been warning of a potential for the perversion of sport. [7]

Another area of discussion at Esalen—broadening the perspectives of physical education as it is frequently taught in schools and colleges—is less problematical. The discussion can best be understood by attending to the story of a lady I shall call Georgia Rickley. Following the birth of one of her children, she wanted to get back into shape, so she took a course in modern dance. As she puts it, "I discovered I had a body." Dance lessons led to lessons in expressive movement. Knowing her body, working on it and with it gradually, became a powerful way to more successful functioning. A podiatrist, for example, noticed a subtle genetic weakness in her feet and those of her daughters. He slipped corrective devices into their shoes. As he predicted, her whole attitude to life changed, because of the subtle changes in the way she stood. She had more energy and a firmer stance, in every sense. From such incidents, Georgia discovered that like most parents, she didn't really look at her children's bodies. So, she went to Hammer State College (again, the name is fictitious) to get a master's degree, planning to teach physical awareness as it relates to personal functioning and to teach it where it would really count, with children. [8]

What Georgia found at Hammer State was not physical education in this sense but rather an overriding and pervasive interest in the technical aspects of sport—the trajectory of the tennis ball, its spin under certain conditions, the correct weight of the racket for a particular arm. Despite intriguing course titles ("The Psychology of Physical Education," "The Social Foundations of Sports"), the real interest of most of her professors seemed to be training people to be as close to Olympic athletes as possible. [9]

Yet, as Georgia knows, a large number of techniques exist that are aimed not at sports performance but at the education of the body in general: *sensory awareness,* experiencing the body very carefully in a meditative attitude; *structural integration,* reviving through manipulation the natural and energetic alignment of the body with gravity; *structural patterning,* studying "preferences" in movement and noting, for example, the enormous cumulative energy wasted as, with each forward step, the left foot swings slightly outward to the side; *body relaxation,* learning an elementary method of physical survival and protection against psychogenic illness; and *expressive movement,* getting to know one's body in full motion. Taken together, such techniques and others hold the promise of a new physical culture with enormous implications for physical education programs. [10]

Furthermore, the notion that the body can be used as a vehicle for the education of the whole person is implicit in a number of these new approaches. It is also at the heart of a number of ancient and Asian disciplines: Tai chi chuan, the increasingly popular meditation-in-movement, originally developed in China; aikido, the modern Japanese martial art that develops from older disciplines like judo but emphasizes centering oneself and becoming aware of physical energy in and outside of oneself; hatha yoga, considered in India as a basic preparation on the path toward the highest. In the West as well, the original intention of athletics was not simply the development of the body. As Socrates said, "The purpose of physical exercise and games is the development of the soul." The Latin notion of "a sound mind in a sound body" also saw the two as interdependent. [11]

Today, many sports do require a kind of integration of the body with emotions and mind. Certainly athletes must *think* and think fast, and they must back up their decisions with emotional conviction, as when a football player finds a hole in the line and pushes his way through it. There is a kind of glow or radiance that successful athletes give off that seems more than physical and that may, perhaps, be the felt emanation of endless practice at integrating mind, body and emotions. But this integration is frequently narrow and limited, so that despite the glow, these men and women fail to correspond to the ancient notion of the well-developed whole person. [12]

Particular sports appear to help or hinder this basic integration. Monotonously rhythmic sports like long distance bicycling, running or swimming help build up the body and teach detachment of the mind from the body in the interest of endurance and rhythmic performance. They may not, however, be integrative in any general way. Mountain climbing, on the other hand, requires instantaneous sensory awareness as well as continually renewed decisiveness and planning. Here, then, more active will and mind may be needed. [13]

Perhaps the biggest task is to study particular sports with the aim of determining just what psychological qualities and character traits each helps to develop. How do different sports affect different people at different times in their personal development? Which sports develop the will; which sports integrate a variety of qualities; what is the role of the mind in particular sports? Is it the mind in the intellectual sense or is it an instinctive, animal awareness that is actually developed in most sports? Which sports are good for whom, when and under what conditions? [14]

Conventional sports can be a powerful psychological searchlight, teaching the player about himself. This knowledge could be consciously used in the development of the whole personality and could become a major focus of sports. Then, instead of being an end in themselves, sports would be back in their rightful place as a means, along with many other human activities, to the full development of a person. [15]

Michael Murphy sounds this theme in *Golf in the Kingdom*, and he recently elaborated it in a conversion with me:

> If we look at life in the largest sense—the return of the human to the divine—then sport is potentially a *vehicle* for this return, because it builds essentially on delight and play, which are at the heart of the universe. Thus the end and means coincide. Today,

> there seems to be so much *work* involved in sports. Certainly we need commitment, thoroughness and wholeheartedness in sport, but there need be no forcing things, no work. [16]

Murphy goes on to propose a change of attitude toward sports. He sees value in sports, even their "negative" elements, because these elements are often symbols of difficult elements in life. Competition, for instance, exists in life, and it exists to be overcome as people evolve higher values. At the simplest level, this means transcending our own competitive drives in the spirit of the "sporting attitude": the thrill of competing, winning or losing, and embracing an opponent. Such acts can be taken as symbolic of the general struggle to reach beyond ourselves in the direction of a higher life. Right now, though, we have no vocabulary in sports for dealing with those transcendent moments when an athlete seems inspired and lifted beyond the possible into incredible feats. [17]

Bob Nadeau, a teacher of aikido and energy awareness, argues that real performance, in sports and in anything else, comes not from technique and intellect ("little mind") but making contact with what the Buddhists call "big mind." In football, for example, the quarterback must gauge distances, obstacles and so on. But if he consciously attempts to make his mind do that work, he is finished. It can't come from trying, Nadeau says, it must come from a letting go to some reality beyond one's little self. [18]

In sum, the game, whatever it is, can be played with or without consciousness of higher meanings. As Murphy puts it, "In a way, sports as they are practiced are like life as practiced: the transcendent moments are there, they happen, but we lose them like sparks in the wind because our attitude isn't right." [19]

The practical task then is how to bring about a harmonious integration of these new dimensions within the world of sports. Sports, with all its striving for technical excellence, may someday become what it ought to be—a means for self-realization. Someday, we may learn to hold the sparks in the wind. [20]

2020 words, 20 paragraphs

Diction

1. The author states that "the dialogue is very much . . . non-dogmatic and open" [4]. "Dialogue" means a conversation between two persons; what is he talking about?

2. Does the use of such **colloquialisms** as "fat kid" [2], "turned off" [3], and "psyche out" [6] add to or detract from the essay?
3. Do the oriental terms in paragraph [10] need further definition? Can they be found in the dictionary?
4. Paragraph [9] uses some italicized terms to name various techniques of bodily education. Are they clear to you? What do you suppose is the source of these terms?
5. What is meant by self-realization [16]?
6. Among the many difficult words in this essay are the following for you to look up: ambiguities [4], emanation [11], empathy [5], implicit [10], intramural [2], nondogmatic (look up "dogmatic") [4], pervasive [8], podiatrist [7], psychotechnologizing [6], transcendent [15].

Rhetoric and Style

1. This essay seems to jump around from descriptions of experiences to quotations to lists of techniques. Can you see an overall organization? Try making an outline.
2. What evidence is there of the "glow" or "radiance" given off by a successful athlete? Do you know what the author means?
3. Paragraph (9) describes some techniques that are aimed at education of the body in general. Could you make use of them from the descriptions given in this essay?
4. Does the description of the experience of Georgia Rickley and her problem at college help to make the point that colleges do not teach physical education effectively? Do such passages generally aid understanding? Comment also on the passage about the volleyball team.
5. Are there any striking **figures of speech** in this selection?
6. The author suggests that training in physical education is badly given and should be used to train the whole person. How does the author solve the problem?

Application and Evaluation

1. Write a brief essay describing some event that happened to you in a physical education class and tell the result it had upon you (either beneficial or detrimental).
2. Ignoring all previous experience you might have had with physi-

cal education, are you convinced by Mr. Miller of his thesis? What is it? How did he convince you or did he fail to do so?

3. Speculate on some reasons other than the ones given for the great number of spectator sports in current society. Make a list of these reasons. Your instructor might ask you to develop an essay.
4. Should participation in physical education class in college be required? Why?
5. What are some of the dangers possible in this new direction sports might take? How could they be overcome?

Erich Fromm (1900–   ) Erich Fromm, a psychoanalyst educated at the University of Heidelberg, Germany, has been a lecturer and faculty member of a great many distinguished colleges and universities in Germany, Mexico, and the United States. He has written more than twenty books about man and his relationship to other men and to the world. He has been elected to most of the major societies in his field and has contributed many papers to learned journals. The following selection has been abstracted from his latest book, *The Anatomy of Human Destructiveness*. Dr. Fromm observes the same events that Ardrey and Lorenz do but from his observations describes a different behavior pattern.

Flight or Fight?

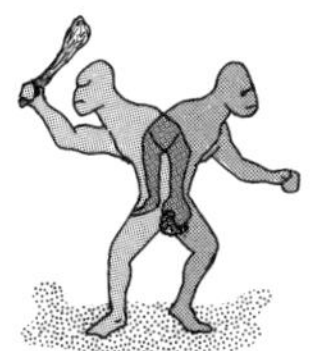

In reviewing both the neurophysiological and the psychological literature on animal and human aggression, the conclusion seems unavoidable that aggressive behavior of animals is a response to *any kind of threat to the survival* or, as I would prefer to say more generally, *to the vital interests of the animal*—whether as an individual or as a member of its species. This general definition comprises many different situations. The most obvious are a direct threat to the life of the individual or a threat to his requirements for sex and food; a more complex form is that of "crowding," which is a threat to the need for physical space and/or to the social structure of the group. But what is common to all conditions for the arousal of aggressive behavior is that they constitute a threat to vital interests. Mobilization of aggression in the corresponding brain areas occurs in the service of life, in response to threats to the survival of the individual or of the species; that is to say, *phylogenetically programmed aggression, as it exists in animals and man, is a biologically adaptive, defensive reaction.* That this should be so is not surprising if we remember the Darwinian principle in regard to the evolution of the brain. Since it is the function of the brain to take care of survival, it would provide for immediate reactions to any threat to survival. [1]

Aggression is by no means the only form of reaction to threats. The animal reacts to threats to his existence either with rage and attack or with fear and flight. In fact, flight seems to be the more frequent form of reaction, except when the animal has no chance to flee and therefore fights—as the *ultima ratio*. . . . [2]

Mark and Ervin summarize the present state of knowledge in the following paragraph:

> Any animal, regardless of its species, reacts to a life-threatening attack with one of two patterns of behavior: either with flight, or with aggression and violence—that is, fight. The brain always acts as a unit in directing any behavior; consequently, the mechanisms in the brain that initiate and limit these two dissimilar patterns of self-preservation are closely linked to one another; as well as to all other parts of the brain; and their proper functioning depends on the synchronization of many complex and delicately balanced subsystems. [3]

The data on fight and flight as defense reactions makes the instinctivistic theory of aggression appear in a peculiar light. The impulse to flee plays—neurophysiologically and behaviorally—the same if not a larger role in animal behavior than the impulse to fight. Neurophysiologically, both impulses are integrated in the same way; there is no basis for saying that aggression is more "natural" than flight. Why, then, do instinctivists talk about the intensity of the innate impulses of aggression, rather then about the innate impulse for flight? [4]

If one were to translate the reasoning of the instinctivists regarding the impulse for fight to that of flight one would arrive at this kind of statement: "Man is driven by an innate impulse to flee; he may try to control this impulse by his reason, yet this control will prove to be relatively inefficient, even though some means can be found that may serve to curb the power of the "flight instinct." [5]

Considering the emphasis that has been given to innate human aggression as one of the gravest problems of social life, from religious positions down to the scientific work of Lorenz, a theory centered around man's "uncontrollable flight instinct" may sound funny, but it is neurophysiologically as sound as that of "uncontrollable aggression." In fact, from a biological standpoint it would seem that flight serves self-preservation better than fight. To political or military leaders it may, in fact, not sound so funny, but rather sensible. They know from experience that man's nature does not seem to incline toward heroism and that many measures have to be taken to motivate man to fight and to prevent him from running away in order to save his life. [6]

The student of history may raise the question whether the instinct for flight has not proven to be at least as powerful a factor as that for fight. He may come to the conclusion that history has been determined not so much by instinctive aggression as by the attempt to suppress man's "flight instinct." He may speculate that a large part of man's social arrangements and ideological efforts have been devoted to this aim. Man had to be threatened with death to instill in him a feeling of awe for the superior wisdom of his leaders, to make him believe in the value of "honor." One tried to terrorize him with the fear of being called a coward or a traitor, or one simply got him drunk with liquor or with the hope of booty and women. Historical analysis might show that the repression of the flight impulse and the apparent dominance of the fight impulse is largely due to cultural rather than to biological factors. . . . [7]

HAS MAN AN INHIBITION AGAINST KILLING?

One of the most important points in the chain of Lorenz's explanations for human aggression is the hypothesis that man, in contrast to predatory animals, has not developed instinctive inhibitions against killing cospecifics; he explains this point by the assumption that man, like all nonpredatory animals, has no dangerous natural weapons like claws, etc., and hence does not need such inhibitions; it is only because he has weapons that his lack of instinctive inhibitions becomes so dangerous. [8]

But is it really true that man has no inhibitions against killing? [9]

Man's historical record is so frequently characterized by killing that at first it would seem unlikely that he has any inhibitions. However, this answer becomes questionable if we reformulate our question to read: Has man any inhibitions against killing living beings, humans, and animals with whom he identifies to a greater or lesser degree, i.e., who are not complete "strangers" to him and to whom he is related by affective bonds? [10]

There is some evidence that such inhibitions might exist and that a sense of guilt may follow the act of killing. [11]

That the element of familiarity and empathy plays a role in the generation of inhibitions against killing animals can easily be detected from reactions to be observed in everyday life. Many people show a definite aversion to killing and eating an animal with which they are familiar or one they have kept as a pet, like a rabbit or a goat. There are a large number of people who would not kill such an animal and to whom the idea of eating it is plainly repulsive. The same people usually have no hesitation in eating a similar animal where this element of empathy is lacking. But there is not only an inhibition against killing with regard to animals that are individually known, but also inasmuch as a sense of identity is felt with the animal as another living being. This seems to be indicated in our language. We use different words for flesh: if the animal is alive, we speak of its *flesh*; if the flesh is to be eaten, we call it *meat*. Quite clearly this differentiation is meant to remove the association between the animal one eats and the living animal. We even give different names to some animals depending on whether they are alive or to be eaten as food. When we speak of the live animal, we speak of cows and bulls; when we eat them, we talk about beef. Pigs to be eaten we call pork, deer we call venison, calf we call veal. While this is not true for all animals, these examples suffice to show the tendency to separate in our minds the categories of living animals from those we eat. All these data would indicate that there might be a conscious or unconscious feeling of guilt related to the destruction of life, especially when there is a certain empathy. This sense of closeness to the animal and need to reconcile oneself to killing it is quite dramatically manifested in the rituals of the bear cult of Paleolithic hunters. [12]

The sense of identity with all living beings that share with man the quality of *life* has been made explicit as an important moral tenet in Indian thinking and has led to the prohibition against killing any animal in Hinduism. [13]

It is not unlikely that inhibitions against killing also exist with regard to other humans, provided there is a sense of identity and empathy. We have to begin with the consideration that for primitive man the "stranger," the person who does not belong to the same group, is often not felt as a fellowman, but as "something" with which one does not identify. There is generally greater reluctance to kill a member of the same group, and the most severe punishment for misdeeds in primitive society often was ostracism, rather than death. (This is still apparent in the punishment of Cain in the Bible.) But we are not restricted to these examples of primitive society. Even in a highly civilized culture like the Greek, the slaves were experienced as not being entirely human. [14]

We find the same phenomenon in modern society. All governments try, in the case of war, to awaken among their own people the feeling that the enemy is not human. One does not call him by his proper name, but by a different one, as in the first World War when the Germans were called "Huns" by the British or "Boches" by the French. This destruction of the humanness of the enemy came to its peak with enemies of a different color. The war in Vietnam provided enough examples to indicate that many American soldiers had little sense of empathy with their Vietnamese opponents, calling them "gooks." Even the word "killing" is eliminated by using the word "wasting." Lieutenant Calley, accused and convicted for murdering a number of Vietnamese civilians, men, women, and children, in My Lai, used as an argument for his defense the consideration that he was not taught to look at the soldiers of the NLF ("Viet Cong") as human beings but only as "the enemy." Whether that is sufficient defense or not is not the question here. It is certainly a strong argument, because it is true and puts into words the underlying attitude toward the Vietnamese peasants. Hitler did the same by calling "political enemies" he wanted to destroy *Untermenschen* ("subhumans"). It seems almost a rule, when one wants to make it easier for one's own side to destroy living beings of the other, to indoctrinate one's own soldiers with a feeling that those to be slaughtered are nonpersons. [15]

Whenever another being is not experienced as human, the act of destructiveness and cruelty assumes a different quality. A simple example will show this. If a Hindu or a Buddhist, for instance, provided he has a genuine and deep feeling of empathy with all living beings, were to see the average modern person kill a fly without the slightest hesitation, he might judge this act as an expression of considerable callousness and destructiveness; but he would be wrong in this judgment. The point is that for many people the fly is simply not experienced as a sentient being and hence is treated as any disturbing "thing" would be; it is not that such people are especially cruel, even though their experience of "living beings" is restricted. [16]

Precisely because man has less instinctive equipment than any other animal, he does not recognize or identify cospecifics as easily as animals. For him different language, customs, dress, and other criteria perceived by the mind rather than by instincts determine who is a cospecific and who is not, and any group which is slightly different is not supposed to share in the same humanity. From this follows the paradox that man, precisely because he lacks instinctive equipment, also lacks the experience of the identity of his species and experiences the stranger as if he belonged to another species; in other words, *it is man's humanity that makes him so inhuman.* [17]

1900 words, 17 paragraphs

Diction

1. Although neither "cospecific" [8 and elsewhere] nor "ultima ratio" [2] are to be found in a standard desk dictionary, you should be able to infer their meaning from **context** and from root words.
2. Who is the Lieutenant Calley referred to in paragraph [15]? Is he a good **example** of the point Dr. Fromm is making?
3. Check both the exact meaning and the derivation, or original language source, of the pairs of words used in paragraph [12]: flesh/meat; cow/beef; pig/pork; deer/venison; calf/veal. Can you offer a theory other than the author's for why we have these pairs of words?
4. The author uses the term "instinctivists" in this selection, but it is not fully **defined**. What does it mean and what are its **connotations**?
5. Here are a few of the words you should be certain to look up: aversion [12], empathy [12], explicit [13], factors [7], inhibitions [8], innate [4], ostracism [14], paradox [17], sentient [16], vital [1].

Rhetoric and Style

1. What is the **rhetorical** function of the first three paragraphs?
2. Paragraph [5] is a rephrasing of the **thesis** of the instinctivists. What must their theory be? Comment on Dr. Fromm's device (using their own words); is it effective?
3. What is the major **emphasis** of this selection, and where is it placed?
4. Paragraph [7] is filled with **generalized** or **abstract** support. Can you think of one specific datum for any one of the generalities?

(Example: any one "social arrangement" that is devoted to suppressing man's "flight instinct.")

5. Please explain the concluding **paradox** [17].

Applications and Evaluation

1. What things will you not eat because of their **classification**? Are there any classes you do not eat that others do eat? A **cause and effect** essay on the subject would be interesting.
2. Can you think of any other times we reclassify something to change our feelings or reactions toward it? (**Euphemisms**?)
3. How is it possible for Ardrey or Lorenz (both have essays in this text) to observe the same creature and develop completely different descriptions from Dr. Fromm's?
4. Do you believe that man has any kind of instinct to flee, to fight, or to do anything?
5. Observe a simple process or a person performing a simple task. See if you can describe the process or act and then develop two **conclusions** that could, logically, account for that process or act. Write your result in an orderly essay (probably four paragraphs: *1.* the event, 2. one reason, 3. the "opposite" reason. 4. your conclusions/summary). Examples: Do small children hit instinctively? Why do children cry when disappointed? Is a smile an instinctive or a learned behavior? Consider why we shake hands, scratch our heads, frown.

Mark Twain (1835–1910) "Mark Twain" was the pen name of Samuel Langhorn Clemens. Both humorist and satirist, Twain is famous for *Tom Sawyer, Huckleberry Finn,* and *Life on the Mississippi.* A working writer or journalist all his life, he is the kind of writer to be read thrice, once foı fun (when the reader is a child), once for wit (when the reader is a student), and once for philosophy (when a reader is mature). This brief selection from *Life on the Mississippi,* a nearly factual account, shows how easy it can be to use a description and synthesize a humorous, false result.

Science!

Dry details are of importance in one particular. They give me an opportunity of introducing one of the Mississippi's oldest peculiarities—that of shortening its length from time to time. If you will throw a long, pliant apple-paring over your shoulder, it will pretty fairly shape itself into an average section of the Mississippi River; that is, the nine or ten hundred miles stretching from Cairo, Illinois, southward to New Orleans, the same being wonderfully crooked, with a brief straight bit here and there at wide intervals. The two-hundred-mile stretch from Cairo northward to St. Louis is by no means so crooked, that being a rocky country which the river cannot cut much. [1]

The water cuts the alluvial banks of the "lower" river into deep horseshoe curves; so deep, indeed, that in some places if you were to get ashore at one extremity of the horseshoe and walk across the neck, half or three-quarters of a mile, you could sit down and rest a couple of hours while your steamer was coming around the long elbow at a speed of ten miles an hour to take you on board again. When the river is rising fast, some scoundrel whose plantation is

From Chapter XVII in *Life on the Mississippi by Mark Twain* (Harper & Row).

back in the country, and therefore of inferior value, has only to watch his chance, cut a little gutter across the narrow neck of land some dark night, and turn the water into it, and in a wonderfully short time a miracle has happened: to wit, the whole Mississippi has taken possesison of that little ditch, and placed the countryman's plantation on its bank (quadrupling its value), and that other party's formerly valuable plantation finds itself away out yonder on a big island; the old watercourse around it will soon shoal up, boats cannot approach within ten miles of it, and down goes its value to a fourth of its former worth. Watches are kept on those narrow necks at needful times, and if a man happens to be caught cutting a ditch across them, the chances are all against his ever having another opportunity to cut a ditch. [2]

Pray observe some of the effects of this ditching business. Once there was a neck opposite Port Hudson, Louisiana, which was only half a mile across in its narrowest place. You could walk across there in fifteen minutes; but if you made the journey around the cape on a raft, you traveled thirty-five miles to accomplish the same thing. In 1722 the river darted through that neck, deserted its old bed, and thus shortened itself twenty-five miles at Black Hawk Point in 1699. Below Red River Landing, Raccourci cut-off was made (forty or fifty years ago, I think). This shortened the river twenty-eight miles. In our day, if you travel by river from the southernmost of these three cut-offs to the northernmost, you go only seventy miles. To do the same thing a hundred and seventy-six years ago, one had to go a hundred and fifty-eight miles—a shortening of eighty-eight miles in that trifling distance. At some forgotten time in the past, cutoffs were made above Vidalia, Louisiana, at Island 92, at Island 84, and at Hale's Point. These shortened the river, in the aggregate, seventy-seven miles. [3]

Since my own day on the Mississippi, cut-offs have been made at Hurricane Island, at Island 100, at Napoleon, Arkansas, at Walnut Bend, and at Council Bend. These shortened the river, in the aggregate, sixty-seven miles. In my own time a cut-off was made at American Bend, which shortened the river ten miles or more. [4]

Therefore the Mississippi between Cairo and New Orleans was twelve hundred and fifteen miles long one hundred and seventy-six years ago. It was eleven hundred and eighty after the cut-off of 1722. It was one thousand and forty after the American Bend cut-off. It has lost sixty-seven miles since. Consequently, its length is only nine hundred and seventy-three miles at present. [5]

Now, if I wanted to be one of those ponderous scientific people, and "let on" to prove what had occurred in the remote past by what had occurred in a given time in the recent past, or what will occur in the far future by what has occurred in late years, what an opportunity is here! Geology never had such a chance, nor such exact data to argue from! Nor "development of species," either! Glacial epochs are great things, but they are vague—vague. Please observe: [6]

In the space of one hundred and seventy-six years the Lower Mississippi has shortened itself two hundred and forty-two miles. That is an average of a trifle over one mile and a third per year. Therefore, any calm person, who is not blind or idiotic, can see that in the Old Oölitic Silurian Period, just a million years ago next November, the Lower Mississippi River was upward of one million three hundred thousand miles long, and stuck out over the Gulf of Mexico like a fishing-rod. And by the same token any person can see that seven hundred and forty-two years from now the Lower Mississippi will be only a mile and three-quarters long, and Cairo and New Orleans will have joined their streets together, and be plodding comfortably along under a single mayor and a mutual board of aldermen. There is something fascinating about science. One gets such wholesale returns of conjecture out of such a trifling investment of fact. [7]

835 words, 7 paragraphs

Diction

1. This section of *Life on the Mississippi* was first printed in 1874, about a hundred years ago; does the language seem old-fashioned or dated in any way?
2. What is the effect on the reader of the naming of the specific islands and bends (see paragraphs [2] and [3] especially).
3. Make an **inference** about the numbering of some of the islands. Why no names?
4. The author says the river is "*wonderfully* crooked" [1] and notes "a *wonderfully* short time" [2]. Why use *wonder*?
5. The following words are interesting enough to look up in a modern dictionary: aggregate [3], alderman [7], alluvial [2], cape [3], epoch [6], pliant [1], ponderous [6], quadruple [2], scoundrel [2], shoal [2].

Rhetoric and Style

1. What seems to be the author's **tone** toward the reader? What evidence is there?
2. Twain is renowned as a humorist; what passages are particularly humorous to you?
3. How does the author maintain **unity** in this brief segment of a longer chapter?
4. Are there any striking **figures of speech** in this passage?
5. Do you note any **dead metaphors?**
6. What is the **logical,** or geological, **fallacy** that permits the author's strange conclusions about data?

Applications and Evaluation

1. Is the author's poking fun at scientific prediction justified?
2. Try to compose a (mildly) humorous essay that takes some data and carries it to an extreme—increasing ratios of television sets per home or automobiles per family, for example.
3. Twain gets great **verisimilitude** because he observes so exactly. Describe a natural phenomenon with the precision that the author uses in his description of the shortening of the Mississippi. Use a natural element in your own locale.
4. Does an essay like this one, one hundred years old, have any real **didactic** value today? Could you develop a brief paragraph about the tendency of certain lessons to repeat themselves?
5. Is **hyperbole** as effective as more sober statement? Less effective? Why?

Vine Deloria, Jr. (1933–   ) Vine Deloria attended both Iowa State University and the Lutheran School of Theology but did not enter either the ministry or the teaching profession. He is a Standing Rock Sioux and has been the National Director of the National Congress of American Indians. Born in one culture, trained in another, he was highly qualified to write *Custer Died for Your Sins*, a most penetrating book from which the following selection is taken. The biting description of the anthropologists helps the white man to understand how the "victim" views the scientist.

Anthropologists

Into each life, it is said, some rain must fall. Some people have bad horoscopes, others take tips on the stock market. McNamara created the TFX and the Edsel. Churches possess the real world. But Indians have been cursed above all other people in history. Indians have anthropologists. [1]

Every summer when school is out a veritable stream of immigrants heads into Indian country. Indeed the Oregon Trail was never so heavily populated as are Route 66 and Highway 18 in the summer time. From every rock and cranny in the East *they* emerge, as if responding to some primeval fertility rite, and flock to the reservations. [2]

"They" are the anthropologists. Social anthropologists, historical anthropologists, political anthropologists, economic anthropologists, all brands of the species, embark on the great summer adventure. For purposes of this discussion we shall refer only to the generic name, anthropologists. They are the most prominent members of the scholarly community that infects the land of the free, and in the summer time, the homes of the braves. [3]

The origin of the anthropologist is a mystery hidden in the historical mists. Indians are certain that all societies of the Near East had anthropologists at one time because all those societies are now defunct. [4]

Indians are equally certain that Columbus brought anthropologists on his ships when he came to the New World. How else could he have made so many wrong deductions about where he was? [5]

While their historical precedent is uncertain, anthropologists can readily be identified on the reservations. Go into any crowd of people. Pick out a tall gaunt white man wearing Bermuda shorts, a World War II Army Air Force flying jacket, an Australian bush hat, tennis shoes, and packing a large knapsack incorrectly strapped on his back. He will invariably have a thin sexy wife with stringly hair, an IQ of 191, and a vocabulary in which even the prepositions have eleven syllables. [6]

He usually has a camera, tape recorder, telescope, hoola hoop, and life jacket all hanging from his elongated frame. He rarely has a pen, pencil, chisel, stylus, stick, paint brush, or instrument to record his observations. [7]

This creature is an anthropologist. [8]

An anthropologist comes out to Indian reservations to make OBSERVATIONS. During the winter these observations will become books by which future anthropologists will be trained, so that they can come out to reservations years from now and verify the observations they have studied. [9]

After the books are written, summaries of the books appear in the scholarly journals in the guise of articles. These articles "tell it like it is" and serve as a catalyst to inspire other anthropologists to make the great pilgrimage next summer. [10]

The summaries are then condensed for two purposes. Some condensations are sent to government agencies as reports justifying the previous summer's research. Others are sent to foundations in an effort to finance the next summer's expedition west. [11]

The reports are spread all around the government agencies and foundations all winter. The only problem is that no one has time to read them. So five-thousand-dollar-a-year secretaries are assigned to decode them. Since the secretaries cannot read complex theories, they reduce the reports to the best slogan possible and forget the reports. [12]

The slogans become conference themes in the early spring, when the anthropologist expeditions are being planned. The slogans turn into battle cries of opposing groups of anthropologists who chance to meet on the reservations the following summer. [13]

Each summer there is a new battle cry, which inspires new insights into the nature of the "Indian problem." One summer Indians will be greeted with the joyful cry of "Indians are bilingual!" The following summer this great truth will be expanded to "Indians are not only bilingual, THEY ARE BICULTURAL!" [14]

Biculturality creates great problems for the opposing anthropological camp. For two summers they have been bested in sloganeering and their funds are running low. So the opposing school of thought breaks into the clear faster than Gale Sayers playing against the little leaguers. "Indians," the losing "anthros" cry, "are a FOLK people!" The tide of battle turns and a balance, so dearly sought by Mother Nature, is finally achieved. [15]

Thus go the anthropological wars, testing whether this school or that school can endure longest. And the battlefields, unfortunately, are the lives of Indian people. [16]

You may be curious as to why the anthropologist never carries a writing instrument. He never makes a mark because he ALREADY KNOWS what he is going to find. He need not record anything except his daily expenses for the audit, for the anthro found his answer in the books he read the winter before. No, the anthropologist is only out on the reservations to VERIFY what he has suspected all along—Indians are a very quaint people who bear watching. [17]

The anthro is usually devoted to PURE RESEARCH. Pure research is a body of knowledge absolutely devoid of useful application and incapable of meaningful digestion. Pure research is an abstraction of scholarly suspicions concerning some obscure theory originally expounded in pre-Revolutionary days and systematically checked each summer since then. A 1969 thesis restating a proposition of 1773 complete with footnotes to all material published between 1773 and 1969 is pure research. [18]

There are, however, anthropologists who are not as clever at collecting footnotes. They depend upon their field observations and write long adventurous narratives in which their personal observations are used to verify their suspicions. Their reports, books, and articles are called APPLIED RESEARCH. The difference, then, between Pure and Applied research is primarily one of footnotes. Pure has many footnotes. Applied has few footnotes. Relevancy to subject matter is not discussed in polite company. [19]

Anthropologists came to Indian country only after the tribes had agreed to live on reservations and had given up their warlike ways. Had the tribes been given a choice of fighting the cavalry or the anthropologists, there is little doubt as to who they would have chosen. In a crisis situation men always attack the biggest threat to their existence. A warrior killed in battle could always go to the Happy Hunting Grounds. But where does an Indian laid low by an anthro go? To the library? [20]

1120 words, 20 paragraphs

Diction

1. The author uses precise **diction** to **satirize** anthropologists. See if you can find two instances. What kinds of words would be nonsatiric? See especially paragraphs [1], [2], and [3].
2. The opening line is a **cliché**. Why does the author use it when he clearly does not have to rely on such **trite** language?
3. Deloria **defines** terms to clarify his essay. Look again at his definition of "research" [18 and 19]. Does it seem to be accurate? It is clearly slanted, but is it invalid?
4. The author states that the anthropologists make "observations." He then traces the development of these observations. Show the eventual conclusion and the steps in between.
5. Are there really as many types of anthropologist as are listed in paragraph [3]? Just what is an anthropologist?
6. Here are some words that should be learned: audit [17], bilingual or bicultural [14], catalyst [10], defunct [4], generic [3], pilgrimage [10], precedent [6], primeval [2], quaint [17], verify [17].

Rhetoric and Style

1. The opening paragraph contains three topical **allusions**. What are they; to what do they refer; and are they effective still?
2. Give an example of the author's effective use of **hyperbole**.
3. Clearly, the **descriptions** are not realistic when the author describes the anthropologist and his wife. What kind of description are they?
4. There are some "verbal echoes" in this essay—phrases that bring to mind other written works. What is brought to mind by the following phrases?
   a. cursed above all other people in history [1]

b. the land of the free and, in summer, the homes of the braves [3]
c. testing whether this school or that school can endure longest [16]

Can you find and explain any others?

5. What elements of culture other than social science does the author **satirize?**
6. According to the author, what is the real function of the anthropologist? At what cost? [see paragraph 16]?
7. How does the author **unify** the essay?

Applications and Evaluation

1. Is there any defense for anthropologists? Write an essay in support of anthropologists.
2. Assume an "anthropologist" from some distant solar system came to your neighborhood to study you. Write your reaction.
3. Pick the other side and describe your neighborhood (or town, or city) as it might be seen by an alien. It would be best to select a particular trait, custom, or scene to avoid looseness in writing.
4. Is there any validity to the author's **argument** that many reports and references are merely revisions of revisions of old propositions? What is the fate of a college paper without footnotes? Comment on the problem.
5. Is the use of ridicule effective in this essay? Is it overdone in your judgment?

Edward Twitchell Hall (1914–   ) Edward Hall is an anthropologist who was educated in Arizona and at Columbia. Dr. Hall has not only taught but also been active in a great many field expeditions. He has, in addition, served as Deputy Director of the Washington Office of Human Relations. He has authored many articles and two books. The following essay is taken from *The Silent Language* and points out how a clear description of the behavior patterns of a group can lead to a better understanding of how they react, what they mean.

The Voices of Time

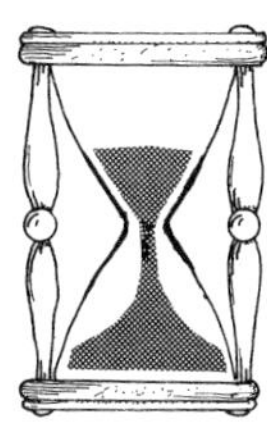

Time talks. It speaks more plainly than words. The message it conveys comes through loud and clear. Because it is manipulated less consciously, it is subject to less distortion than the spoken language. It can shout the truth where words lie. [1]

Different parts of the day, for example, are highly significant in certain contexts. Time may indicate the importance of the occasion as well as on what level an interaction between persons is to take place. In the United States if you telephone someone very early in the morning, while he is shaving or having breakfast, the time of the call usually signals a matter of utmost importance and extreme urgency. The same applies for calls after 11:00 P.M. A call received during sleeping hours is apt to be taken as a matter of life and death, hence the rude joke value of these calls among the young. [2]

How troublesome differing ways of handling time can be is well illustrated by the case of an American agriculturalist assigned to duty as an attaché of our embassy in a Latin country. After what seemed to him a suitable period he let it be known that he would like to call on the minister who was his counterpart. For various reasons, the suggested time was not suitable; all sorts of cues came back to the effect that the time was not yet ripe to visit the minister. Our friend, however, persisted and forced an appointment which was reluctantly granted. Arriving a little before the hour (the American respect pattern), he waited. The hour came and passed; five minutes —ten minutes—fifteen minutes. At this point he suggested to the secretary that perhaps the minister did not know he was waiting in the outer office. This gave him the feeling he had done something concrete and also helped to overcome the great anxiety that was stirring inside him. Twenty minutes—twenty-five minutes—thirty minutes—forty-five minutes (the insult period)! [3]

He jumped up and told the secretary that he had been "cooling his heels" in an outer office for forty-five minutes and he was "damned sick and tired" of this type of treatment. This message was relayed to the minister, who said, in effect, "Let him cool his heels." The attaché's stay in the country was not a happy one. [4]

The principal source of misunderstanding lay in the fact that in the country in question the five-minute-delay interval was not significant. Forty-five minutes, on the other hand, instead of being at the tail end of the waiting scale, was just barely at the beginning. To suggest to an American's secretary that perhaps her boss didn't know you were there after waiting sixty seconds would seem absurd, as would raising a storm about "cooling your heels" for five minutes. Yet this is precisely the way the minister registered the protestations of the American in his outer office! He felt, as usual, that Americans were being totally unreasonable. [5]

Throughout this unfortunate episode the attaché was acting according to the way he had been brought up. At home in the United States his responses would have been normal ones and his behavior legitimate. Yet even if he had been told before he left home that this sort of thing would happen, he would have had difficulty not *feeling* insulted after he had been kept waiting forty-five minutes. If, on the other hand, he had been taught the details of the local time system just as he should have been taught the local spoken language, it would have been possible for him to adjust himself accordingly. [6]

What bothers people in situations of this sort is that they don't realize they are being subjected to another form of communication, one that works part of the time with language and part of the time independently of it. The fact that the message conveyed is couched in no formal vocabulary makes things doubly difficult, because neither party can get very explicit about what is actually taking place. Each can only say what he thinks is happening and how he feels about it. The thought of what is being communicated is what hurts. [7]

People of the Western world, particularly Americans, tend to think of time as something fixed in nature, something around us and from which we cannot escape; an ever-present part of the environment, just like the air we breathe. That it might be experienced in any other way seems unnatural and strange, a feeling which is rarely modified even when we begin to discover how really differently it is handled by some other people. Within the West itself certain cultures rank time much lower in over-all importance than we do. In Latin America, for example, where time is treated rather cavalierly, one commonly hears the expression, "Our time or your time?" "*Hora americana, hora mejicana?*" [8]

As a rule, Americans think of time as a road or a ribbon stretching into the future, along which one progresses. The road has segments or compartments which are to be kept discrete ("one thing at a time"). People who cannot schedule time are looked down upon as impractical. In at least some parts of Latin America, the North American (their term for us) finds himself annoyed when he has made an appointment with somebody, only to find a lot of other things going on at the same time. An old friend of mine of Spanish cultural heritage used to run his business according to the "Latino" system. This meant that up to fifteen people were in his office at one time. Business which might have been finished in a quarter of an hour sometimes took a whole day. He realized, of course, that the Anglo-Americans were disturbed by this and used to make some allowance for them, a dispensation which meant that they spent only an hour or so in his office when they had planned on a few minutes. The American concept of the discreteness of time and the necessity for scheduling was at variance with this amiable and seemingly confusing Latin system. However, if my friend had adhered to the American system he would have destroyed a vital part of his prosperity. People who came to do business with him also came to find out things and to visit each other. The ten to fifteen Spanish-Americans and Indians who used to sit around the office (among whom I later found myself after I had learned to relax a little) played their own part in a particular type of communications network. [9]

Not only do we Americans segment and schedule time, but we look ahead and are oriented almost entirely toward the future. We like new things and are preoccupied with change. We want to know how to overcome resistance to change. In fact, scientific theories and even some pseudo-scientific ones, which incorporate a striking theory of change, are often given special attention. [10]

Time with us is handled much like a material; we earn it, spend it, save it, waste it. To us it is somewhat immoral to have two things going on at the same time. In Latin America it is not uncommon for one man to have a number of simultaneous jobs which he either carries on from one desk or which he moves between, spending a small amount of time on each. [11]

While we look to the future, our view of it is limited. The future to us is the foreseeable future, not the future of the South Asian that may involve centuries. Indeed, our perspective is so short as to inhibit the operation of a good many practical projects, such as sixty- and one-hundred-year conservation works requiring public support and public funds. Anyone who has worked in industry or in the government of the United States has heard the following: "Gentlemen, this is for the long term! Five or ten years." [12]

For us a "long time" can be almost anything—ten or twenty years, two or three months, a few weeks, or even a couple of days. The South Asian, however, feels that it is perfectly realistic to think of a "long time" in terms of thousands of years or even an endless period. A colleague once described their conceptualization of time as follows: "Time is like a museum with endless corridors and alcoves. You, the viewer, are walking through the museum in the dark, holding a light to each scene as you pass it. God is the curator of the museum, and only He knows all that is in it. One lifetime represents one alcove." [13]

The American's view of the future is linked to a view of the past, for tradition plays an equally limited part in American culture. As a whole, we push it aside or leave it to a few souls who are interested in the past for very special reasons. There are, of course, a few pockets, such as New England and the South, where tradition is emphasized. But in the realm of business, which is the dominant model of United States life, tradition is equated with *experience*, and experience is thought of as being very close to if not synonymous with know-how. Know-how is one of our prized possessions, so that when we look backward it is rarely to take pleasure in the past itself but usually to calculate the know-how, to assess the prognosis for success in the future. [14]

Promptness is also valued highly in American life. If people are not prompt, it is often taken either as an insult or as an indication that they are not quite responsible. There are those, of a psychological bent, who would say that we are obsessed with time. They can point to individuals in American culture who are literally time-ridden. And even the rest of us feel very strongly about time because we have been taught to take it so seriously. We have stressed this aspect of culture and developed it to a point unequaled anywhere in the world, except, perhaps, in Switzerland and north Germany. Many people criticize our obsessional handling of time. They attribute ulcers and hypertension to the pressure engendered by such a system. Perhaps they are right. [15]

1680 words, 15 paragraphs

Diction

1. The author uses several **clichés** in the opening paragraphs of this essay. What are they, and do they help or hinder his communicating [1, 3, 4, and 5]?
2. Test your linguistic ability; translate the Spanish phrase at the end of paragraph [8]. Does the use of foreign words or phrases bother you?
3. What is the meaning of the term "time-ridden" [15], for time cannot ride? Infer the origin of the **metaphor**.
4. In paragraph [9] the author states, "a dispensation which meant they [Anglo-Americans] had to spend only an hour or so in the office." Why is "dispensation" a stronger word than, say, "arrangement"? What are its **connotations?**
5. At what "grade level," generally, would you place the vocabulary in this essay? High school, freshman, senior, graduate, or average adult? On what basis?
6. Here are some words that may help you to answer question 5. Determine their meaning: adhered [9], amiable [9], attaché [2], cavalierly [8], curator [13], discrete [9], explicit [7], inhibit [12], oriented [10], prognosis [14].

Rhetoric and Style

1. This essay opens with a striking **figure of speech.** What kind is it, and does it help clarify the **thesis?**
2. The author describes the way Americans use time to help understand other cultures; in his description he uses other **rhetorical** devices. Find examples of **narration, analogy, definition, exposi-**

tion (**comparison, contrasting**), and **example** that he uses to make his description more effective.

3. This essay is held together (see **Coherence**) by several of the standard transitional devices. See if you can locate the paragraphs linked by repetition of key word; by pronoun reference; by transitional phrases (for example, "also").
4. At the end of paragraph [9] the author seems to be relaxing among the Indians. Why among Indians?
5. The American concept of time as a road [9] is clearly a **metaphor,** but what is the Asian concept of time as a museum [13]?
6. Nowhere in this selection does Dr. Hall mention the names of countries, people, places; would doing so make the ideas more acceptable?

Applications and Evaluation

1. Do you have a telephone timetable? When is a call urgent? Is Hall's idea still valid, or is it going out of style?
2. What standards of promptness are current in your social group? When do you arrive for a date or a party that is scheduled for 7:30? For an 8:00 A.M. business appointment?
3. How long should two people wait to get married? Until the day after they meet? For a year?
4. Does your use of time differ from that of your friends, or do they determine how you use time?
5. Can you develop a better **analogy** for time than "a road"?
6. Using one of the ideas in the first five questions, write a descriptive essay examining it in some detail.

Robert Kirsch (1922–) Robert Kirsch attended The University of California at Los Angeles, where he later returned as a lecturer in Journalism. Mr. Kirsch has written several novels, one of the more recent is *Knight of the Scimitar*. He has also coauthored a history of the western United States, *West of the West*. He has been a reporter, an editor, a columnist, and is currently the Literary Editor of the *Los Angeles Times*. In this selection he uses description as an aid to understanding the book he is reviewing.

1984—Not All That Bad?

"What we need is a technology of behavior," says B. F. Skinner in BEYOND FREEDOM AND DIGNITY (Knopf: $6.95). "We could solve our problems quickly enough if we could adjust the growth of the world's population as precisely as we adjust the course of a spaceship, or improve agriculture and industry with some of the confidence with which we accelerate high-energy particles, or move toward a peaceful world with something like the steady progress with which physics has approached absolute zero (even though both remain presumably out of reach)." [1]

Skinner, the foremost proponent of behaviorism, writes eloquently and forthrightly but the world he posits is for most of us charged with overtones of 1984. He does not intend it, for his confidence in the technology of behavior is so absolute that those oddballs who value freedom, dignity and privacy, the heretics he calls autonomous men, would not be around to cause trouble. [2]

Those who speak of freedom and dignity, says Skinner, are anachronisms in the scientific age ("the literatures of freedom and dignity were once brilliant exercises in countercontrol, but the measures they proposed are no longer appropriate to the task"), hangovers of a belief in attitudes, feelings, inner capacities of man. [3]

Skinner assures us the behaviorists do not deny these "non-physical" things, but their concern is in the physical expression, i.e., how they bring about physical changes in the physical world. But they are not really important, Skinner goes on to say, when we consider genetic matters and conditioning, environment and control, contingencies and countercontrol. The behaviorists, he claims, do not want to "abolish" man, "certainly not as a species or as an individual achiever. It is the autonomous inner man who is abolished and that is a step forward . . . A scientific view of man offers exciting possibilities. We have not yet seen what man can make of man." [4]

Repressive Nightmare

So he says. But in the scientific age we have seen what man has made of man. There are systems in the world today in which the technology of behavior operates to abolish the autonomous inner man, and despite all of Skinner's promises, these systems are nightmares of repression. [5]

And there is more which echoes as I read it, the essence of totalitarianism, the sacrifice of self for the state (Skinner calls it the culture). "The individualist can find no solace in reflecting upon any contribution which will survive him. He has refused to act for the good of others and is therefore not reinforced by the fact that others whom he has helped will outlive him. He has refused to be concerned for the survival of his culture and is not reinforced by the fact that the culture will survive him. In the defense of his own freedom and dignity he has denied the contributions of the past and must therefore relinquish all claim upon the future." [6]

Nostalgia and Vanity

Skinner has a good deal to say about nostalgia and vanity. "The traditional conception of man is faltering; it confers reinforcing privileges. It is therefore easily defended and can be changed only with difficulty. It was designed to build up the individual as an instrument of countercontrol, and it did so effectively but in such a way as to limit progress. We have seen how the literatures of freedom and dignity, with their concern for autonomous man, have perpetuated the use of punishment and condoned the use of only weak nonpunitive techniques . . ." [7]

If the adherents of freedom and dignity are called out of date, selfish and antiscientific, the same charges may be made against Skinner. His faith in science and technology (though he concedes "that things grow steadily worse, and it is disheartening to find that technology itself is increasingly at fault") is impressive but in my view naive. The only solution he can really offer is that physical technology is not enough. His talk of a technology of behavior raises far more questions than he can satisfactorily answer for me. [8]

Politics, art, music, philosophy, the humanistic disciplines, values, are touched but really thrust aside. Skinner is a man caught and hardened in amber, worshiping the promise of science, assuming that position that Krutch criticized when he argued that whereas the traditional view supports Hamlet's exclamation, "How like a God!," Pavlov, the behavioral scientist, emphasized, "How like a dog!" [9]

Skinner says: "But that was a step forward. A god is the archetypal pattern of an explanatory fiction, of a miracle-working mind, of the metaphysical. Man is much more than a dog, but like a dog he is within range of a scientific analysis." [10]

What Skinner does not seem equipped to see is that "much more" is the difference between manipulating the world and directing the course of the spaceship. Simplifying the magnitude and complexity of the problem may bring more peril than help. [11]

750 words, 11 paragraphs

Diction

1. The title of this book review is "1984—Not All That Bad?" Why does the author use the specific date 1984?
2. Why does the author use Hamlet, a literary creation, and Pavlov, a Russian psychologist, as **illustration?** What are the **connotations** of each?
3. What does the phrase "Skinner is a man caught and hardened in amber" mean? Why is the reference to amber?
4. *Beyond Freedom and Dignity* is an interesting title; what might it mean? Why do you suppose Dr. Skinner selected it for the title of his book? What are its **connotations?**
5. Here are some words used in the review that should be looked

up: adherents [8], anachronism [3], archetypal [10], autonomous [2], behaviorist [4], condone [7], metaphysical [10], posit [2], solace [6], totalitarian [7].

Rhetoric and Style

1. How does Mr. Kirsch tie his **introduction** and **conclusion** together?
2. How does the author let the reader know when he is stating the words of Dr. Skinner and when he is stating his own opinion and judgment?
3. What seems to be Mr. Kirsch's **tone** toward the author of the book he is reviewing—B. F. Skinner?
4. In what way does Kirsch show his **attitude** (or **tone**)?
5. Does there seem to be a pattern to this review? What is it, if there is?

Applications and Evaluation

1. Do you think that the reviewer's hostility toward the content of the book is **validated** by the examples given?
2. Make a list of the complimentary comments about the book and another list of the derogatory comments. Which list is longer?
3. The reviewer concentrates on the content of *Beyond Freedom and Dignity*. What does he say about the **style** or the literary value?
4. Combining questions 2 and 3 above, write an **evaluation** of the review; use the two lists as data.
5. Try to write a **review** of one of the other essays in this book following Kirsch's pattern (quotation plus comment).

John Ronald Reuel Tolkien (1892–1973) J. R. R. Tolkien was born in South Africa but was sent to England when a child and educated at Oxford. His contribution to scholarship is impressive, including *A Middle-English Vocabulary* and such papers as "Beowulf: the Monster and the Critics." However well known Professor Tolkien was as a philologist, his monumental fame rests on his creation of an entire world peopled by strange beings who wage the eternal struggle between good and evil. This selection, a classification of one of these peoples, is from the first volume of the trilogy *The Lord of the Rings.*

Concerning Hobbits

Hobbits are an unobtrusive but very ancient people, more numerous formerly than they are today; for they love peace and quiet and good tilled earth: a well-ordered and well-farmed countryside was their favourite haunt. They do not and did not understand or like machines more complicated than a forge-bellows, a water-mill, or a handloom, though they were skilful with tools. Even in ancient days they were, as a rule, shy of the 'the Big Folk', as they call us, and now they avoid us with dismay and are becoming hard to find. They are quick of hearing and sharp-eyed, and though they are inclined to be fat and do not hurry unnecessarily, they are nonetheless nimble and deft in their movements. They possessed from the first the art of disappearing swiftly and silently, when large folk whom they do not wish to meet come blundering by; and this art they have developed until to Men it may seem magical. But Hobbits have never, in fact, studied magic of any kind, and their elusiveness is due solely to a professional skill that heredity and practice, and a close friendship with the earth, have rendered inimitable by bigger and clumsier races. [1]

For they are a little people, smaller than Dwarves: less stout and stocky, that is, even when they are not actually much shorter. Their height is variable, ranging between two and four feet of our measure. They seldom now reach three feet; but they have dwindled, they say, and in ancient days they were taller. According to the Red Book, Bandobras Took (Bullroarer), son of Isengrim the Second, was four foot five and able to ride a horse. He was surpassed in all Hobbit records only by two famous characters of old; but that curious matter is dealt with in this book. [2]

As for the Hobbits of the Shire, with whom these tales are concerned, in the days of their peace and prosperity they were a merry folk. They dressed in bright colours, being notably fond of yellow and green; but they seldom wore shoes, since their feet had tough leathery soles and were clad in a thick curling hair, much like the hair of their heads, which was commonly brown. Thus, the only craft little practised among them was shoe-making; but they had long and skilful fingers and could make many other useful and comely things. Their faces were as a rule good-natured rather than beautiful, broad, bright-eyed, red-cheeked, with mouths apt to laughter, and to eating and drinking. And laugh they did, and eat, and drink, often and heartily, being fond of simple jests at all times, and of six meals a day (when they could get them). They were hospitable and delighted in parties, and in presents, which they gave away freely and eagerly accepted. [3]

It is plain indeed that in spite of later estrangement Hobbits are relatives of ours: far nearer to us than Elves, or even than Dwarves. Of old they spoke the languages of Men, after their own fashion, and liked and disliked much the same things as Men did. But what exactly our relationship is can no longer be discovered. The beginning of Hobbits lies far back in the Elder Days that are now lost and forgotten. Only the Elves still preserve any records of that vanished time, and their traditions are concerned almost entirely with their own history, in which Men appear seldom and Hobbits are not mentioned at all. Yet it is clear that Hobbits had, in fact, lived quietly in Middle-earth for many long years before other folk became even aware of them. And the world being after all full of strange creatures beyond count, these little people seemed of very little importance. [4]

Before the crossing of the mountains the Hobbits had already become divided into three somewhat different breeds: Harfoots, Stoors, and Fallohides. The Harfoots were browner of skin, smaller, and shorter, and they were beardless and bootless; their hands and feet were neat and nimble; and they preferred highlands and hillsides. The Stoors were broader, heavier in build; their feet and hands were larger, and they preferred flat lands and riversides. The Fallohides were fairer of skin and also of hair, and they were taller and slimmer than the others; they were lovers of trees and of woodlands. [5]

The Harfoots had much to do with Dwarves in ancient times, and long lived in the foothills of the mountains. They moved westward early, and roamed over Eriador as far as Weathertop while the others were still in Wilderland. They were the most normal and representative variety of Hobbit, and far the most numerous. They were the most inclined to settle in one place, and longest preserved their ancestral habit of living in tunnels and holes. [6]

The Stoors lingered long by the banks of the Great River Anduin, and were less shy of Men. They came west after the Harfoots and followed the course of the Loudwater southwards; and there many of them long dwelt between Tharbad and the borders of Dunland before they moved north again. [7]

The Fallohides, the least numerous, were a northerly branch. They were more friendly with Elves than the other Hobbits were, and had more skill in language and song than in handicrafts; and of old they preferred hunting to tilling. They crossed the mountains north of Rivendell and came down the River Hoarwell. In Eriador they soon mingled with the other kinds that had preceded them, but being somewhat bolder and more adventurous, they were often found as leaders or chieftains among clans of Harfoots or Stoors. [8]

At no time had Hobbits of any kind been warlike, and they had never fought among themselves. In olden days they had, of course, been often obliged to fight to maintain themselves in a hard world; but that was very ancient history. [9]

Nonetheless, ease and peace had left this people still curiously tough. They were, if it came to it, difficult to daunt or to kill; and they were, perhaps, so unwearyingly fond of good things not least because they could, when put to it, do without them, and could survive rough handling by grief, foe, or weather in a way that astonished those who did not know them well and looked no further than their bellies and their well-fed faces. Though slow to quarrel, and for sport killing nothing that lived, they were doughty at bay, and at need could still handle arms. They shot well with the bow, for they were keen-eyed and sure at the mark. Not only with bows and arrows. If any Hobbit stooped for a stone, it was well to get quickly under cover, as all trespassing beasts knew very well. [10]

All Hobbits had originally lived in holes in the ground, or so they believed, and in such dwellings they still felt most at home; but in the course of time they had been obliged to adopt other forms of abode. Actually in the Shire it was, as a rule, only the richest and the poorest Hobbits that maintained the old custom. The poorest went on living in burrows of the most primitive kind, mere holes indeed, with only one window or none; while the well-to-do still constructed more luxurious versions of the simple diggings of old. But suitable sites for these large and ramifying tunnels (or *smials* as they called them) were not everywhere to be found; and in the flats and the low-lying districts the Hobbits, as they multiplied, began to build above ground. Indeed, even in the hilly regions and the older villages, such as Hobbiton or Tuckborough, or in the chief township of the Shire, Michel Delving on the White Downs, there were now many houses of wood, brick, or stone. These were specially favoured by millers, smiths, ropers, and cartwrights, and others of that sort; for even when they had holes to live in, Hobbits had long been accustomed to build sheds and workshops. [11]

The habit of building farm-houses and barns was said to have begun among the inhabitants of the Marish down by the Brandywine. The Hobbits of that quarter, the East-farthing, were rather large and heavy-legged, and they wore dwarf-boots in muddy weather. But they were well known to be Stoors in a large part of their blood, as indeed was shown by the down that many grew on their chins. No Harfoot or Fallohide had any trace of a beard. Indeed, the folk of the Marish, and of Buckland, east of the River, which they afterwards occupied, came for the most part later into the Shire up from south-away; and they still had many peculiar names and strange words not found elsewhere in the Shire. [12]

The craft of building may have come from Elves or Men, but the Hobbits used it in their own fashion. They did not go in for towers. Their houses were usually long, low, and comfortable. The oldest kind were, indeed, no more than built imitations of *smials,* thatched with dry grass or straw, or roofed with turves, and having walls somewhat bulged. That stage, however, belonged to the early days of the Shire, and hobbit-building had long since been altered, improved by devices, learned from Dwarves, or discovered by themselves. A preference for round windows, and even round doors, was the chief remaining peculiarity of hobbit-architecture. [13]

The houses and the holes of Shire-hobbits were often large, and inhabited by large families. (Bilbo and Frodo Baggins were as bachelors very exceptional, as they were also in many other ways, such as their friendship with Elves.) Sometimes, as in the case of the Tooks of Great Smials, or the Brandybucks of Brandy Hall, many generations of relatives lived in (comparative) peace together in one ancestral and many-tunnelled mansion. All Hobbits were, in any case, clannish and reckoned up their relationships with great care. They drew long and elaborate family-trees with innumerable branches. In dealing with Hobbits it is important to remember who is related to whom, and in what degree. It would be impossible in this book to set out a family-tree that included even the more important members of the more important families at the time which these tales tell of. The genealogical trees at the end of the Red Book of Westmarch are a small book in themselves, and all but Hobbits would find them exceedingly dull. Hobbits delighted in such things, if they were accurate: they liked to have books filled with things that they already knew, set out fair and square with no contradictions. [14]

1820 words, 14 paragraphs

Diction

1. The author writes of "Middle-earth" [4]; whence the name? What does it mean?
2. The author lends a feeling of antiquity to the description by the types of machines and weapons he mentions. What are they? Are any of them still in use?
3. Obviously, many of the names of places and creatures are the inventions of Professor Tolkien. Find the place names and names of creatures (kinds of "people" for example) that are not invented.
4. We still use the words "dwarves" and "elves." Why does the author capitalize them? Do we use them the way he does?
5. Some of the words used in this selection give a slightly archaic flavor to the writing. What do they mean? Comely [2], deft [1], doughty [10], dwindle [2], elusiveness [1], estrangement [4], geneology [14], haunt [1], inimitable [1], nimble [5].

Rhetoric and Style

1. Hobbits are **classified** generally as people. How are they differentiated from the other people in the selection?
2. *The Lord of the Rings* is, of course, fantasy. What **tone** does the

author maintain as he presents this fantasy to the reader? How does he maintain the **tone?**

3. A creature of fantasy must be mostly believable, must have generally real qualities. What is the one quality of the Hobbits that is completely unreal?
4. In this description the author has a plan. He uses four main divisions to tell us about Hobbits. Can you see them? What are they?
5. Can you locate any of the standard **figures of speech** in this highly descriptive passage?

Applications and Evaluation

1. Try a description by **classification** (place in a *genus* and show *differentia*) of a mythological creature such as a unicorn, a mermaid, or a griffin.
2. Now make an effort to create your own creature. Perhaps it could be another subclass of man. As you describe, maintain the same serious tone that Professor Tolkien used.
3. In the complete trilogy Tolkien has created an entire world. Have you ever invented a world, or part of one—perhaps an improved version of here and now? Describe the kind of world you would like to create.
4. *The Lord of the Rings* has proven immensely popular; thirty-six printings, Tolkien clubs, parodies, even master's and doctoral theses written about it. Why is it so popular? Of what use is a fantasy **epic?**
5. If you are of a philosophical turn you might write a brief essay indicating man's need for fantasy. Try to use examples from contemporary literature including such elements as cartoon films, comic strips, television.

Frank J. Anderson (1912–   ) Frank J. Anderson is assistant to the Librarian at the New York Botanical Garden. He is a graduate of the Pratt Institute of Fine and Applied Arts. He also edits the Botanical Garden's Newsletter. This particular selection first appeared in *Natural History* Magazine. The need for clear, precise description as an aid to proper classification is most clearly shown by the possibility of reclassifying something because of a minor omission. Notice how the medieval writers and tale-tellers did by accident what Edgar Allan Poe did by design in his short story "The Sphinx."

Medieval Beasties

Having persisted through a long hard night of disbelief, mythology is once again gaining credit in a few respectable circles. Archaeology and psychology, two of its newfound friends, are now busy removing the tarnish from its reputation. This process began when Heinrich Schliemann rediscovered Troy by placing his confidence in ancient worn-out tales. The modern Israelis, following the same method, have also uncovered sites thought to be merely legendary. And psychiatry, through the voice of one of its major prophets, Carl Jung, has even suggested a science of mythology. [1]

The natural sciences, too, have supplied a few samples as evidence in favor of the reliability of myth. Most of these have risen out of exaggerated or misinterpreted reports that were based on poor observation. Examples that immediately come to mind are the manatees and dugongs, which wishful sailors transformed into mermaids, and the common oranges that became the golden apples of the Hesperides. Almost all myths are constructed after the same fashion: a hard kernel of fact is overlaid with layers of decoration and padding, much like a slightly larcenous expense account. [2]

One of the great myth-making periods ran from postclassic times to the sixteenth century, but at the time of their creation, few of the legends were regarded as fiction by either their creators or their perpetuators. Most of these fables were based on hearsay information, which when circulated in manuscript form lent themselves to further misinterpretation. A busy scribe with little time to check over what he had set down, was often guilty of errors of both sight and hearing; some works were copied by dictating to an enormous battery of scribes, and one error could easily beget another as easily as amoebas can establish a family. As a consequence, medieval manuscripts abound in puzzlements and oddities. Creatures were fathered out of a combination of ignorance and illegibility, assisted by an inexhaustible passion for the miraculous. [3]

Three such garbled progeny seem to be endowed more than others with their creator's passion for the miraculous. The first of the trio is called Zytiron, the Fish-tailed Knight, monstrous terror of the seas. Helmeted in steel and encased in armor, he looked the very figure of the noble knight, complete with shield and gauntlet. But below his waistline a curious change occurred, for his lower half was that of a fish. [4]

For some unaccountable reason, this odd being enjoyed a wave of popular appeal in Flanders and Germany during the final decades of the fifteenth century. He is found gracing the border of a Flemish Book of Hours from the Ghent-Bruges area and is also the subject of a carving on the choir stalls at Saint Sulpice in Diest. Hieronymus Bosch depicts Zytiron confronting a mermaid in the central panel of the fantastic *Garden of Earthly Delights*, and he is described and pictured in the many editions of the famous medieval herbal *Hortus Sanitatis* or *Garden of Health*. He was, in short, the kind of fellow who got around. [5]

But for all his fame, Zytiron's antecedents are a little hazy, a condition that was not altogether uncommon in the Middle Ages. The firmest birthdate that can presently be assigned to him is 1491, the year in which he appeared in the first edition of the *Hortus*. The text in that massive Latin work speaks of him as being armored like a knight of old and calls him "great and out of measure strong." He is said to wear a helmet, while pendent from his neck is a shield bound to his body by many sinews. Upon his hand he wears a gauntlet, divided only at the thumb, and with this "he stryketh ryght sore." [6]

But matters don't end with mere identification, for certain characteristics make it very interesting for an iconographer. Hieronymus Bosch, penetrating Zytiron's disguise in the *Hortus Sanitis,* seized on his transfigured form as a fresh symbol of sinfulness, one that combined anger and lust. Anger was a way of life for Zytiron and was reflected in the warlike pose of the merknight. Lust could be attributed to almost any creature that was loathsome and unclean, and this was the verdict of the Scripture itself on the creature, its place in iconology was fixed. [7]

The second member of our mythical threesome is a citizen of two worlds, the animal and the vegetable. Variously known as the Tartarian, Scythian, or Vegetable Lamb, it is also called by the Tartar name of Barometz, and is a considerably more innocent creature than the merknight. [8]

Although its ancestry goes back to ancient Hebrew writings in the Talmud of Jerusalem, the Lamb did not enter European literature until the Middle Ages. Friar Odoric of Pordenone first made mention of it in 1330 while he was describing his travels to the Orient, and some thirty years later Sir John Mandeville recounted much the same tale. [9]

This peculiar plant-animal was described as being a full-sized lamb fixed at its navel to a stalk that rose out of the ground. It fed by bending and stretching to reach the grass that grew around it, and when the supply failed, it died—unless, of course, the wolves got to it sooner. Barometz was, therefore, a perfect model of meekness, living out its life without harm to any other creature. For this reason, many medieval churchmen saw it as a prefiguration of the true Christian, an archetype of the Mystic Lamb, and argued that it was to be found growing in Paradise. It did, in fact, turn up in the very center of Paradise on one occasion, but that was only in the frontispiece to Parkinson's *Paradise in Sole, Paradisus Terrestris.* He also wrote of it in another of his works, the *Theatrum Botanicum* of 1640, but few others believed in it by that time. Still, Erasmus Darwin, writing about a century later, gave it a place in his *Loves of the Plants,* although he changed both its location and color. After Darwin, all is either silence or derision, for the legendary plant-animal was never discovered. [10]

The reason, of course, lies in the misleading description of an Asiatic plant as a "wool-bearing tree," one that bore as its fruit "fleeces surpassing those of sheep in beauty and excellence." And it was scarcely any less puzzling to the Tartars themselves. They were constantly being asked the whereabouts of the Barometz, which in their language meant a plain, ordinary four-legged sheep. But these inquiring strangers wanted a different Barometz, one that grew on a stalk or a shrub. And what could be done with people who insisted that something of that sort was to be found in the neighborhood when every sensible person knew better? The only logical thing, of course, was to send them on to the source of all good legends—some place farther down the road. [11]

The last of the fabulous creatures on our list enjoyed the most mixed ancestry of all. It began on a tree, passed through a marine stage as a barnacle, and then ended up as a fowl. This magnificently impossible being, known as the barnacle goose, was once a common article of sale in the medieval Lenten markets, for the bird was real even if its pedigree was not. [12]

Giraldus Cambrensis, writing the history of Ireland in 1186 was the first to chronicle this legend, which had circulated for some time among Irish and Scottish fisherfolk. He described the bird's manner of generation in rotted timbers floating in the sea, and related how it hung by its beak within a heart-shaped shell until it was mature enough to fly or swim away. If Giraldus had stopped there, the legend might have remained no more than a local myth, but he went on to state that some of the Irish clergy made "no scruple of eating these birds on fasting days, as not being flesh, because they are not born of flesh." This news delighted ordinary men who found the rigors of Lenten fasting just a bit too demanding, and churchmen suddenly found themselves with a rather thorny problem on their hands. [13]

Concurrent with the quandary that beset the Christian community, rabbis also found themselves faced with an unusual puzzle. If these geese originated as shellfish, they were obviously unclean, but if the shellfish had been engendered from wood, what then? And if that last question was answered so as to satisfy dietary laws, an even nastier one lurked beyond. How, exactly, were these geese to be killed so as to render them ritually clean? Nowhere in the dietary laws was there a ruling on the case, and nobody wanted the responsibility of declaring one. In the meantime, the goose graced as many tables among the Jewish brethren as it did among the Christian. [14]

The legend was still alive in the early part of the seventeenth-century. John Gerard wrote about these fowl in his *Herball* of 1597, and even showed the veritable goose-tree, together with the geese being born of barnacles. Ulisse Aldrovandi, an Italian naturalist writing at the same time, also took the story seriously. But doubt was growing on every side. Another Italian naturalist, Fabio Colonna, firmly stated that the goose-barnacle did *not* have its origin on land, and that geese did not rise from it, and that it was entirely a marine specimen and remained so all its life. He was right in line with Aeneas Silvius, who a century earlier had been skeptical of these birds. Seeking their place of origin while he was on a diplomatic mission to Scotland, Silvius was forever referred to yet another place, and concluded that "miracles will always flee farther and farther away." [15]

Nevertheless, the fishermen did have a certain amount of reason on their side. For one thing, these birds always flew in from the northern seas, and nobody ever saw them breed in any corner of Europe. What were the Irish and Scottish observers to think when, ignorant of the fact that the barnacle goose, *Branta leucopsis,* actually bred in the Arctic barrens out of the sight of man? They were also aware that a small, white, goose-shaped form could be found inside opened barnacle shells and that a kind of feathery appendage protruded from the shell's mouth. To them this was clear evidence that, if its feathers were to be found sticking out, the goose was most certainly being formed within. Unaware that this was the means by which the barnacle swept food from the water, they added two and two together and got infinity as an answer, something not entirely unknown in human history. [16]

So the next time you encounter a description of a seemingly impossible beastie, don't dismiss it altogether. Hidden beneath the camouflage there is very likely to be something real or something odd, but always something to tell us a little more about the workings of the human mind. [17]

The Answers

Our armored knight of the sea loses his verbal disguise woven out of simile and metaphor and dwindles down to nothing more awesome than the gourmet's delight, the lobster. The shield hanging from his neck and fastened to his body is simply a carapace, while the singly divided gauntled is just as plainly a claw—with which he can strike very sore indeed. [18]

The snowy fleeces were nothing but the opened bolls of the cotton plant, for that was the true Tartarian Lamb, a purely vegetable product with no taint of the animal about it. Growing in India, it was woven there and reached markets to the west by way of Tartary. There it was often sold side by side with the Tartar's own woolen goods and lambskins thereby setting the stage for myth making. Thus there arose an understandable, charming, and colorful error that puzzled Europeans for centuries. [19]

The dietary injunction against the lobster or the barnacle is in Leviticus 11:10 "And all that have not fins and scales in the seas, and in the rivers, of all that move in the waters, and of any living thing which is in the waters, they shall be an abomination unto you." [20]

1925 words, 20 paragraphs

Diction

1. The author uses the phrase "three such garbled progeny" [4]. Is it possible for progeny—descendents—to be garbled—confused or distorted? Whose progeny were these?
2. Do you find any instances of **jargon** or **slang** in this essay? How about "beasties" [title and 17]?
3. **Infer** from the two terms "mermaid" and "merknight" what the prefix probably means. Create, without checking a dictionary, some similar terms that might be used.
4. Why does the author use so many Latin titles in the essay (such as *Hortus Sanitatis, Theatrum Botanicum,* and *Paradisus Terrestris*)?
5. There seems to be an excessive number of hyphenated words in this particular essay: plant-animal, full-sized, lobster-knight, myth-making, wool-bearing, heart-shaped, goose-shaped, goose-barnacle (but not in "barnacle goose"), and goose-tree. Why so many? What is the rule for using hyphens, if there is such a rule?
6. There are some words or phrases that might not be found in a college dictionary; see if you can determine the meaning of "Book of Hours" and "dietary laws." Find the meaning of the following words: archetype [10], concurrently [14], derision [10], engendered [14], gauntlet [4], iconography, -ology [7], prefiguration [10], quandary [14], rigors [13], Talmud [9].

Rhetoric and Style

1. The author starts his essay with a **metaphor** and continues to use **figures of speech** freely in the first three paragraphs. Point

out at least one example each of **metaphor, simile,** and **personification** in those paragraphs. Speculate as to their purpose.

2. What are the **connotations** of the phrase "And psychiatry, through the voice of one of its major prophets, Carl Jung . . ."?
3. There are seven sentences beginning with "And" or "But" in this essay. Isn't it wrong to begin a sentence with them?
4. What seems to be the author's **attitude** toward his subject, and how does the reader know?
5. This essay is **unified** and coherent. **Unity** is gained by the overall plan and **coherence** by standard methods explained in the Glossary. A close examination might help the student writer.
   a. How are paragraph [3], [4], [5], and [6] linked together?
   b. Take a close look at paragraph [10]. What devices does the author use to make the eight sentences cohere? Make a list from 1 to 8, write the transition word, and classify it.
6. How does the author classify the term "myth"? Does his **classification** differ from the one in the glossary of this book? Does it differ from the one in your dictionary? Comment?

Applications and Evaluation

1. Can you think of any other mythological creatures that might have originated in faulty observations or incomplete descriptions (consider failure to mention size and leaving out sections)? Are there any mythological creatures made of combined forms like the barnacle goose?
2. Has man lost his myth-making ability? Do you know of any contemporary **myths?** Any mythical beings? Could you develop a paragraph or essay showing the similarity of the myth-making ability and prejudice?
3. Do you agree or disagree with the author's **thesis?** State thesis and make a comment of agreement or disagreement.
4. Make a list of American unnatural history. You might include such items of folklore as the hoop-snake, or toads as the cause of warts, for example. Be prepared to write a paragraph or essay putting your items in some **class** or another and coming to a **conclusion** about them.
5. Write a descriptive essay about a commonly observed item, but take great care with the **detail.** Perhaps you might omit one important element or distort one element in order to confuse the reader. Create your own Zytiron.

6. Write a brief essay reclassifying a standard myth or legend—for example, Adam and Eve as male chauvinism; Pandora's box as women being the cause of woe; Paul Bunyan as a legend of environmental waste.

Robert A. Hall, Jr. (1911–) Robert Hall was educated at Princeton, the University of Chicago, and the University of Rome. Primarily interested in linguistic research, he has studied the Romance languages and various pidgin dialects. A great part of his writing has been about these studies; he has produced essays on linguistics, a history of Italian literature, and *Linguistics and Your Language*, from which this selection is taken. Notice how careful description is used as a basis for a reclassification of the term "correct."

Right vs. Wrong

Our problem is, to look at some of the ways in which we are supposed to be speaking wrongly, and to see whether there really exists a choice between "right" and "wrong," and, if so, what "right" and "wrong" consist of. [1]

Our first approach may be made through very ordinary, everyday instances of "mistakes" like *I ain't, he don't, we seen him, you done it* or *hisn*. Most of us know that these are pretty widely condemned as "errors," when used instead of the corresponding *I am not* or *I'm not, he doesn't, we saw him, you did it, his*. But what is it that makes them "mistakes" or "errors?" If we drive through a traffic light, steal somebody's property, or kill someone, we know exactly what provides sanctions against these actions: the law of the land; and we know what will punish us if we disobey the law: the government. Is there any law of the land to set up rules about our speech, or any branch of the government that will enforce them? Obviously not. There are books that contain rules for speaking and writing, and there are people who will raise objections and criticize us if we fail to follow these rules; but those books and those people

From *Linguistics and Your Language* by Robert A. Hall, Jr. (Linguistics). Reprinted by permission of the author.

have no legal authority over us (outside of the rather special and limited situation in the schoolroom, where of course the teacher can give us a bad mark for not obeying the rules). Not only have they no legal authority, they have no authority whatsoever conferred on them by any power. Some countries, it is true, have had regulators of language with a kind of authority, such as the national Academies of France and Spain, which were set up by the king with the specific duty of "regulating and preserving the purity of the language." Even in those countries, very few people ever took the Academies' authority over language too seriously; but, technically speaking, their authority did exist in a way. But no such authority has ever existed in any English-speaking country, nor does it seem likely that speakers of English would ever be willing to accept the decrees of an Academy or similar institution, or of a Ministry of Education. [2]

And yet, if we say *I ain't, you done it,* or *hisn,* we *are* likely to run into trouble. Trouble with whom?—with everybody? No. A foreigner using some completely abnormal turn of phrase, such as *this must we first do,* will confuse the ordinary speaker of English considerably, and will run no chance of finding anybody who would accept that as normal English. He would have trouble with everybody. But with *I ain't* and the like, some people would not be in the slightest upset; in fact, more than a few would find those "incorrect" forms more normal than the supposedly "correct" usage that they "ought" to be following themselves and insisting on in others. With some other people, however, our use of *he don't* and similar expressions may get us into more or less serious trouble. Our hearers may correct us on the spot, and tell us "Don't say *I ain't,* say *I'm not;* not *hisn,* but *his*"; or, even though they may not correct our usage then and there, they are nevertheless likely to hold it against us, and to allow it to determine their attitude toward us in one way or another. They may, perhaps, not consider us their social equals; they may not invite us to their home again; they may object to our marrying into their family; they may pick someone else, who says *I'm not* and *his,* to give a job or a promotion to; or some other form of unfavorable reaction may result from our using a form or word which is the wrong one for the given situation. [3]

Notice also that the forms themselves are of equal worth as expressions of the ideas you are trying to communicate. *You done it* is just as good an expression of "doing" something, in past time, as *you did it,* and no present-day speaker of English will ever be confused as to what you mean. The same is true for *he don't* instead of *he doesn't;* for *we seen him* instead of *we saw him;* and for a host of others. In some cases, one might even argue that the "incorrect" form is actually somewhat preferable from the point of view of clarity or simplicity. The form *his*, in "correct" speech, is both an adjective (*his book*) and a pronoun (*that's his*); whereas the "incorrect" form *hisn* and the others parallel to it ending in *-n* (*hern, ourn, yourn, theirn*) are clearly marked, by their ending, as being possessive pronouns and nothing else. The argument runs similarly for *ain't*. To make the present-tense forms of the verb *be* negative, we must use, in "correct" speech, three different forms: *I'm not, he isn't, we* (*you, they*) *aren't;* whereas the "incorrect" *ain't* offers us one single form, exactly parallel to *can't, won't* or *don't*, and equally convenient. *He doesn't* instead of *he don't* is also an extra complication, seen to be needless when compared with *can't* or *won't*. We might make similar arguments in favor of other "incorrect" forms as well. [4]

What is it, then, that makes some forms "incorrect" and others not? This is not a matter of legal or quasi-legal authority, as we have seen. It is not a matter of universal condemnation, nor yet of incomprehensibility; in fact, some "incorrect" forms, as we have just pointed out, would be clearer or simpler than the corresponding "correct" forms. It all boils down, really, to a question of acceptability in certain classes of our society, in those classes which are socially dominant and which set the tone for others. Whether a form is accepted or rejected does not depend on its inherent merit nor yet on any official approval given it, but purely on whether its hearers like it or not—on whether they will react favorably or unfavorably towards a person they hear using it. "Correct" can only mean "socially acceptable," and apart from this has no meaning as applied to language. [5]

The social acceptability, and hence "correctness," of any form or word is determined, not by reason or logic or merit, but solely by the hearer's emotional attitude towards it—and emotional attitudes naturally differ from person to person, from group to group, from social class to social class. Forms and words also change in social acceptability in the course of time: in the early seventeenth century, conservative speakers and purists objected violently to *ye* and *you*, used in speaking to one person, instead of the earlier *thou* and *thee;* and there must have been a time when *cows*, instead of the older plural *kine*, seemed an objectionable innovation. [6]

Nevertheless, the difference in social acceptability between *I ain't* and *I am not*, between *hern* and *hers*, and so forth, is a real fact. If my child is likely to run into trouble later on for saying

I done it or *hisn,* I will try to keep him from getting into the habit of using those forms which are actually not acceptable socially and which may cause others to react unfavorably towards him. But, if I am sensible about it, I will realize that the reason I want him to avoid these "incorrect" forms is not any inherent badness or evil character that they may have, but a purely practical consideration, that of their social acceptability. His choice of language will be used by others as a purely arbitrary means of classifying him socially among the sheep or the goats. All we need to do in the case of *I ain't,* etc., is to re-word the traditional instructions, and say that we avoid using such turns of speech, not because they are "bad" or "wrong" or "ungrammatical," but because they are socially unacceptable. Of course, as soon as people in any given group stop treating, say, *he don't* as socially unacceptable, it automatically becomes "correct." [7]

There is a close parallel between acceptable usage in language and "correct" behavior in other social customs, such as personal garb or table manners. What is it that makes it perfectly good manners to eat some things, such as bread-and-jam, with the fingers, and not others, like meat or vegetables? Certainly not the decree of any official or self-appointed authority; and certainly not any inherent feature or characteristic of what we eat or do not eat with the fingers. Some things that we eat with our fingers are much more messy than others that we would always take up with knife and fork. Here again, it is social acceptability that determines whether we may or may not eat a given item of food with our fingers, or wear a four-in-hand tie with a tuxedo. This acceptability varies from place to place, and from one period of time to another. Thus, in England it is perfectly good manners to pile your peas up on the back of your fork, using your knife as a pusher, and to eat the peas from the back of the fork; but it is very much frowned upon to keep changing the fork from the left hand to the right and back again, as Americans normally do. And the permissibility of, say, table behavior is constantly changing; for instance, I was brought up always to eat bacon with knife and fork or in a sandwich, whereas by now it has become much more widely "correct" to eat it with the fingers. [8]

"Right" and "wrong," then, have no meaning, as applied to language, apart from the situations in which language is used. That is, by definition, we can never be wrong in our own language, when we use it as we have grown up speaking it, among our own family and friends. The ditch-digger who says *him and me ain't got none* and who uses swear-words and "four-letter" words freely is absolutely right—in his own language. His type of speech is not necessarily right for the language of other groups, just through the very fact that they speak differently. But when we condemn the ditch-digger's speech, we do so, not because of any inherent demerit of the way he talks, but because we take his speech as being characteristic of his social class. This fact in our speech attitudes is a relic from earlier, antidemocratic times, which accords very poorly with other aspects of our modern aspirations to true democracy. [9]

When a person who has grown up using *him and me ain't got none* speaks in his normal, natural way and is told he is "wrong," therefore, all that this really means is that he is using these forms in a situation where his usage would make things harder rather than easier for him. But most often—in fact, we can say usually—neither the person making the "error" nor the one criticizing him understands this. As a result, speakers who have not been brought up speaking "correctly" are made to feel inferior, and either have to make a strong (and often poorly guided) effort to change their habits of speech, or else take shelter behind defensive feelings of hostility, mockery, etc., towards the approved type of speech. Current prescriptions of "right" and "wrong" thus serve only to divide our society, and to increase further the split between upper and lower, favored and unfavored classes—just at the time when greater unity, not greater division, is our crying need. [10]

2000 words, 10 paragraphs

Diction

1. Professor Hall is a linguist. Does he use professional **jargon** or special **definitions** in this essay? Why?
2. The author does use some **figures of speech** that are not too new and sprightly, "classifying him socially among *the sheep or the goats*" [7]; "it *all boils down*, really, *to* a question of acceptability" [5]; and "*set the tone* for others" [5]. Where did they come from? What do they mean? Why "sheep from goats" for example? If you do not know, guess.
3. The author mentions an "abnormal turn of phrase" [3], and "such turns of speech" [7]. Why "turns"? Speech doesn't "turn." What could the phrase possibly mean?
4. Professor Hall uses the word "parallel" in paragraph [4] to com-

pare forms of words and again in paragraph [8] to introduce a similarity. What are **"parallel forms"?**

5. In his example in paragraph [8] Hall says we would not "wear a four-in-hand tie with a tuxedo." What kind of a tie is that and why not wear it with a tuxedo? If you do not know, make an **inference** before you check.
6. An understanding of the precise meanings of the following words will increase your comprehension of this essay: arbitrary [7], decrees [2], demerit [9], host [4], incomprehensibility [5], inherent [5, 7, 8, and 9], purist [6], quasi-legal (especially the prefix) [5], relic [9], sanctions [2].

Rhetoric and Style

1. The author develops his **definition** by use of **example,** yet there are two paragraphs that have no examples in them. Which ones are they, and why are there no examples?
2. In addition to examples, the author uses **analogy** in his description of language. What is one analogy?
3. Hall complains that prescriptions of "right" and "wrong" are undemocratic [10]. He also expects a ditch-digger to say "him and me ain't got none" and to curse. Any comment?
4. Does the statement that people can "never be wrong in . . . [their] own language" [9] contradict his admission [7] that he would have his child use socially accepted forms?
5. The author actually is reclassifying "correct English" by carefully describing the way words are used. What does "correct" mean to him?
6. What is the **rhetorical** effect of placing the **thesis** in the middle of the essay [5] instead of at the beginning?

Application and Evaluation

1. Write an essay describing the different standards of "correct" dress, eating habits, speech patterns, or formality between two different cultures or two different generations. You may wish to point out the conflict these standards cause (and the waste of time).
2. Does Professor Hall convince you of his **thesis**? Why? Explain briefly.

3. Why would an American Academy of Language be a benefit to the country—or why wouldn't it?
4. Should people be allowed to talk in any manner they choose?
5. If everybody accepted Hall's **thesis,** would English teachers and linguists be out of work?

George Orwell (1903–1950) Eric Arthur Blair—Orwell's real name—was born in India, educated at Eton in England, and served for five years in the Burmese Imperial Police. A first-rate essayist, he is perhaps better known in America for his terrifying picture of the future in the novel *Nineteen Eighty-four* and the fable about communism, *Animal Farm.* The following selection may well be considered a classic; it shows Orwell's concern with the way politicians use language and is as timely today as when it was first written.

Politics and the English Language

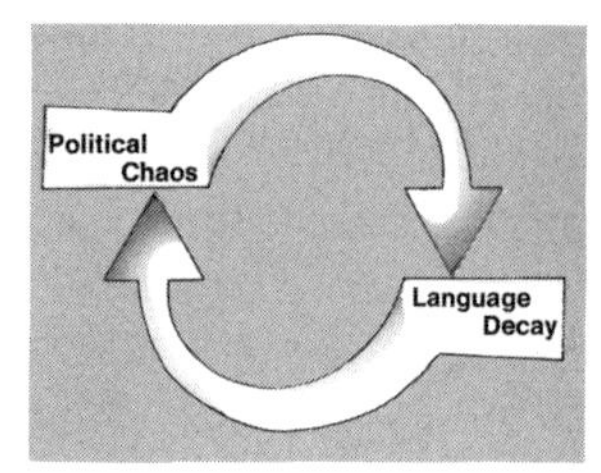

Most people who bother with the matter at all would admit that the English language is in a bad way, but it is generally assumed that we cannot by conscious action do anything about it. Our civilization is decadent and our language—so the argument runs—must inevitably share in the general collapse. It follows that any struggle against the abuse of language is a sentimental archaism, like preferring candles to electric light or hansom cabs to aeroplanes. Underneath this lies the half-conscious belief that language is a natural growth and not an instrument which we shape for our own purposes. [1]

Now, it is clear that the decline of a language must ultimately have political and economic causes: it is not due simply to the bad influence of this or that individual writer. But an effect can become a cause, reinforcing the original cause and producing the same effect in an intensified form, and so on indefinitely. A man may take to drink because he feels himself to be a failure, and then fail all the more completely because he drinks. It is rather the same thing that is happening to the English language. It becomes ugly and inaccurate because our thoughts are foolish, but the slovenliness of our language makes it easier for us to have foolish thoughts. The point is that the process is reversible. Modern English, especially written English, is full of bad habits which spread by imitation and which can be avoided if one is willing to take the necessary trouble. If one gets rid of these habits one can think more clearly, and to think clearly is a necessary first step towards political regeneration: so that the fight against bad English is not frivolous and is not the exclusive concern of professional writers. I will come back to this presently, and I hope that by that time the meaning of what I have said here will have become clearer. Meanwhile, here are five specimens of the English language as it is now habitually written. [2]

These five passages have not been picked out because they are especially bad—I could have quoted far worse if I had chosen—but because they illustrate various of the mental vices from which we now suffer. They are a little below the average, but are fairly representative samples. I number them so that I can refer back to them when necessary:

> (1) I am not, indeed, sure whether it is not true to say that the Milton who once seemed not unlike a seventeenth-century Shelley had not become, out of an experience ever more bitter in each year, more alien [*sic*] to the founder of that Jesuit sect which nothing could induce him to tolerate.
>
> *Professor Harold Laski*
> (Essay in *Freedom of Expression*).

> (2) Above all, we cannot play ducks and drakes with a native battery of idioms which prescribes such egregious collocations of vocables as the Basic *put up with* for *tolerate* or *put at a loss* for *bewilder*.
>
> *Professor Lancelot Hogben* (*Interglossa*).

> (3) On the one side we have the free personality: by definition it is not neurotic, for it has neither conflict nor dream. Its desires, such as they are, are transparent, for they are just what institutional approval keeps in the forefront of consciousness; another institutional patteern would alter their number and intensity; there is little in them that is natural, irreducible, or culturally dangerous. But *on the other side*, the social bond itself is nothing but the mutual reflection of these self-secure integrities. Recall the

definition of love. Is not this the very picture of a small academic? Where is there a place in this hall of mirrors for their personality or fraternity?

Essay on psychology in *Politics* (New York).

(4) All the "best people" from the gentlemen's clubs, and all the frantic fascist captains, united in common hatred of Socialism and bestial horror of the rising tide of the mass revolutionary movement, have turned to acts of provocation, to foul incendiarism, to medieval legends of poisoned wells, to legalize their own destruction of proletarian organizations, and rouse the agitated petty-bourgeoisie to chauvinistic fervor on behalf of the fight against the revolutionary way out of the crisis.

Communist pamphlet.

(5) If a new spirit *is* to be infused into this old country, there is one thorny and contentious reform which must be tackled, and that is the humanization and galvanization of the B.B.C. Timidity here will bespeak canker and atrophy of the soul. The heart of Britain may be sound and of strong beat, for instance, but the British lion's roar at present is like that of Bottom in Shakespeare's *Midsummer Night's Dream*—as gentle as any sucking dove. A virile new Britain cannot continue indefinitely to be traduced in the eyes or rather ears, of the world by the effete languors of Langham Place, brazenly masquerading as "standard English." When the Voice of Britain is heard at nine o'clock, better far and infinitely less ludicrous to hear aitches honestly dropped than the present priggish, inflated, inhibited, school-ma'amish arch braying of blameless bashful mewing maidens!

Letter in *Tribune* [3]

Each of these passages has faults of its own, but, quite apart from avoidable ugliness, two qualities are common to all of them. The first is staleness of imagery; the other is lack of precision. The writer either has a meaning and cannot express it, or he inadvertently says something else, or he is almost indifferent as to whether his words mean anything or not. This mixture of vagueness and sheer incompetence is the most marked characteristic of modern English prose, and especially of any kind of political writing. As soon as certain topics are raised, the concrete melts into the abstract and no one seems able to think of turns of speech that are not hackneyed: prose consists less and less of *words* chosen for the sake of their meaning, and more and more of *phrases* tacked together like the sections of a prefabricated hen-house. I list below, with notes and examples, various of the tricks by means of which the work of prose-construction is habitually dodged: [4]

Dying metaphors. A newly invented metaphor assists thought by evoking a visual image, while on the other hand a metaphor which is technically "dead" (e.g. *iron resolution*) has in effect reverted to being an ordinary word and can generally be used without loss of vividness. But in between these two classes there is a huge dump of worn-out metaphors which have lost all evocative power and are merely used because they save people the trouble of inventing phrases for themselves. Examples are: *Ring the changes on, take up the cudgels for, toe the line, ride roughshod over, stand shoulder to shoulder with, play into the hands of, no axe to grind, grist to the mill, fishing in troubled waters, on the order of the day, Achilles' heel, swan song, hotbed.* Many of these are used without knowledge of their meaning (what is a "rift," for instance?), and incompatible metaphors are frequently mixed, a sure sign that the writer is not interested in what he is saying. Some metaphors now current have been twisted out of their original meaning without those who use them even being aware of the fact. For example, *toe the line* is sometimes written *tow the line*. Another example is *the hammer and the anvil,* now always used with the implication that the anvil gets the worst of it. In real life it is always the anvil that breaks the hammer, never the other way about: a writer who stopped to think what he was saying would be aware of this, and would avoid perverting the original phrase. [5]

Operators or *verbal false limbs.* These save the trouble of picking out appropriate verbs and nouns, and at the same time pad each sentence with extra syllables which give it an appearance of symmetry. Characteristic phrases are *render inoperative, militate against, make contact with, be subjected to, give rise to, give grounds for, have the effect of, play a leading part (role) in, make iself felt, take effect, exhibit a tendency to, serve the purpose of, etc., etc.* The keynote is the elimination of simple verbs. Instead of being a single word, such as *break, stop, spoil, mend, kill,* a verb becomes a *phrase,* made up of a noun or adjective tacked on to some general-purposes verb such as *prove, serve, form, play, render.* In addition, the passive voice is wherever possible used in preference to the active, and noun constructions are used instead of gerunds (*by examination of* instead of *by examining*). The range of verbs is further cut down by means of the *-ize* and *de-* formations, and the banal statements are given an appearance of profundity by means of the *not un-* formation. Simple conjunctions and prepositions are replaced by such phrases as *with respect to, having regard to, the fact that, by dint of, in view of, in the interests of, on the hypothesis that;* and the ends of sentences are saved by anticlimax by such resounding common-places as *greatly to be desired, cannot be left out of account, a development to be expected in the near future, deserving of serious consideration, brought to a satisfactory conclusion,* and so on and so forth. [6]

Pretentious diction. Words like *phenomenon, element, individual* (as noun), *objective, categorical, effective, virtual, basic, primary, promote, constitute, exhibit, exploit, utilize, eliminate, liquidate,* are used to dress up simple statement and give an air of scientific impartiality to biased judgments. Adjectives like *epoch-making, epic, historic, unforgettable, triumphant, age-old, inevitable, inexorable, veritable,* are used to dignify the sordid processes of international politics, while writing that aims at glorifying war usually takes on an archaic color, its characteristic words being: *realm, throne, chariot, mailed fist, trident, sword, shield, buckler, banner, jackboot, clarion.* Foreign words and expressions such as *cul de sac, ancien régime, deus ex machina, mutatis mutandis, status quo, gleichschaltung, weltanschauung,* are used to give an air of culture and elegance. Except for the useful abbreviations *i.e., e.g.,* and *etc.,* there is no real need for any of the hundreds of foreign phrases now current in English. Bad writers, and especially scientific, political and sociological writers, are nearly always haunted by the notion that Latin or Greek words are grander than Saxon ones, and unnecessary words like *expedite, ameliorate, predict, extraneous, deracinated, clandestine, subaqueous* and hundreds of others constantly gain ground from their Anglo-Saxon opposite numbers.[1] The jargon peculiar to Marxist writing (*hyena, hangman, cannibal, petty bourgeois, these gentry, lacquey, flunkey, mad dog, White Guard,* etc.) consists largely of words and

[1] An interesting illustration of this is the way in which the English flower names which were in use till very recently are being ousted by Greek ones, *snapdragon* becoming *antirrhinum, forget-me-not* becoming *myosotis, etc.* It is hard to see any practical reason for this change of fashion: it is probably due to an instinctive turning-away from the more homely word and a vague feeling that the Greek word is scientific.

phrases translated from Russian, German or French; but the normal way of coining a new word is to use a Latin or Greek root with the appropriate affix and, where necessary, the size formation. It is often easier to make up words of this kind (*deregionalize, impermissible, extramarital, non-fragmentary* and so forth) than to think up the English words that will cover one's meaning. The result, in general, is an increase in slovenliness and vagueness. [7]

Meaningless words. In certain kinds of writing, particularly in art criticism and literary criticism, it is normal to come across long passages which are almost completely lacking in meaning.[2] Words like *romantic, plastic, values, human, dead, sentimental, natural, vitality,* as used in art criticism, are strictly meaningless, in the sense that they not only do not point to any discoverable object, but are hardly ever expected to do so by the reader. When one critic writes, "The outstanding feature of Mr. X's work is its living quality," while another writes, "The immediately striking thing about Mr. X's work is its peculiar deadness," the reader accepts this as a simple difference of opinion. If words like *black* and *white* were involved, instead of the jargon words *dead* and *living,* he would see at once that language was being used in an improper way. Many political words are similarly abused. The word *Fascism* has now no meaning except in so far as it signifies "something not desirable." The words *democracy, socialism, freedom, patriotic, realistic, justice,* have each of them several different meanings which cannot be reconciled with one another. In the case of a word like *democracy,* not only is there no agreed definition, but the attempt to make one is resisted from all sides. It is almost universally felt that when we call a country democratic we are praising it: consequently the defenders of every kind of régime claim that it is a democracy, and fear that they might have to stop using the word if it were tied down to any one meaning. Words of this kind are often used in a consciously dishonest way. That is, the person who uses them has his own private definition, but allows his hearer to think he means something quite different. Statements like *Marshal Pétain was a true patriot, The Soviet Press is*

[2] Example: "Comfort's catholicity of perception and image, strangely Whitmanesque in range, almost the exact opposite in aesthetic compulsion, continues to evoke that trembling atmospheric accumulative hinting at a cruel, an inexorably serene timelessness. . . . Wrey Gardiner scores by aiming at simple bull's-eyes with precision. Only they are not so simple, and through this contented sadness runs more than the surface bitter-sweet of resignation." (*Poetry Quarterly.*)

the freest in the world, The Catholic Church is opposed to persecution, are almost always made with intent to deceive. Other words used in variable meanings, in most cases more or less dishonestly, are: *class, totalitarian, science, progressive, reactionary, bourgeois, equality.* [8]

Now that I have made this catalogue of swindles and perversions, let me give another example of the kind of writing that they lead to. This time it must of its nature be an imaginary one. I am going to translate a passage of good English into modern English of the worst sort. Here is a well-known verse from *Ecclesiastes:* [9]

"I returned and saw under the sun, that the race is not to the swift, nor the battle to the strong, neither yet bread to the wise, nor yet riches to men of understanding, nor yet favour to men of skill; but time and chance happeneth to them all." [10]

Here it is in modern English: [11]

"Objective considerations of contemporary phenomena compels the conclusion that success or failure in competitive activities exhibits no tendency to be commensurate with innate capacity, but that a considerable element of the unpredictable must invariably be taken into account." [12]

This is a parody, but not a very gross one. Exhibit (3), above, for instance, contains several patches of the same kind of English. It will be seen that I have not made a full translation. The beginning and ending of the sentence follow the original meaning fairly closely, but in the middle the concrete illustrations—race, battle, bread—dissolve into the vague phrase "success or failure in competitive activities." This had to be so, because no modern writer of the kind I am discussing—no one capable of using phrases like "objective consideration of contemporary phenomena"—would ever tabulate his thoughts in that precise and detailed way. The whole tendency of modern prose is away from concreteness. Now analyse these two sentences a little more closely. The first contains forty-nine words but only sixty syllables, and all its words are those of everyday life. The second contains thirty-eight words of ninety syllables: eighteen of its words are from Latin roots, and one from Greek. The first sentence contains six vivid images, and only one phrase ("time and chance") that could be called vague. The second contains not a single fresh, arresting phrase, and in spite of its ninety syllables it gives only a shortened version of the meaning contained in the first. Yet without a doubt it is the second kind of sentence that is gaining ground in modern English. I do not want to exaggerate. This kind of writing is not yet universal, and outcrops of simplicity will occur here and there in the worst-written page. Still, if you or I were told to write a few lines on the uncertainty of human fortunes, we should probably come much nearer to my imaginary sentence than to the one from *Ecclesiastes.* [13]

As I have tried to show, modern writing at its worst does not consist in picking out words for the sake of their meaning and inventing images in order to make the meaning clearer. It consists in gumming together long strips of words which have already been set in order by someone else, and making the results presentable by sheer humbug. The attraction of this way of writing is that it is easy. It is easier—even quicker, once you have the habit—to say *In my opinion it is not an unjustifiable assumption that* than to say *I think.* If you use ready-made phrases, you not only don't have to hunt about for words; you also don't have to bother with the rhythms of your sentences, since these phrases are generally so arranged as to be more or less euphonious. When you are composing in a hurry—when you are dictating to a stenographer, for instance, or making a public speech—it is natural to fall into a pretentious, Latinized style. Tags like *a consideration which we should do well to bear in mind* or *a conclusion to which all of us would readily assent* will save many a sentence from coming down with a bump. By using stale metaphors, similes and idioms, you save much mental effort, at the cost of leaving your meaning vague, not only for your reader but for yourself. This is the significance of mixed metaphors. The sole aim of a metaphor is to call up a visual image. When these images clash—as in *The Fascist octopus has sung its swan song, the jackboot is thrown into the melting pot*—it can be taken as certain that the writer is not seeing a mental image of the objects he is naming; in other words he is not really thinking. Look again at the examples I gave at the beginning of this essay. Professor Laski (1) uses five negatives in fifty-three words. One of these is superfluous, making nonsense of the whole passage, and in addition there is the slip *alien* for akin, making further nonsense, and several avoidable pieces of clumsiness which increase the general vagueness. Professor Hogben (2) plays ducks and drakes with a battery which is able to write prescriptions, and, while disapproving of the everyday phrase *put up with,* is unwilling to look *egregious* up in the dictionary and see what it means; (3), if one takes an uncharitable attitude towards it, is simply meaningless: probably one could work out its intended meaning by reading the whole of the article in which it occurs. In (4), the writer knows more or less what he wants to say, but an accumulation of stale phrases chokes him like tea leaves blocking a sink. In (5), words and meaning have almost parted company. People who write in this manner usually have a general emotional meaning—they dislike one thing and want to express solidarity with another—but they are not interested in the detail of what they are saying. A scrupulous writer, in every sentence that he writes, will ask himself at least four questions, thus: What am I trying to say? What words will express it? What image or idiom will make it clearer? Is this image fresh enough to have an effect? And he will probably ask himself two more: Could I put it more shortly? Have I said anything that is avoidably ugly? But you are not obliged to go to all this trouble. You can shirk it by simply throwing your mind open and letting the ready-made phrases come crowding in. They will construct your sentences for you—even think your thoughts for you, to a certain extent—and at need they will perform the important service of partially concealing your meaning even from yourself. It is at this point that the special connection between politics and the debasement of language becomes clear. [14]

In our time it is broadly true that political writing is bad writing. Where it is not true, it will generally be found that the writer is some kind of rebel, expressing his private opinions and not a "party line." Orthodoxy, of whatever color, seems to demand a lifeless, imitative style. The political dialects to be found in pamphlets, leading articles, manifestos, White Papers and the speeches of under-secretaries do, of course, vary from party to party, but they are all alike in that one almost never finds in them a fresh, vivid, home-made turn of speech. When one watches some tired hack on the platform mechanically repeating the familiar phrases—*bestial atrocities, iron heel, bloodstained tyranny, free peoples of the world, stand shoulder to shoulder*—one often has a curious feeling that one is not watching a live human being but some kind of dummy: a feeling which suddenly becomes stronger at moments when the light catches the speaker's spectacles and turns them into blank discs which seem to have no eyes behind them. And this is not altogether fanciful. A speaker who uses that kind of phraseology has gone some distance towards turning himself into a machine. The appropriate noises are coming out of his larynx, but his brain is not involved as it would be if he were choosing his words for himself. If the speech he is making is one that he is accustomed to make over and over again, he may be almost unconscious of what he is saying, as one is when one utters the responses in church. And this reduced state of consciousness, if not indispensable, is at any rate favorable to political conformity. [15]

In our time, political speech and writing are largely the defence of the indefensible. Things like the continuance of British rule in India, the Russian purges and deportations, the dropping of the atom bombs on Japan, can indeed be defended, but only by arguments which are too brutal for most people to face, and which do not square with the professed aims of political parties. Thus political language has to consist largely of euphemism, question-begging and sheer cloudy vagueness. Defenceless villages are bombarded from the air, the inhabitants driven out into the countryside, the cattle machine-gunned, the huts set on fire with incendiary bullets: this is called *pacification*. Millions of peasants are robbed of their farms and sent trudging along the roads with no more than they can carry: this is called *transfer of population* or *rectification of frontiers*. People are imprisoned for years without trial, or shot in the back of the neck or sent to die of scurvy in Arctic lumber camps: this is called *elimination of unreliable elements*. Such phraseology is needed if one wants to name things without calling up mental pictures of them. Consider for instance some comfortable English professor defending Russian totalitarianism. He cannot say outright, "I believe in killing off your opponents when you can get good results by doing so." Probably, therefore, he will say something like this: [16]

"While freely conceding that the Soviet régime exhibits certain features which the humanitarian may be inclined to deplore, we must, I think, agree that a certain curtailment of the right to political opposition is an unavoidable concomitant of transitional periods, and that the rigors which the Russian people have been called upon to undergo have been amply justified in the sphere of concrete achievement." [17]

The inflated style is itself a kind of euphemism. A mass of Latin words falls upon the facts like soft snow, blurring the outlines and covering up all the details. The great enemy of clear language is insincerity. When there is a gap between one's real and one's declared aims, one turns as it were instinctively to long words and exhausted idioms, like a cuttlefish squirting out ink. In our age there is no such thing as "keeping out of politics." All issues are political issues, and politics iteslf is a mass of lies, evasions, folly, hatred and schizophrenia. When the general atmosphere is bad, language must suffer. I should expect to find—this is a guess which I have not sufficient knowledge to verify—that the German, Russian and Italian languages have all deteriorated in the last ten or fifteen years, as a result of dictatorship. [18]

But if thought corrupts language, language can also corrupt

thought. A bad usage can spread by tradition and imitation, even among people who should and do know better. The debased language that I have been discussing is in some ways very convenient. Phrases like *a not unjustifiable assumption, leaves much to be desired, would serve no good purpose, a consideration which we should do well to bear in mind,* are a continuous temptation, a packet of aspirins always at one's elbow. Look back through this essay, and for certain you will find that I have again and again committed the very faults I am protesting against. By this morning's post I have received a pamphlet dealing with conditions in Germany. The author tells me that he "felt impelled" to write it. I open it at random, and here is almost the first sentence that I see: "[The Allies] have an opportunity not only of achieving a radical transformation of Germany's social and political structure in such a way as to avoid a nationalistic reaction in Germany itself, but at the same time of laying the foundations of a co-operative and unified Europe." You see, he "feels impelled" to write—feels, presumably, that he has something new to say—and yet his words, like cavalry horses answering the bugle, group themselves automatically into the familiar dreary pattern. This invasion of one's mind by ready-made phrases (*lay the foundations, achieve a radical transformation*) can only be prevented if one is constantly on guard against them, and every such phrase anaesthetizes a portion of one's brain. [19]

I said earlier that the decadence of our language is probably curable. Those who deny this would argue, if they produced an argument at all, that language merely reflects existing social conditions, and that we cannot influence its development by any direct tinkering with words and constructions. So far as the general tone or spirit of a language goes, this may be true, but it is not true in detail. Silly words and expressions have often disappeared, not through any evolutionary process but owing to the conscious action of a minority. Two recent examples were *explore every avenue* and *leave no stone unturned,* which were killed by the jeers of a few journalists. There is a long list of flyblown metaphors which could similarly be got rid of if enough people would interest themselves in the job; and it should also be possible to laugh the *not un-* formation out of existence,[3] to reduce the amount of Latin and Greek in the average sentence, to drive out foreign phrases and strayed scientific words,

[3] One can cure herself of the *not un-* formation by memorizing this sentence: *A not unblack dog was chasing a not unsmall rabbit across a not ungreen field.*

and, in general, to make pretentiousness unfashionable. But all these are minor points. The defence of the English language implies more than this, and perhaps it is best to start by saying what it does *not* imply. [20]

To begin with it has nothing to do with archaism, with the salvaging of obsolete words and turns of speech, or with the setting up of a "standard English" which must never be departed from. On the contrary, it is especially concerned with the scrapping of every word or idiom which has outworn its usefulness. It has nothing to do with correct grammar and syntax, which are of no importance so long as one makes one's meaning clear, or with the avoidance of Americanisms, or with having what is called a "good prose style." On the other hand it is not concerned with fake simplicity and the attempt to make written English colloquial. Nor does it even imply in every case preferring the Saxon word to the Latin one, though it does imply using the fewest and shortest words that will cover one's meaning. What is above all needed is to let the meaning choose the word, and not the other way about. In prose, the worst thing one can do with words is to surrender to them. When you think of a concrete object, you think wordlessly, and then, if you want to describe the thing you have been visualizing you probably hunt about till you find the exact words that seem to fit it. When you think of something abstract you are more inclined to use words from the start, and unless you make a conscious effort to prevent it, the existing dialect will come rushing in and do the job for you, at the expense of blurring or even changing your meaning. Probably it is better to put off using words as long as possible and get one's meaning as clear as one can through pictures or sensations. Afterwards one can choose—not simply *accept*—the phrases that will best cover the meaning, and then switch round and decide which impression one's words are likely to make on another person. This last effort of the mind cuts out all stale or mixed images, all prefabricated phrases, needless repetitions, and humbug and vagueness generally. But one can often be in doubt about the effect of a word or a phrase, and one needs rules that one can rely on when instinct fails. I think the following rules will cover most cases:

(i) Never use a metaphor, simile or other figure of speech which you are used to seeing in print.

(ii) Never use a long word where a short one will do.

(iii) If it is possible to cut a word out, always cut it out.

(iv) Never use the passive where you can use the active.

(v) Never use a foreign phrase, a scientific word or a jargon word if you can think of an everyday English equivalent.

(vi) Break any of these rules sooner than say anything outright barbarous. [21]

These rules sound elementary, and so they are, but they demand a deep change of attitude in anyone who has grown used to writing in the style now fashionable. One could keep all of them and still write bad English, but one could not write the kind of stuff that I quoted in those five specimens at the beginning of this article. [22]

I have not here been considering the literary use of language, but merely language as an instrument for expressing and not for concealing or preventing thought. Stuart Chase and others have come near to claiming that all abstract words are meaningless, and have used this as a pretext for advocating a kind of political quietism. Since you don't know what Fascism is, how can you struggle against Fascism? One need not swallow such absurdities as this, but one ought to recognize that the present political chaos is connected with the decay of language, and that one can probably bring about some improvement by starting at the verbal end. If you simplify your English, you are freed from the worst follies of orthodoxy. You cannot speak any of the necessary dialects, and when you make a stupid remark its stupidity will be obvious, even to yourself. Political language—and with variations this is true of all political parties, from Conservatives to Anarchists—is designed to make lies sound truthful and murder respectable, and to give an appearance of solidity to pure wind. One cannot change this all in a moment, but one can at least change one's own habits, and from time to time one can even, if one jeers loudly enough, send some worn-out and useless phrase—some *jackboot, Achilles' heel, hotbed, melting pot, acid test, veritable inferno* or other lump of verbal refuse—into the dustbin where it belongs. [23]

5900 words, 23 paragraphs

Sir Francis Bacon, Baron Verulam, Viscount St. Albans (1561–1626) Bacon has been called the Father of Modern Science, not so much because he was a great scientist, but because, in *The Advancement of Learning* and other works, he proposed the inductive method as the way to truth. Known for his famous essays, he also wrote *Novum Organon,* in which he notes the hinderances we must overcome before we can think clearly. The selection here is based on the standard nineteenth-century translation but has been revised from Bacon's original list of aphorisms to meet modern American usage.

Idols of the Mind

It is idle to expect any great advancement from science from the grafting of new things upon the old. We must begin anew from the very foundations, unless we would revolve forever in a circle. The idols and false notions that already preoccupy the human understanding are deeply rooted in it and so beset men's minds that truth can scarcely find an entrance. Even when it does, they will again trouble us unless, being forewarned, we fortify ourselves against their assaults. [1]

Four classes of Idols beset men's minds; to these, for distinction's sake, I have assigned names, calling the first, *Idols of the Tribe*; the second, *Idols of the Den*; the third, *Idols of the Market-place*; the fourth, *Idols of the Theatre.* The use of true induction in the formation of ideas and axioms is the only fitting way of clearing away and keeping free of these Idols; however, it is of great service to point them out. [2]

The Idols of the Tribe have their foundation in human nature, in the tribe or race of men. It is a false assertion that man's senses are the measure of all things. For man's perceptions, both of the senses and the mind, bear reference to man and not to the universe. The human mind resembles those uneven mirrors which distort and disfigure images by mingling their own natures with the reflections. [3]

The Idols of the Den are those of the individual man. For everybody (in addition to the errors common to the tribe of man) has a cave or den of his own, which refracts and distorts the light of nature according to his own peculiar nature, or to his education and conversation with others, or to his reading of books and acceptance of the authority of those he esteems and admires, or to the differences impressions make upon his mind depending on whether the mind is tranquil or troubled, preoccupied or predisposed. The spirit of man is a thing variable and full of perturbation, and governed, as it were, by chance. As Heraclitus said, men look for sciences in their own lesser worlds and not in the greater world. [4]

There are also Idols formed by the association and intercourse of men with each other, which I call *Idols of the Marketplace* from the commerce and consort of men there. For men converse by means of language; but words are formed by the use of the majority; and there arises from the ill and unfit choice of words a wonderful obstruction to understanding. Nor can the definitions or explanations with which learned men are wont to guard and defend themselves always set the matter straight, for words can overrule the understanding, throw everything into confusion, and lead mankind into empty controversies and idle fancies. [5]

Lastly there are Idols which have crept into man's minds from the various dogmas of strange philosophies and from twisted rules of demonstration. These I call *Idols of the Theatre*, because all of these systems are so many stage plays representing unreal, scenic worlds of their own creation. Nor is it only of the systems now in vogue, nor only of the systems of the ancients that I speak; for many more plays of the same kind may be yet composed and, in a similar artificial manner, be presented and made to agree with each other, the causes of most errors being alike. Nor do I mean only entire systems, but also parts of systems such as those axioms and principles accepted by science which have become accepted through tradition, credulity, and neglect. [6]

But of these several kinds of Idols I must speak more largely and exactly, that the understanding may be duly cautioned. [7]

The human understanding of its own nature imposes a greater order and a regularity upon the world than it actually finds there. Although many things in the world singular and unattached, yet man finds for them parallels and conjugates and relatives that do not exist. Hence the fiction that all celestial bodies move in perfect circles and spirals. Hence too the element of fire being brought in to make a perfect square with the other three which the sense perceives. Hence also the ratio of the density of the so-called elements is arbitrarily fixed at ten to one. And so on of other dreams, for the human understanding when once it has adopted an opinion draws all things else to support and agree with it. Though there be a greater number and weight of instances to be found on the other side, yet these it either neglects and despises, or else by some distinction sets aside and rejects. And therefore it was a good answer that was made by the one who, when shown in a temple a picture of those who paid their vows having escaped being shipwrecked and being asked would he not now accept the power of the gods—"Aye," he asked, "but where are they painted that were drowned after their vows?" And such is the way of all superstitions: astrology, dreams, omens or the like where men mark the event when it is fulfilled, but neglect and pass by when the event is not fulfilled. [8]

But by far the greatest hinderance and aberration of the human understanding is caused by the dullness, incompetency, and deceptions of the senses. Things which srtike the senses outweigh things that do not immediately strike them, though they might be more important. Hence it is that speculation commonly ceases where sight ceases. The subtle changes of form go unobserved, and yet, unless they are brought to light, nothing great can be achieved. For the sense by itself is infirm and erring; neither can instruments for enlarging and sharpening the senses do much. Such, then, are the Idols of the Tribe which take their rise from the shape and substance of the human form and spirit. [9]

The Idols of the Den take their rise from the peculiar mental or physical constitution of each individual; and also from the education, habit, and accidental events which have befallen each man. For example, men become attached to certain particular sciences and speculations, either because they are the inventors or because they have bestowed great pains upon them. Then they will distort any new philosophy to comply with their former fancy. Aristotle, thus, made his natural philosophy a mere bond servant to his logic, thereby rendering it well nigh useless. The race of chemists, out of a few experiments of the furnace, have built up a fantastic philosophy framed with reference to new things. Gilbert, after he had worked most laboriously with the loadstone, constructed an entire system in accordance with his favorite subject. Let our provision and prudence for dislodging the Idols of the Den be to take this as a rule: Whatever the mind seizes and dwells on with most satisfaction is to be held in greatest suspicion. [10]

But the Idols of the Marketplace are the most troublesome of all—idols which have crept into the mind through the alliance of words and names. For men believe that their reason governs words; but it is also true that words react upon the understanding. Now, words are usually developed and applied according to the capacity of the common man, follow those lines of division which are most obvious to the common man. When the need arises to change or shift those lines of division, words stand in the way and resist change. It often comes to pass that the high and formal discussion of learned men often ends in disputes about words and names. According to the use and wisdom of the mathematicians, it would be more prudent to begin by means of definition. Yet, even definitions cannot cure this evil for definitions themselves are words, and those words beget others. It is always necessary to recure to individual instances in due series and order. [11]

The idols imposed by words are of two kinds: the names of things which do not exist or the names of things which exist, but yet are confused, or ill-defined or hastily and irregularly derived from realities. Of the former kind are Fortune, the Prime Mover, Planetary Orbits, Element of Fire and like fictions. This class of idol is easily gotten rid of by steadily rejecting and dismissing theories as obsolete. But the other class springs from a faulty and unskilled abstraction and is intricate and deeply rooted. [12]

The Idols of the Theatre are not inate, nor do they steal into the understanding secretly, but are plainly impressed and received into the mind from the playbooks of the philosophical systems and twisted rules of demonstration. To attempt refutation of the demonstrations would be useless; the question would evolve only as to who kept the right way. For, as the saying is, the lame man who keeps the right road outstrips the runner who takes the wrong road. Nay, it is clear that when a man runs the wrong way, the swifter and more active he is, the more he will go astray. [13]

Idols of the Theatre, or of systems, are many, and there can be and perhaps will be many more. For as on the phenomena of the Heavens many hypotheses may be constructed, so likewise (and more so) many dogmas may be constructed on the phenomena of philosophy. And of the plays of this philosophical theatre one may observe the same thing that is found in plays of the theatre, that stories invented for the stage are more compact and elegant and more as one would wish them to be than true stories out of history. [14]

1575 words, 14 paragraphs

Writing Suggestions for Description

Descriptive writing rarely occurs by and for itself. "The Domain of Arnheim" by Edgar Allan Poe is, with the pendant "Landor's Cottage," one of the few pieces of extended description. More often, the descriptive unit is a purposeful part of a longer **essay** or **narrative.** While a purely descriptive essay is rare, a descriptive paragraph is commonplace.

The Descriptive Paragraph

A. Realistic Description

1. From top to bottom
2. From left to right
3. From distant to close
4. Reversal of the above

Be sure to keep the sequence consistent so the reader will not become confused. Do not jump about. Do not describe illogical items (like things behind closed doors).

B. Impressionistic Description

1. Select and list details
2. Relate interpretations
3. Tell feelings aroused
4. Combine 1 and 3

The impressionistic description will use more connotative words, although it may follow the same pattern in space as the realistic.

C. Either or Both

1. Select dominant impression
   a. one sense (e.g., sound)
   b. size or shape (e.g., tiny or huge)
   c. attribute (e.g., ugly or lovely)
2. Observe keenly; relate exactly
   a. the parts
   b. their relationship to whole

The purpose is to picture in words either the sense impressions, the reaction to them, or the conclusions drawn from them. Be as accurate as possible.

Selected Topics for Description

1. Observe a tree. Describe it. Look at it upside down between your legs. You will be surprised at how much more you will see.
2. Observe the traffic pattern on the campus, in a building, or around an eating area. Describe the general flow of people. Can you make a generalized theory from your description?
3. Write a simple description of a room in your house or dormitory. Do not move from your selected spot and do not describe anything you cannot sense. Does your description have a dominant mood?
4. Try a few one-liners; answer the questions "How fat was he?" "How small was it?" or "How ________ was ________?" with a smashing **simile** of your own creation.
5. Select an occupation (like plumbing or bookkeeping) and write an exaggerated description of a person engaged in that trade with his attendant paraphernalia. (Reread Deloria or Twain.)
6. Describe, **impressionistically** and emotionally, one of the pseudosciences like astrology, tarot reading, numerology, or seance holding.
7. Describe in a **realistic** fashion one of the tribal folkways of the American people (marriage, divorce, eating taboos, for example).
8. Write a brief description in which one sense dominates. (Examples: life near an airport, in a boiler factory, beside a stockyard.)
9. Now write a second paragraph showing the way you or another might interpret that description (from question 8).
10. Although it is admittedly very difficult, try to create a dominant impression; fear, awe, anger, huge size, foreboding, hilarity, joy. To do so you will have to select the **details** of your description carefully. It can be done by describing a room, for instance, with **connotative** rather than **denotative** words.
11. Describe a person by listing only his good qualities. Write another paragraph listing only his bad qualities. For each paragraph write a brief statement about how this person might be **classified**. It is easier to use a real person.
12. Try the technique used in Question 11 to describe a thing. Use a building, perhaps, or a functioning mechanical contrivance of some type. If you decide to reclassify it, try to see it as your great grandfather might.
13. The process of **classification** is based on accurate observation and clear description. Agree or disagree (as your instructor sug-

gests) with each of the following classifications by your description of the thing being classified. Devote one paragraph to each description.

a. A sixteen-year-old human being is an adult.
b. A college football player is an amateur.
c. Aspirin is a drug.
d. The practice of medicine is a trade.

14. How many **classes** do you fit into? (Consider sex, race, general age, schooling, home, marital status, for example.) Make a valid **induction**—generalize from your own situation—about people and then write a well-organized paragraph on this subject.

exposition

Exposition is the informative mode; it informs or shows; it exposes. If narration answers the question, "What happened to it?" and description answers the question, "What did it look like?" **exposition** answers the rest of the questions that might be asked about an object, an event, or an idea.

What is it?
What is it for?
What good is it?
What does it mean?
How does it work?
How is it put together?

What caused it?

What will it cause?

Obviously, *expository writing* is the type most used by college students, for the bulk of college writing is meant to answer questions and to explain ideas and processes. As noted before, it is rare for any of the four modes of rhetoric to be used in a pure form. Exposition may have some description to clarify or a bit of argumentation to pursuade or some narration to enhance. So when expository prose is referred to, the reference is to prose that is *primarily* expository in nature.

There are four main methods of writing exposition; the competent writer usually selects the method that best suits his purpose, his material, and his audience. Each of these methods is more fully explained in the Glossary.

1. **Analysis**
   a. **Technical analysis** How is it put together?
   b. **Functional analysis** How does it work? Shows the working of the parts, singly or together.
   c. **Process analysis** How is it made? Usually shows the action of an agent.
   d. **Causal analysis** What caused it?
2. **Comparison** (showing the similarities) and **Contrast** (showing the differences). Comparing and contrasting are often used in a single essay as well as separately.
3. **Definition.** Definition is primarily a request to share experiences. The glossary shows the basic ways of developing this method.
4. **Illustration.** Illustration is the use of one instance as typical of the whole.

In this section "The Lessons of Watergate" and "My Wood" are causal analyses, while "To Build a World" is a process analysis. "Witchdoctors and the Universality of Healing" compares two types of healing. "Apache Riches" contrasts (with some comparison) two concepts of wealth. "Of Men and Mockingbirds" indicates the similarities between the two creatures. The final trio of essays show different uses and types of **analogy.** "The Enforcer" emphasizes the analogy of sport to combat; "Is This Education?" suggests an analogy as a possible explanation of a seeming mystery; "The Population Bomb" is one great analogy: population as a bomb.

Some writers insist that analogy is merely a special type of **comparison.** Others maintain that analogy is really the basis of **metaphor** or a kind of **parable.** However it is classified, it is most useful to the writer, for it may be used to aid a definition, to illustrate an exposition, to clarify an argument.

Although there are no separate sections showing the use of definition and illustration, note that each of the authors makes use of those two methods in his essay. As has been noted before, in practice these methods of development and modes of rhetoric tend to overlap. They are isolated or emphasized to make explanation and understanding easier.

Ralph Nader (1934–   ) Since his book *Unsafe at Any Speed* brought his concern for public welfare vividly to the attention of America, Ralph Nader has been recognized as our most uncompromising (and uncompromised) investigator and consumer defender. Educated at Princeton and with a law degree from Harvard, Mr. Nader is the author of many articles and essays. He is credited with the passage of federal laws imposing standards on cars, meat and poultry products, and coal mining, and other laws setting safety rules for radiation and gas. He is the founder of Public Interest Research Group (1970), which investigates and does research on consumer problems and issues. In this essay he analyzes the lessons of Watergate and outlines what each citizen can do to see that it never happens again.

The Lessons of Watergate

And all the people gathered themselves together as one man into the street that was before the water gate; and they spake unto Ezra the scribe to bring the book of the law of Moses. . . . And Ezra the priest brought the law before the assembly both of men and women and all that could hear with understanding.

—Nehemiah 8:1-3

How could the Watergate conspiracy and related crimes have happened? Our founding fathers tried to build a constitutional system of government with institutional safeguards against the frailties of men in positions of political power. Having expelled King George III, they were in no mood to replace a foreign monarchy with a domestic one. That is why they provided Congress with the pre-eminent authorities in government—the power to tax, to spend, and to make war. That is why they provided for an independent court system and freedom of the press under the First Amendment. And that is why they accorded citizens the Bill of Rights as protection from the tyranny of the state and as tools to advance justice. [1]

But in recent decades—spurred by wars, expanded government duties, weak Congressional leadership and the use of mass communications—the power of the Presidency has grown and the arrogance of Presidents has swollen accordingly. [2]

As Presidents are given and take more power, and as they become less accountable, it is not surprising that they become more royal in their thinking and behavior. It was Louis XIV of France who said "*L'état c'est moi*" (I am the state). Increasingly, until Watergate, too many people looked upon the White House and the Presidency with reverence instead of earned respect, with faith instead of reason. This drift toward royalty has been cultivated by inhabitants of the White House, who do not hesitate to issue policies as edicts, to shield activity from scrutiny, and to wave the flag vigorously to keep down the reaction when troubles and tragedies ensue. [3]

Both the Congress and the press have been cowed by these Presidential techniques, which only further emboldens the White House to occupy more remote pedestals. Such a state of affairs was clearly not what Thomas Jefferson or Benjamin Franklin had in mind. Nor should we. [4]

The belief that neither the Congress nor the courts could reach into the White House set the stage for the Watergate conspiracy. Two more ingredients were needed, however. One was money, and the Nixon supporters had no difficulty raising many millions of dollars from business sources who wanted something from the government or wanted the government to be lenient. The other was a cadre of political operatives who could pass orders from one to another in a context of blind loyalty to the President and his aides. As Herbert Porter, one of the lower-level operatives, said to the Senate Committee when asked why he did not protest his superior's suggestion that he perjure himself: "I have been guilty of a deep sense of loyalty to the President of the United States." To which Republican Senator Howard Baker of Tennessee replied that loyalty can never excuse the abdication of one's conscience. Such loyalty to men rather than to the laws and the Constitution was apparent all the way up the ladder to the President and his chief aides. These aides have considerable power but escape Senatorial confirmation and Congressional interrogation through their White House status as part of the President's official family. [5]

The public exposure of the Watergate conspiracy began when the conditions that nourished this conspiracy began to crumble. First, ironically enough for a law-and-order administration, the police caught the burglars at the Watergate; they were then brought before a tough judge and convicted. The press, most notably the *Washington Post,* never gave up probing deeper into this sordid episode at a time in late 1972 and early 1973 when the coverup almost seemed to succeed. That sleeping giant of democracy, Congress, began to exercise its constitutional duties and investigate the subversion of the national elections. The tight web of slavish loyalty began to unravel when a few of the culprits put their interests above that of the "Nixon team's," and began to tell the truth as the law held them more personally responsible for their behavior. They could no longer get along by going along. Citizen groups, such as Common Cause, began to flush out incriminating facts through court suits. Public opinion forced the appointment of a special federal prosecutor to bring the Watergate criminals to justice. [6]

Welcome as these democratic initiatives are for law enforcement purposes, they come too late to prevent the harm done to last year's Presidential election. The Watergate activities and coverup strove to deny Americans, in Walter Cronkite's words, the "right to choose their President fair and square." In this, the coverup succeeded. The importance of keeping the White House's Watergate involvement secret was unquestioned. As coverup participant Jeb Magruder told the Senate hearing in June: "I honestly think his [President Nixon's] election probably would have been negated." [7]

Looking backward is constructive if it helps us to look forward. Like exercise for a human muscle, Watergate can be the political exercise for our society to deepen its understanding of our constitutional freedoms and responsibilities—but only if we put them into practice. As voters and citizens, we have tolerated for too long over the past generation government lawlessness, influence peddling by economic interests, the huge role of money in elections, and the nonenforcement of laws that tame the excesses of powerful groups. Against this background, Watergate is a symptom of a malaise underlying the failure of government to stand up adequately for the interests of the people: consumers, taxpayers, workers, women, and minorities. In both the short and long run, the quality of a democracy depends on the quality of citizenship. And whether it is to head off another Watergate or actively to foster good government, we must help make the following changes: [8]

1. Citizens should not be cynical toward officials holding public office, particularly high public office. If people expect politicians to

behave badly (as reflected in the phrase "that's politics"), then it is more likely that such behavior will continue. Rather, public office holders should be held to high standards of expectation, so that their activities can be measured accordingly. There is little more destructive than a public attitude that the Watergate scandal was "just politics." It undermines public support for thorough law enforcement against political crimes—support that would deter any would-be violators in the future. [9]

2. We must insist on an open government that provides accurate and timely information to the public about its activities. Presently, secrecy envelops government (far beyond any needs of national security) in order to prevent the people from knowing about and evaluating their public servants. Information is the currency of democracy. Its denial must always be suspect and the burden of proof to explain any such denial must always rest on government. Without information, the press cannot begin to do its job, voters will not know what they are voting for, and manipulative techniques and emotional slogans will continue to be on the White House's political menu. [10]

3. The reform and strengthening of Congress should be a top priority for Americans of all political persuasions. As a continually elected body, a people-oriented Congress, willing to use its estimable constitutional powers to supervise the Executive branch, can do more to clean up government than any other institution. High on its reform agenda should be changing the existing secretive way of financing political campaigns by special interests, as well as improving the Congress's own procedures and facilities so that it can meet its responsibilities promptly in the public interest. It is the Congress's historic duty to stop the steady usurpation of its powers by the Presidency, to set right the system of checks and balances, and to open itself to the participation of citizens in its deliberations. While it may take some time to improve the accountability of the 2,500,000-strong federal bureaucracy, it need not take long at all for voters to improve the ability of Congress to open up the bureaucracy to efficient and accountable performance. The Watergate jolt can be a strong assist in this direction. [11]

4. Citizens should be able to enforce the law against public office holders and civil servants who do not observe the law. Unless illegal activity (either positive illegality such as Watergate or systematic refusal to enforce the laws and administer programs) is reachable by those Americans who are harmed or defrauded (as taxpayers), there will not be a responsive, just government. The tech-

nical barriers that now insulate the government from the people have no justification other than to keep government derelictions above the law. We should keep in mind: "Who guards the guards?" In a democracy, the answer is: the people. This means that from the President on down, the law must be supreme if public officials are not to be a law unto themselves. The citizens should be able to invoke these laws more speedily if standards of proper government behavior are to be observed more promptly. [12]

5. Finally, the bedrock of an embracing democracy is a growing number of active and skilled citizens. In our country, we have more problems than we deserve—and more solutions than we use. What is so necessary is to develop the engines that put these solutions to work. Citizen action is the fuel for those engines—the *only* fuel. We can no longer abdicate nor delegate our citizen obligations unless we wish to perpetuate the same governmental and business sickness that gave rise to Watergate and many other public injustices in the consumer, environmental, housing, tax, and other areas. [13]

As a democracy, this nation is both vulnerable and resilient. Watergate brought out both traits in a very dramatic and detailed way. But if Americans are to find motivation for more citizen involvement because of their resolution at Watergate-type scandals —and they often occur on a smaller scale at the state and local levels— each individual has to spend time and energy on the causes or problems of her or his choice. A new way of life—the citizen way— is badly needed as an antidote to that helpless feeling so many people harbor against the injustices that fester but can be prevented. [14]

It is my belief that citizen action can be both important and fun. It can overcome the feelings of loneliness, alienation, or boredom that plague so many people—while at the same time constructively help people to harness their potential power to do good. And like other areas of human endeavor, practice makes perfect. [15]

1850 words, 15 paragraphs

Diction

1. Check the use of "embolden" [4] and "presently" [10]; are they used in a standard fashion? What does the prefix "em-" mean?
2. Why is the phrase "Who guards the guards?" [12] in quotation marks?
3. What is the meaning of "blind loyalty" [5]? Why is some kind

of loyalty called "blind"? What is the difference between "blind loyalty" and "unswerving devotion"?

4. The headnote calls Mr. Nader "uncompromising (and uncompromised)." What does the phrase mean?
5. In paragraph [8] the author calls Watergate "a symptom of a malaise." What does he actually mean?
6. Always look up the meanings of any new or difficult words in a good up-to-date dictionary. Here are some to start with: accorded [1], estimable [11], foster [8], incriminating [6], manipulative [10], resilient [14], sordid [6], strove [7], usurpation [12], vulnerable [14].

Rhetoric and Style

1. What is the purpose of the quotation from the Bible at the beginning of this selection?
2. Why would Mr. Nader call Congress "the sleeping giant of democracy" [6]? Explain the **metaphor.**
3. Can you find any other **metaphors** used to make the meaning of the ideas more clear? List two or three; are they effective?
4. This essay is a two-part presentation. The first part **analyzes,** and the second part offers a solution to a problem. Where is the division? How are the two parts tied together?
5. What seem to be the author's **tone** and **attitude** toward his subject? How can you tell?
6. Mr. Nader usually offers some exact directions and gives places to seek information. In this essay he appended the following items of information. It might be interesting to follow through.

   For information about how to obtain material describing the Congress and members of Congress that will assist citizen involvement, write to Grossman Publishers, Box 19281, Washington, D.C. 20036.

   For a collection of community problems that citizens can work to diminish *A Public Citizen's Action Manual* by Donald Ross (1973) at your library or bookstore.

Applications and Evaluation

1. The author compares the growth of presidential power to royalty. Is such a **comparison** fair or valid? Exactly what powers of

royalty are shown by an elected official? What royal powers does he lack?

2. Three conditions were necessary for the Watergate conspiracy to develop [5]. If those conditions continued to exist, what caused the conspiracy to crumble? In your opinion does Mr. Nader adequately explain the collapse? Discuss.
3. Might there be circumstances when our elected officials should be able to break the law? Consider grave national emergencies, need for sudden action, or other possible problems, and write a brief paper either defending the need for breaking the law or condemning any attempt to break the law by elected officials.
4. Mr. Nader offers five specific changes that will help to foster good government. He has presented a problem and is offering a solution. Write an essay in which you follow the same pattern of **analysis** and solution. Here are some topics: taping or recording of private conversations by government agencies; the growth of government (2½ million employees?); the general apathy of voters; campaign contributions by large corporations who expect, and get, special consideration later.
5. What is the **thesis** of this essay? Write it in one sentence.

Edward M. Forster (1879–1971) was a British novelist, essayist, short-story writer, and literary critic. Educated at Cambridge, he is probably best known in America for his novel *Passage to India,* to which he refers in this essay. His short novel *Howard's End* and his study of fiction, *Aspects of the Novel,* gained him much respect on both sides of the Atlantic. He is noted for his subtle use of irony. This particular essay is from *Abinger Harvest,* a collection. In it Forster analyzes the effect of property on himself and, by implication, on anybody. It is a tightly organized essay, filled with allusions.

My Wood

A few years ago I wrote a book which dealt in part with the difficulties of the English in India. Feeling that they would have had no difficulties in India themselves, the Americans read the book freely. The more they read it the better it made them feel, and a cheque to the author was the result. I bought a wood with the cheque. It is not a large wood—it contains scarcely any trees, and it is intersected, blast it, by a public footpath. Still, it is the first property that I have owned, so it is right that other people should participate in my shame, and should ask themselves, in accents that will vary in horror, this very important question: What is the effect of property upon the character? Don't let's touch economics; the effect of private ownership upon the community as a whole is another question—a more important question, perhaps, but another one. Let's keep to psychology. If you own things, what's their effect on you? What's the effect on me of my wood? [1]

In the first place, it makes me feel heavy. Property does have this effect. Property produces men of weight, and it was a man of weight who failed to get into the Kingdom of Heaven. He was not wicked, that unfortunate millionaire in the parable, he was only stout; he stuck out in front, not to mention behind, and as he wedged himself this way and that in the crystalline entrance and bruised his well-fed flanks, he saw beneath him a comparatively slim camel passing through the eye of a needle and being woven into the robe of God. The Gospels all through couple stoutness and slowness. They point out what is perfectly obvious, yet seldom realized: that if you have a lot of things you cannot move about a lot, that furniture requires dusting, dusters require servants, servants require insurance stamps, and the whole tangle of them makes you think twice before you accept an invitation to dinner or go for a bathe in the Jordon. Sometimes the Gospels proceed further and say with Tolstoy that property is sinful; they approach the difficult ground of asceticism here, where I cannot follow them. But as to the immediate effects of property on people they just show straightforward logic. It produces men of weight. Men of weight cannot, by definition, move like the lightening from the East unto the West, and the ascent of a fourteen-stone bishop into a pulpit is thus the exact antithesis of the coming of the Son of Man. My wood makes me feel heavy. [2]

In the second place, it makes me feel it ought to be larger. [3]

The other day I heard a twig snap in it. I was annoyed at first, for I thought someone was blackberrying, and depreciating the value of the undergrowth. On coming nearer, I saw it was not a man who had trodden on the twig and snapped it, but a bird, and I felt pleased. My bird. The bird was not equally pleased. Ignoring the relation between us, it took fright as soon as it saw the shape of my face, and flew straight over the boundary hedge into a field, the property of Mrs. Henessy, where it sat with a loud squawk. It had become Mrs. Henessy's bird. Something seemed grossly amiss here, something that would not have occurred had the wood been larger. I could not afford to buy Mrs. Henessy out, I dared not murder her, and limitations of this sort beset me on every side. Ahab did not want that vineyard—he only needed it to round off his property, preparatory to plotting a new curve—and all the land around my wood has become necessary to me in order to round off the wood. A boundary protects. But—poor little thing—the boundary ought in its turn to be protected. Noises on the edge of it. Children throw stones. A little more, and then a little more, until we reach the sea. Happy Canute! Happier Alexander! And after all, why should even the world be the limit of possession? A rocket containing a Union Jack, will, it is hoped, be shortly fired at the moon. Mars, Sirius. Beyond which . . .

But these immensities ended by saddening me. I could not suppose that my wood was the destined nucleus of universal dominion—it is so very small and contains no mineral wealth beyond the blackberries. Nor was I comforted when Mrs. Henessy's bird took alarm for the second time and flew clean away from us all, under the belief that it belonged to itself. [4]

In the third place property makes its owner feel that he ought to do something to it. Yet he isn't sure what. A restlessness comes over him, a vague sense that he has a personality to express—the same sense which, without any vagueness, leads the artist to an act of creation. Sometimes I think I will cut down such trees as remain in the wood, at other times I want to fill up the gaps between them with new trees. Both impulses are pretentious and empty. They are not honest movements toward money-making or beauty. They spring from a foolish desire to express myself and from an inability to enjoy what I have got. Creation, property, enjoyment form a sinister trinity in the human mind. Creation and enjoyment are both very, very good, yet they are often unattainable without a material basis, and at such moments property pushes itself in as a substitute saying, "Accept me instead—I'm good enough for all three." It is not enough. It is, as Shakespeare said of lust, "The expense of spirit, in a waste of shame"; it is "Before, a joy proposed; behind a dream." Yet we don't know how to shun it. It is forced on us by our economic system as the alternative to starvation. It is also forced upon us by an internal defect in the soul, by the feeling that in property may lie the germs of self-development and of exquisite or heroic deeds. Our life on earth is, and ought to be, material and carnal. But we have not yet learned to manage our materialism and carnality properly; they are still entangled with the desire for ownership, where (in the words of Dante) "Possession is one with loss." [5]

And this brings us to our fourth and final point: the blackberries. [6]

Blackberries are not plentiful in this meagre grove, but they are easily seen from the public footpath which traverses it, and all too easily gathered. Foxgloves, too—people will pull up the foxgloves, and ladies of an educational tendency even grub for toadstools to show them on the Monday in class. Other ladies, less educated, roll down the bracken in the arms of their gentlemen friends. There is paper, there are tins. Pray, does my wood belong to me or doesn't it? And, if it does, should I not own it best by allowing no one else to walk there? There is a wood near Lyme Regis, also cursed by a public footpath, where the owner has not hesitated on this point. He has built high stone walls on each side of the path, and has spanned it by bridges, so that the public circulate like termites while he gorges on the blackberries unseen. He really does own his wood, this able chap. Dives in hell did pretty well, but the gulf dividing him from Lazarus could be traversed by vision, and nothing traverses it here. And perhaps I shall come to this in time. I shall wall in and fence out until I really taste the sweets of property. Enormously stout, endlessly avaricious, pseudo-creative, intensely selfish, I shall weave upon my forehead the quadruple crown of possession until those nasty Bolshies come and take it off again and thrust me aside into the outer darkness. [7]

1250 words, 7 paragraphs

Diction

1. The author is obviously English. What are some of his word choices that an American would not make?
2. Are there any spellings that also indicate the author's non-American background?
3. He uses the phrase "servants require insurance stamps" in paragraph [2]. **Infer** what "insurance stamps" must be from the **context**.
4. He uses the term "nasty Bolshies" in paragraph [7]. To whom does he refer? Why are they nasty? Why will they take away his crown? What would be a more common term for "Bolshies"?
5. Paragraph [7] states in part that "ladies of an educational tendency" will grub for toadstools "to show them on the Monday class." What is he writing about? Why is it not more clear?
6. Check the meanings of the following words as used in this essay: antithesis [2], asceticism [2], bracken [7], carnal [5], fourteen-stone (check *stone* separately) [2], the Gospels [2], nucleus [4], pretentious [5], sinister [5], Union Jack [4].

Rhetoric and Style

1. E. M. Forster makes several references to specific **parables** in the Bible. What are they? How is it possible to locate these **allusions** in the Bible?
2. Are there any other **allusions** to the Bible other than those to the **parables**? What are they?

3. Of what benefit are such **allusions**?
4. The author connects Ahab, Canute, and Alexander in paragraph[4]. Why these three, and why in that order?
5. By what obvious device does the author give **unity** to this essay?
6. What seems to be the author's **tone**, and how does he express it?

Applications and Evaluation

1. Can ownership of property have no good or beneficial effects upon a man? What might such effects be?
2. Forster quotes Dante as having said, "Possession is one with loss." Would it be possible to apply that quotation to a relationship between people, such as love?
3. Did anybody own the bird? Does anybody "own" you? Write an analytical essay with the tentative title "My Owners."
4. It is possible that possessions tie one down. Try an essay with the topic "Man is owned by his possessions."
5. Would this essay, with its emphasis on Christian **allusions** and morality be effective to a non-Christian? Does it lose anything by traversing the Atlantic?
6. Read the entire Sonnet 129 by Shakespeare, and decide whether or not Forster uses the lines the way Shakespeare meant them.

Konrad Z. Lorenz (1903–   ). Konrad Lorenz, a Nobel Prize-winning Austrian zoologist, was educated and has taught both in Europe and in the United States. He is generally regarded as a pioneer in the field of modern ethology (the scientific study of animal behavior). He is the author of many books, including *King Solomon's Ring*, of which the following selection is a chapter. The work was translated from German by Marjorie Kerr Wilson. Dr. Lorenz writes with clarity and simplicity heightened by entertaining illustrations. This essay is the type technically called a "process analysis" and less technically called a "how-to-do-it" paper.

Build A World

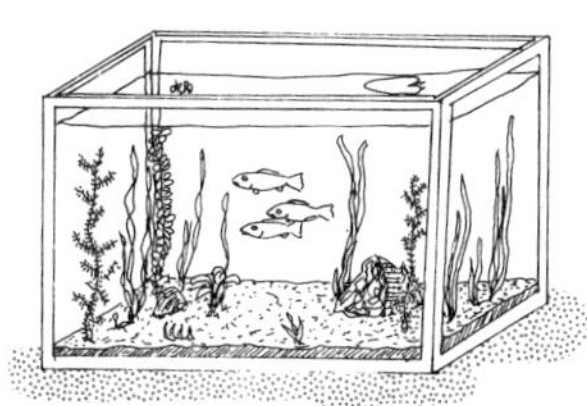

Wie alles sich zum Ganzen webt
Eins in dem anderen wirkt und lebt.
GOETHE, *Faust*

It costs almost nothing and is indeed wonderful: cover the bottom of a glass tank with clean sand, and insert in this foundation a few stalks of ordinary water plants. Pour in carefully a few pints of tap water and stand the whole thing on a sunny window-sill. As soon as the water has cleared and the plants have begun to grow, put in some little fishes, or, better still, go with a jam jar and a small net to the nearest pond—draw the net a few times through the depth of the pool, and you will have a myriad interesting organisms. [1]

The whole charm of childhood still lingers, for me, in such a fishing net. This should preferably not be a complicated contraption with brass rim and gauze bag, but, according to Altenbergian tradition, should rather be home-made in a matter of ten minutes: the rim an ordinary bent wire, the net a stocking, a piece of curtain or a baby's napkin. With such an instrument, I caught, at the age of nine, the first Daphnia for my fishes, thereby discovering the wonder-world of the freshwater pond which immediately drew me under its spell. In the train of the fishing net came the magnifying glass; after this again a modest little microscope, and therewith my fate was sealed; for he who has once seen the intimate beauty of nature cannot tear himself away from it again. He must become either a poet or a naturalist and, if his eyes are good and his powers of observation sharp enough, he may well become both. [2]

So you skim with your net through the water plants in the pond, generally filling your shoes with water and mud in the process. If you have chosen the right pond and found a place where "something is up," the bottom of the net will soon be swarming with glassily transparent, wriggling creatures. Tip up the base of the net and wash it out in the jam jar which you have already filled with water. Arrived home, you empty your catch carefully in the aquarium and contemplate the tiny world now unfolding its secrets before your eyes and magnifying glass. [3]

The aquarium is a world; for, as in a natural pond or lake, indeed as all over our whole planet, animal and vegetable beings live together in biological equilibrium. The carbon dioxide which the animals breathe out is assimilated by the plants which, in their turn exhale oxygen. Nevertheless it is false to say that plants do not breathe like animals but "the other way round." They breathe in oxygen and breathe out carbon dioxide, just as animals do, but, apart from this, the growing green plant assimilates carbon dioxide, that is, it uses the carbon for the building up of its body substance: indeed, one might say that, independently of its breathing, the plant *eats* carbon dioxide. During this process it excretes oxygen in excess of its own breathing and, from this surplus, man and animals breathe. Finally, plants are able to assimilate the products of dead bodies decomposed by bacteria and to make them again available to the great cycle of life which thus consists of three interlocking links: the constructors—the green plants, the consumers—the animals, and the decomposers—the bacteria. [4]

In the restricted space of the aquarium, this natural cycle of metabolism is easily disturbed and such a disturbance has catastrophic results for our little world. Many aquarium keepers, children and adults alike, are unable to resist the temptation of slipping just one more fish into the container, the capacity of whose green plants is already overburdened with animals. And just this one more fish may be the final straw that breaks the camel's back. With too many animals in the aquarium, a lack of oxygen ensues. Sooner or later some organism will succumb to this and its death may easily pass unnoticed. The decomposing corpse causes an enormous multiplication of bacteria in the aquarium, the water becomes turbid, the oxygen content decreases rapidly, then further animals die and, through this vicious circle, the whole of our carefully tended little world is doomed. Soon even the vegetation begins to decompose—and what some days ago was a beautiful, clear pool with healthy growing plants and lively animals becomes a horrid, stinking brew. [5]

The advanced aquarium keeper counteracts such dangers by aerating the water artificially. Such technical aids, however, detract from the intrinsic value of the aquarium, whose deeper meaning lies in the fact that this little water-world is self-supporting and, apart from the feeding of the animals and the cleaning of the front pane of the container (the algae on all other panes are carefully left alone as valuable suppliers of oxygen!), needs no biological care. As long as the right equilibrium is maintained, the aquarium itself needs no cleaning. If one denies oneself the larger fishes, particularly those that stir up the bottom, it does not matter if a layer of mud is gradually formed from the excreta of animals and from dying plant tissues. This is even to be desired, since it suffuses and fertilizes the sandy bottom which was originally sterile. In spite of the mud, the water itself remains as crystal clear and odourless as any of our alpine lakes. [6]

From a biological, as also from a decorative point of view, it is best to arrange the aquarium in spring time and to set it only with a few sprouting plants. Only plants that have grown in the aquarium itself are able to adapt themselves to the special conditions of the particular container and thrive, while all plants which one puts full-grown into an aquarium lose much of their original beauty. [7]

Two aquaria, separated from each other by only a few inches, have individual characters just as sharply defined as two lakes many miles apart. That is the attractive part about a new aquarium. When one is setting it up, one never knows how it will develop and what it will look like by the time it has reached its own particular stage of equilibrium. Suppose that one establishes, at the same time, and with the same inorganic material, three containers which one places close together on the same stand and plants all three with water thyme (*Elodea canadensis*) and water milfoil (*Myriophyllum verticillatum*): in the first, a dense jungle of Elodea may soon be flourishing which more or less eliminates the Myriophyllum, in the second the opposite may take place and, in the third, the plants may har-

Myriophyllum

monize, and apparently from nothing there may spring a delightful vegetation of *Nitella flexilis*, a decorative green alga, branched like a chandelier. Thus the three containers can each produce an entirely different landscape. They would also have completely different biological properties, and be propitious for different types of animals. In short, although prepared under the same conditions, each aquarium develops its own little individual world. A certain amount of restraint and self-control is necessary to prevent oneself from interfering with the natural development of an aquarium. Even well-meant adjustments on the part of the owner may cause much damage. It is, of course, possible to set up a "pretty" aquarium with artificial foundations and carefully distributed plants; a filter would prevent any mud formation and artificial aeration permit the keeping of many more fish than would otherwise be possible. In this case the plants are merely ornamental, the animals do not require them since they derive from the artificial aeration enough oxygen for their maintenance. It is purely a matter of taste, but I personally think of an aquarium as of a living community that regulates its own equilibrium. The other kind is a "cage," an artificially cleaned container which is not an end in itself, but purely a means of keeping certain animals. [8]

It is a real art to determine in advance the type of animal and plant community which one wants to develop in an aquarium, and to do this requires much experience and biological tact in choosing the right materials for the bottom, the situation of the tank, the heat and light conditions, and finally the plant and animal inmates themselves. A past master of this art was my tragically deceased friend Bernhard Hellman who was able to copy, at will, any given type of pond or lake, brook or river. One of his masterpieces was a large aquarium which was a perfect model of an Alpine lake. The tank was very deep and cool, and was placed not too near the light, the vegetation in the crystal-clear water consisted of glassily transparent, pale green pond weed (*Potamogeton*), the stony bottom was covered with dark green Fontinalis and decorative stonewort (*Chara*). Of the non-microscopic animals the only representatives were some minute trout and minnows, a few freshwater shrimps and a little crayfish. Thus, the animal inhabitants were so few that they hardly required feeding, since they were able to subsist on the natural microfauna of the aquarium. [9]

Fontinalis

If one wishes to breed some of the more delicate water animals, it is essential, in the construction of an aquarium, to reproduce

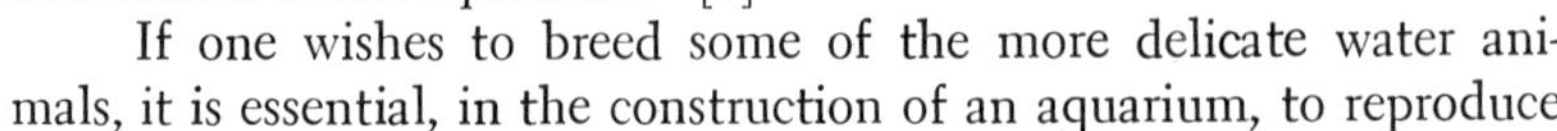

the whole of the natural habitat with its entire community of living macro- and micro-organisms. Even the commonest of tropical aquarium fishes are dependent on this condition, but their natural habitat is that of a small and not too clean pond which harbours exactly the sort of life community which automatically develops in the average aquarium. The conditions of our European waters, exposed to the variations of our climate, are much more difficult to reproduce indoors, and that is the reason why the majority of our native fishes are harder to keep and to breed than tropical species. You will now understand why I advised you to fetch your first water organisms out of the nearest pond with the traditional homemade fishing net. I have kept hundreds of aquaria of the most varied types, but the cheapest and most ordinary pond aquarium has always appealed to me particularly since its walls enclose the most natural and perfect life community that can be attained under artificial conditions. [10]

A man can sit for hours before an aquarium and stare into it as into the flames of an open fire or the rushing waters of a torrent. All conscious thought is happily lost in this state of apparent vacancy, and yet, in these hours of idleness, one learns essential truths about the macrocosm and the microcosm. If I cast into one side of the balance all that I have learned from the books of the library and into the other everything that I have gleaned from the "books in the running brooks," how surely would the latter turn the scales. [11]

1930 words, 11 paragraphs

Diction

1. Notice the Latin plural "aquaria" [8 and 10] and the singular "aquarium" (used throughout). What other English words can you think of that still use the Latin forms for singular and plural?
2. How can you tell that the author is not an American? Look for phrases, word uses, and references.
3. What do you suppose is the purpose of giving the Latin names for plants (in parentheses)?
4. The author states that "in the train of the fishing net came a magnifying glass." Explain the use of "train" in this **context**.
5. What kind of a net would a baby's napkin [2] make? What do you **infer** a baby's napkin to be?
6. A knowledge of the following words will make the essay more

easily understood: assimilate [4], equilibrium [4], habitat [10], intrinsic [6], macrocosm [11], metabolism [5], microcosm [11], myriad [1], propitious [8], turbid [5].

Rhetoric and Style

1. The **conclusion** to this essay is of a type not covered in the Glossary, yet it is most effective. How would you **classify** it?
2. Although seemingly an afterthought, the **conclusion** actually picks up an idea from paragraph [2]. Locate it.
3. The author states, "The aquarium is a world" [4]. Is this phrase a **metaphor** or a **fact**?
4. What is Lorenz' **tone** and attitude toward aquaria that use artificial aids? How does he show this attitude? Be specific.
5. Can you cite any **examples** that show the author's attitude toward the reader of his essay (see **Tone**)?
6. Can you find any indications that this essay is a translation from German to English?

Applications and Evaluation

1. The author suggests that we "go with a jam jar and a small net to the nearest pond." To many people the nearest pond is miles away or surrounded with fences or walls. Is there any other way to observe the world of nature? Write an essay on alternatives to aquaria.
2. The **paradox** of paragraph [11], that of gaining insight without the appearance of actual thought, needs resolution. How is such a process possible? Explain in a well-organized essay.
3. This expository essay is personal; the author relates his personal experiences as he gives directions and advice. Write a **process analysis** ("how to") essay in which you deliberately strive for a personal **tone**.
4. It is possible to buy in aquarium stores plastic plants, colored gravel, heaters, thermostats, air pumps, and other paraphernalia to maintain an aquarium. How does the plastic aquarium reflect our larger culture?
5. The "cycle of life" [4] consists of three interlocking links—in Dr. Lorenz **metaphor**. In what way has man upset the cycle? Use specific **examples** from your own observation.

Edwin Fuller Torrey (1937–   ) E. Fuller Torrey, M.D. was educated at Princeton and at McGill University Medical School. He took psychiatric training at Stanford and is now with the National Institute of Mental Health. Dr. Torrey has written for many professional publications and has edited two books. His most recent work is *The Mind Game: Witchdoctors and Psychiatrists,* which presents quite fully the material introduced in this brief extract. This selection is an excellent example of exposition by the method of comparison.

Witchdoctors and the Universality of Healing

Witch doctors and psychiatrists perform essentially the same function in their respective cultures. They are both therapists; both treat patients, using similar techniques; and both get similar results. Recognition of this should not downgrade psychiatrists—rather it should upgrade witchdoctors. [1]

The term "witchdoctor" is Western in origin, imposed on healers of the Third World by 18th and 19th century explorers. The world was simpler then, and the newly discovered cultures were quickly assigned their proper status in the Order of Things. We were white, they were black. We were civilized, they were primitive. We were Christian, they were pagan. We used science, they used magic. We had doctors, they had witchdoctors. [2]

American psychiatrists have much to learn from therapists in other cultures. My own experience observing and working with them includes two years in Ethiopia and briefer periods in Sarawak, Bali, Hong Kong, Colombia, and with Alaskan Indians, Puerto Ricans, and Mexican-Americans in this country. What I learned from these

Abridged from *The Mind Game: Witchdoctors and Psychiatrists* by E. Fuller Torrey, M.D. (New York: Emerson Hall, 1972). Reprinted by permission of the author.

doctor-healers was that I, as a psychiatrist, was using the same mechanisms for curing my patients as they were—and, not surprisingly, I was getting about the same results. The mechanisms can be classified under four categories. [3]

The first is the naming process. A psychiatrist or witchdoctor can work magic by telling a patient what is wrong with him. It conveys to the patient that someone—usually a man of considerable status—understands. And since his problem can be understood, then, implicitly, it can be cured. A psychiatrist who tells an illiterate African that his phobia is related to a fear of failure, or a witchdoctor who tells an American tourist that his phobia is related to possession by an ancestral spirit will be met by equally blank stares. And as therapists they will be equally ineffective. This is a major reason for the failure of most attempts at cross-cultural psychotherapy. Since a shared world-view is necessary for the naming process to be effective, then it is reasonable to expect that the best therapist–patient relationships will be those where both come from the same culture or subculture. The implications for our mental health programs are obvious. [4]

The second healing component used by therapists everywhere is their personality characteristics. An increasing amount of research shows that certain personal qualities of the therapist—accurate empathy, nonpossessive warmth, genuineness—are of crucial importance in producing effective psychotherapy. Clearly, more studies are needed in this area, but if they substantiate the emerging trend, then radical changes in the selection of therapists will be in order. Rather than selecting therapists because they can memorize facts and achieve high grades, we should be selecting them on the basis of their personality. Therapists in other cultures are selected more often for their personality characteristics; the fact that they have not studied biochemistry is not considered important. [5]

The third component of the healing process that appears to be universal is the patients' expectations. Healers all over the world use many ways to raise the expectations of their patients. The first way is the trip itself to the healer. It is a common observation that the farther a person goes to be healed, the greater are the chances that he will be healed. This is called the pilgrimage. Thus, sick people in Topeka go to the Leahy Clinic in Boston. The resulting therapeutic effects of the trip are exactly the same as have been operating for centuries at Delphi or Lourdes. The next way to raise patients' expectations is the building used for the healing. The more impressive it is, the greater will be the patients' expectations. This has been called the edifice complex. Therapists in different cultures use certain paraphernalia to increase patient expectations. In Western cultures nonpsychiatric healers have their stethoscope and psychotherapists are supposed to have their couch. Therapists in other cultures have their counterpart trademark, often a special drum, mask or amulet. Another aspect of patients' expectations rests upon the therapist's training. Some sort of training program is found for healers in almost all cultures. Blackfoot Indians, for instance, had to complete a seven-year period of training in order to qualify as medicine men. [6]

Finally, the same techniques of therapy are used by healers all over the world. Let me provide a few examples: Drugs are one of the techniques of Western therapy of which we are most proud. However, drugs are used by healers in other cultures as well. Rauwulfia root, for example, which was introduced into Western psychiatry in the 1950s as reserpine, a major tranquilizer, has been used in India for centuries as a tranquilizer, and has also been in wide use in West Africa for many years. Another example is shock therapy. When electric shock therapy was introduced by Cerletti in the 1930s, he was not aware that it had been used in some cultures for up to 4000 years. The technique of applying electric eels to the head of the patient is referred to in the writings of Aristotle, Pliny, and Plutarch. [7]

What kind of results do therapists in other cultures—witchdoctors—achieve? A Canadian psychiatrist, Dr. Raymond Prince spent 17 months studying 46 Nigerian witchdoctors, and judged that the therapeutic results were about equal to those obtained in North American clinics and hospitals. [8]

It would appear, then, that psychiatrists have much to learn from witchdoctors. We can see the components of our own therapy system in relief. We can learn why we are effective—or not effective. And we can learn to be less ethnocentric and arrogant about our own therapy and more tolerant of others. If we can learn all this from witchdoctors, then we will have learned much. [9]

890 words, 9 paragraphs

Diction

1. The author mentions healers of the Third World [2]. What is the Third World? (What are the first two worlds?)
2. In the same paragraph [2], "Order of Things" is capitalized. Explain why.

3. The Leahy Clinic is a well-known medical center in Massachusetts, but what are Delphi and Lourdes [6]?
4. A horse doctor tends horses; a baby doctor helps babies. How do we know that a witchdoctor does not make sick witches well? Can you think of any other odd phrases like that?
5. Check this brief essay carefully for **clichés, slang,** and **jargon** words. Make a list and comment.
6. Here are a few words you might not know the precise meaning of: amulet [6], component [5], empathy [5], ethnocentric [9], implicitly [4], paraphernalia [6], phobia [4], pilgrimage [6], radical [5], therapy (also check others like "therapist," "therapeutic" [1].

Rhetoric and Style

1. Which of the two main methods of **comparison** does Dr. Torrey use in this essay?
2. How does he maintain **coherence**?
3. The author deliberately uses **parallel structure** in a series of sentences to increase his effectiveness. Find the section. Could it be written in another way? Explore in some detail.
4. What kind of specifics does the author use to **validate** his **coordinate points**? Offer one or two examples.
5. The author's **tone** is generally serious, but whimsey or humor peeps through from time to time. Note an example of the lightness that prevents this essay from becoming a sermon.

Applications and Evaluation

1. Dr. Torrey mentions that personality characteristics are more necessary than ability to achieve high grades [5]. Recently Dr. Eli Ginsberg of Columbia University surveyed 342 graduate students from the 1940s. He found that the ones who made the highest grades were not in the highest professional levels.
   a. Write an essay suggesting alternatives to high grades for entrance to professional schools.
   b. Why do you think we still believe high college grades are indicative of valuable people.
   c. Suggest other means of grading than answers on tests. (A grade for "empathy" for example?)

2. Read the essay "Voices of Time" and write a brief paper comparing it to this selection. Use either shape of **comparison** essay.
3. Do you know of any medicines or therapeutic techniques, in addition to those mentioned in this essay, Western man has derived from witchdoctors?
4. Outline an essay that would apply one of the main ideas of this essay to the field of education. (Examples: primitive techniques that might work in a modern city; a teacher's need for an understanding of his students' world-view, especially in the teaching of minority students.)

Herbert Gold (1924–   ) A novelist and a teacher, Herbert Gold has written many novels about contemporary America. His first was *Birth of a Hero* and his most recent, *My Last 2,000 Years*, was published in 1972. He was educated at Columbia, won a Guggenheim Fellowship, and has been a visiting professor at Cornell, University of California at Berkeley, and Harvard. He has also written many articles and short stories. The following selection contrasts tribal wealth and individual poverty, what many call the great Indian paradox.

Apache Riches

Not long ago the Jicarilla Apache tribe of Dulce (N.M.) entered the history of the cinema by putting up $2-million to back a Johnny Cash–Kirk Douglas Western called "A Gunfight." With payments now coming in from Paramount, the tribe's officers think it's turning out to be a pretty good deal, despite poor business in Cleveland. "The word from Spain is outstanding and we sold the European rights," says Charlie A. Vigil, who is president of the Tribal Council. [1]

And now the Tribal Council is meeting in the Administration Building to deal with a number of the normal questions which come up during the month, such as water and feed planning, complaints about telephone service, difficulties in the alcoholism and family-planning projects—and a proposal to buy an adjacent 73,000-acre ranch for $950,000. Presiding is Charlie Vigil, who hates to be called

Abridged from *How Rich Is a Rich Apache?* by Herbert Gold, published in *The New York Times Magazine*, February 13, 1972.

Chief because he's president of an independent nation, and also present are most of the elected Tribal Council members. [2]

It's a Real Estate Showdown. Facing the Indians on their raised platform is a delegation of ranchers and real-estate men. C. W. Berry, rancher, says: "I'm a businessman and you people are businessmen and this is a business venture. Either you want the ranch or you don't. I've talked with my people and we'd like an answer today. Nine hunnert and ninety-five thousand dollars." [3]

C. W. Berry stands before the council and waits. President Vigil says, "I want a secret ballot right now—yes or no." [4]

Tom Olson, the tribal lawyer, up from Albuquerque, passes out little folded slips of paper. Kenneth A. Kruhm, vice president and senior trust officer of the First National Bank of Albuquerque, whispers to me: "See that fellow on the extreme left? I can see he wrote 'No.' I can tell from how it wiggles." [5]

Mr. Olson collects the slips of paper and reads the results aloud. No. . . . No. . . . Yes. . . . Yes. . . . Yes. . . . No. . . . Yes. . . . Yes. . . . Yes. . . . "Well," he says to the council, "you just got yourself a piece of property." [6]

Is a multimillionaire Apache tribe really rich? [7]

When I walked over to the Arriba Inn of Dulce from the $200,000 private airstrip which the tribe recently built, the first moving vehicle I saw was a pale green Fiat sports car, driven pell-mell by a lovely nut-brown maiden, another lovely nut-brown maiden as her passenger, their long straight hair flying in the dry mountain air of northern New Mexico. I had come to confirm the stories of this tribe's wealth, and lo! everything was falling into place. [8]

But everything was not as it seemed. The two girls turned out to be volunteer social workers from Kansas City, here to study problems of alcoholism, joblessness, childhood retardation, adolescent boredom and distraction; *identity crisis,* as they put it, *anomie.* [9]

The word *Jicarilla* (pronounced Hickarelya) refers to basket-weaving; the Zuni word Apache means "enemy," because they were strangers and warriors; so these are the basket-weaving enemies, an odd name for a tribe of land investors, movie producers and security analysts. They are not quite what the articles in business magazines say. Geronimo himself was not the bloodthirsty brave of children's history. He died instructing children in moral behavior in Oklahoma, to which he had been exiled after the usual dreary treacheries on the part of white men and renegade Apaches. [10]

After the wars, fought with incomparable energy and intelligence—Geronimo's band of braves numbered only about 100 fighters—the Apaches sank into the lethargy and melancholy of a defeated, shamed people. About a generation ago, the Jicarillas revived. Now their self-governing institutions, cooperatives, the Tribal Council, credit unions, plans and projects serve as a model of modern mixed control of money and resources. They went from hunting and warfare to handouts from the Government, from charity to serious sheep and cattle raising, from desultory stripping of the land to shrewd sale of gas, oil and timber leases and hunting rights, and, as the few hundred remaining Jicarillas increased toward the present 1,800, to directing their resources through a cooperative commonwealth toward a general tribal accumulation of power. [11]

They took an initial Government loan of $85,000 and with this bought local properties and handled the goods needed locally. The loan was paid off within five years. Individual Jicarillas returned their private lands to the group. Oil and gas were discovered; there was money in oil and gas. Tribal and individual holdings in sheep and cattle were developed; there is money in beef and wool. The elk attracted hunters. The streams attracted fishermen. The mountains attracted sightseers. There is money in hunting licenses, fishing licenses and lodging for the night. Group control of resources and income, plus conservative management by a consortium of four banks, plus continued money for development from Washington, made the tribal funds grow nicely, increasing and multiplying. [12]

Capitalism works well when you have oil, gas, timber, cows, sheep and beautiful sunsets. The First National Bank of Albuquerque gave good counsel. The Jicarilla tribe leapt from the condition of a backward, primitive, Stone Age, worse than Stone Age, defeated people to a modern cooperative enterprise, partaking equally of Chase National and Kibbutz Nir David. Jesus Saves, but now the Great Spirit Invests. A graffito in the men's room of the Administration Building: "Indians, dare to be great again! Get into hedge funds!" [13]

It turns out that there is a million-dollar scholarship fund, but few of the students return to enrich the tribe with professional help. "We are stressing toward that end," says President Vigil in his serious, elegant way, but the young talents either leave the reservation forever or come back defeated by white eyes. There is a serious effort to organize work in Dulce, but Jicarilla Apache Tribe Industries employs only some 60 Indians at present, filling contracts for leather mailbags, electronic wiring, oxygen tubes, Marine scabbards. [14]

Hated prohibition has been ended, and there are take-out stores and bars on the reservation, making the roads safer for everyone—no longer need to drive great distances for drink, and then perilously home again—but alcoholism is a problem for men, women and children. Winning "the Battle of the Bottle" is said to be a condition for political success in the tribe. The main street in Dulce has no credit jeweler, but it is an Anglo-run strip consisting of the Square D shopping center, a busy beauty parlor, bank, post office, and Marine recruiting office with its poster outside depicting a college boy in V-neck sweater and a black in a cardigan about to sign up for the Marines future. [15]

Apache families line up nearby for medical help, and the pickup trucks spin back and forth in the dust. One truck has both a Confederate flag and "Go Navy" stickers on it, and a boy with a peace-insignia sweatshirt riding behind. [16]

There is a sense of sadness, withdrawal, coolness, depression despite the flickering wit and enthusiasm of Charlie Vigil, with his pair of telephones on his desk, another private-line telephone in a drawer, and a baby-blue hotline phone along with the coffee-can ashtray and the giant cigar lighter in front of him at council meetings. [17]

The reservation looks poor despite public affluence. They are prospering, but not prospering individually. "They're caught between being Indians and the dominant white society," says a social worker, but that's both obvious and insufficient. They live for the present, perhaps, but the present isn't really beautiful. Kenneth Kruhm of the First National Bank of Albuquerque says: "They have a very advanced form of fiduciary management. Let me put it this way: Essentially, they're still poor as individuals, though the tribe is rich. I hope you can understand that. They get income distributions, a few hundred dollars a year per person; it doesn't amount to much." [18]

"I can understand that."

"So if they don't have work, which they don't mostly, and they have problems, they're not really rich." [19]

One night I was invited to a religious ceremony taking place miles up the canyon in a little clearing lit by fires, with a roof of green branches constructed overhead. It was a traditional initiation rite. At the feast, an old Indian, uncle to the girl being honored and inducted on the occasion of her first menstruation, took me into the tepee where the girl and her symbolic mate, a boy with face chalked white, were dancing—and would dance for four nights. We danced, too, while an old man chanted and clapped his hands. Later we ate sheep stew, roasting cow, drank pot coffee and tasted fried corn bread, and he had a question to ask me. "White man go to the moon now?" [20]

"Yes." [21]

"And not come back alive?" [22]

"It seems that way for some." [23]

He clapped both hands to his thighs and came up laughing in advance to prepare me for the joke: "Then he'll leave the earth to the Indians again!" [24]

Coming back, we drove home a young woman who had lost her husband at the feast. "He got drunk; I want a divorce," she said. "I met a Mescalero Apache I like better, you know?" [25]

"Is he giving you a hard time?" [26]

"I don't know; I give him the worse of it. I just drink a little teswin and I give him the worst of it. You got any teswin?" This is the traditional native brew, and it's not very strong. It's just for thirst. "Teswin didn't do this to me. I'm sad, that's all—and maybe the two six-packs I drank, too." [27]

The exact figures are hard to come by. There are about $8-million—some say $12-million—invested and producing dividends. There's that million-dollar scholarship fund. There are about $8-million or $9-million coming from a longtime settlement due from the Government. The lands of the reservation themselves are not valued. Cattle. Timber. Leases. There is impressive income from fishing and hunting licenses, $100,000 last year—elk, deer, plus the spring and fall turkey season—and much more to come when the new Elk Park resort is finished. [28]

The average family income at present, however, is less than $4,000 a year. But how to project what this is worth? They are relieved of many taxes. They get all sorts of services—medical, dental, credit, subsidized housing. They get those windfall dividends. "They're taken care of real good," says one veteran official. "Listen, one year they had to pay a carnival $300 to come here, next year it was $200, now the carnival pays *them*. They don't look it, they don't act it. They're well off." [29]

"STESWIN APACHE GO-GO BAND PLAYS TONITE! APACHE HAVEN." I headed for the Apache Haven, a bar in Dulce near the ravine just past the gas station, to take in the Steswin Apache Go-Go. The beautiful green and coppery land streched in waves of hills in all directions, a chameleon spread of clouds reflecting the final colors of the sunset—yellows, oranges and finally a deep and mournful gray-blue. It's surely a land for ancient dreams. What are the dreams of this ancient people? [30]

A young man I'll call Fernando came out to greet me as I paused at the door. "Beautiful, isn't it?" he asked. [31]

"So I was thinking." [32]

He pointed to the wrecked cars nearby, the shacks, a worked-over dry terrain, and began to laugh. "We're rich," he said, "we're friends of Johnny Cash. Welcome. I'll buy you a beer." Of course he had a story to tell, and I'll abridge it here: "Graduated from high school in, let's see, 1961. Ain't had much in the way of work since, but I can read and write, and let me tell you, what they write about us—it's all rumors and the rumors of rumors. We may be rich for Indians, but we're not what you'd call satisfactory off." [33]

I had visited stores, homes, the eating place at the Arriba Inn, the Laundromat, and now the Apache Haven, and the feeling was melancholy. This is, of course, a subjective judgment by a traveling man sleeping in a motel away from home. But I was beginning to understand the mood which creates a high incidence of alcoholism and a suicide rate 30 times the national average. A B.I.A. official explained: "Well, they don't say too much. Can't talk it out. So they're fond of suicide because then they go to the great happy hunting ground in the sky—don't they?" [34]

Fernando said, "Now take me. I'm losing the Battle of the Bottle. But you been talking to fellows who won it, haven't you?" [35]

We finished our beers. [36]

A host of Anglo managers and counselors have a bright future dealing in the Indians' riches. A few of the technicians and tribal councilmen will stay and work with their people, hoping eventually to replace the domination of white eyes with Jicarilla lawyers, doctors, accountants, engineers. They might even seek to make better contact with the rest of the Indian nation. "One day in the future," said President Vigil, "we might all work together again, but in the meantime we have our own work, and that sort of makes you separate." [37]

Rich in resources as they are, earnest and concerned about development as they have proven to be, the individual members of the Jicarilla Apache tribe still turn and turn in the traditional Indian dilemmas of rootlessness and frustration. Even if they get a better percentage of the gross from the next movie, they are not quite living the rumored corporate dream of widening profit horizons and American fiscal rapture. [38]

2280 words, 38 paragraphs

Diction

1. Why are the quotations by the Indians not quite standard American usage? [20–23, 27, and 33]
2. The author uses the phrase "white eyes" more than once. What does it mean?
3. The sense in paragraph [3] is not instantly apparent. What are Chase National and Kibbutz Nir David? Why the reference to Jesus Saves?
4. At what **level of usage** would you place this essay? Why?
5. Paragraph [34] mentions a B.I.A. official. What do you suppose B.I.A. stands for? Why are the officials not specified by name?
6. Write down what you think the following words mean; compare your definitions with the precise meaning you find in a good dictionary—you might be surprised: consortium [12], dilemma [38], desultory [11], fiduciary [18], graffitto [13], lethargy [11], melancholy [10, 34], renegade [10], rite [20], venture [3].

Rhetoric and Style

1. Although written in semi-**narrative** form, this essay is primarily a **comparison/contrast** selection. What general pattern does the author follow?
2. In addition to the main **contrast** (which you should state) there are a half-dozen lesser contrasts; list three or five.
3. Identify the **irony** in paragraph [37].
4. Although not rich in **figurative language**, this essay does have some colorful descriptions; list a few.
5. What seems to be the function of paragraphs [8] and [9] in the essay? Why would the author bother to show the kind of car and a detailed description of the social workers in this one instance only?
6. Can you **classify** the kind of **introduction** used? Will the reference be valid in twenty years?

Application and Evaluation

1. The Jicarilla Apache still perform a rite when a young girl becomes a woman. Do you know of any other "rites of passage" from childhood to adulthood? Should we have one in our general American culture?
2. How is it possible for a tribe of 1800 people to be worth millions and still be individually poor? Speculate.
3. Do you think it is possible to retain a cultural heritage (like Indian, Italian, Oriental, or any other) and still compete in the mainstream of American culture? Write an essay in which you **compare**—or **contrast**—possible points of conflict.
4. State the author's **thesis** in a single declarative sentence, and tell whether he convinced you of it or not. Why was he or was he not convincing? You have just started an **evaluation**; your instructor may wish you to write it in a well-organized essay.
5. Prepare an outline for an essay showing the change (if any) in feeling in America toward the native American. Pick a distinct time for reference such as 1880 or 1920; get some data other than John Wayne movies.

Robert Ardrey (1908–   ) Robert Ardrey was educated in anthropology at the University of Chicago and lectured on that subject at the Chicago World's Fair. He soon turned to drama and wrote many plays, including *Thunder Rock* and *Shadow of Heros*. Almost twenty years later he became interested in anthropology again and championed the cause of certain men in the book *African Genesis*. This book was followed by *The Territorial Imperative*, both of which he introduces as personal inquiries into man's relationships with his animal origins. The selection that follows was taken from the second book. He has written a third, *The Social Contract*, offering further thoughts and evidence on the same general theme.

Of Men and Mockingbirds

A territory is an area of space, whether of water or earth or air, which an animal or group of animals defends as an exclusive preserve. The word is also used to describe the inward compulsion in animate beings to possess and defend such a space. A territorial species of animals, therefore, is one in which all males, and sometimes females too, bear an inherent drive to gain and defend an exclusive property. [1]

In most but not all territorial species, defense is directed only against fellow members of the kind. A squirrel does not regard a mouse as a trespasser. In most but not all territorial species—not in chameleons, for example—the female is sexually unresponsive to an unpropertied male. As a general pattern of behavior, in territorial species the competition between males which we formerly believed was one for the possession of females is in truth for possession of property. [2]

We may also say that in all territorial species, without exception, possession of a territory lends enhanced energy to the proprietor. Students of animal behavior cannot agree as to why this should be, but the challenger is almost invariably defeated, the intruder expelled. In part, there seems some mysterious flow of energy and resolve which invests a proprietor on his home grounds. But likewise, so marked is the inhibition lying on the intruder, so evident his sense of trespass, we may be permitted to wonder if in all territorial species there does not exist, more profound than simple learning, some universal recognition of territorial rights. [3]

The concept of territory as a genetically determined form of behavior in many species is today accepted beyond question in the biological sciences. But so recently have our observations been made and our conclusions formed that we have yet to explore the implications of territory in our estimates of man. Is *Homo sapiens* a territorial species? Do we stake out property, chase off trespassers, defend our countries because we are sapient, or because we are animals? Because we choose, or because we must? Do certain laws of territorial behavior apply as rigorously in the affairs of men as in the affairs of chipmunks? That is the principal concern of this inquiry, and it is a matter of considerable concern, I believe, to any valid understanding of our nature. But it is a problem to be weighed in terms of present knowledge, not past. [4]

How recently our information about animal territory has come to us is very well illustrated by reflections recorded only thirty years ago by the anthropologist Julian H. Steward, now of the University of Illinois. "Why are human beings the only animals having land-owning groups?" he wondered. And he brought together observations of twenty-four different hunting peoples so primitive that their ways differ little, in all probability, from the ways of paleolithic man. Their homes were isolated and far-spread—in Philippine and Congo forests, in Tasmania and Tierra del Fuego, in Canada's Mackenzie basin, in the Indian Ocean's Andaman Islands, in southwestern Africa's Kalahari Desert. So remote were they from each other that there seemed small likelihood that any one could have learned its ways from others. Yet all formed social bands occupying exclusive, permanent domains. [5]

How could it be that such a number of peoples in such varying environments so remote from each other should all form similar social groups based on what would seem to be a human invention, the ownership of land? Steward came to a variety of conclusions, but one line of speculation was denied him. Even in 1936 he could not know that his assumption was false, since many animals form land-owning groups. Lions, eagles, wolves, great-horned owls are all hunters, and all guard exclusive hunting territories. The lions and wolves, besides, hunt in cooperative prides and packs differing little from the bands of primitive man. Ownership of land is scarcely a human invention, as our territorial propensity is something less than a human distinction. [6]

Man, I shall attempt to demonstrate in this inquiry, is as much a territorial animal as is a mockingbird singing in the clear California night. We act as we do for reasons of our evolutionary past, not our cultural present, and our behavior is as much a mark of our species as is the shape of a human thigh bone or the configuration of nerves in a corner of the human brain. If we defend the title to our land or the sovereignty of our country, we do it for reasons no different, no less innate, no less ineradicable, than do lower animals. The dog barking at you from behind his master's fence acts for a motive indistinguishable from that of his master when the fence was built. [7]

Neither are men and dogs and mockingbirds uncommon creatures in the natural world. Ring-tailed lemurs and great-crested grebes, prairie dogs, robins, tigers, muskrats, meadow warblers and Atlantic salmon, fence lizards, flat lizards, three-spined sticklebacks, nightingales and Norway rats, herring gulls and callicebus monkeys—all of us will give everything we are for a place of our own. Territory, in the evolving world of animals, is a force perhaps older than sex. [8]

The survival value that territory brings to a species varies as widely as do the opportunities of species themselves. In some it offers security from the predator, in others security of food supply. In some its chief value seems the selection of worthy males for reproduction, in some the welding together of a group, and in many, like sea birds, the prime value seems simply the excitement and stimulation of border quarrels. And there are many species, of course, for which the territorial tie would be a handicap to survival. Grazing animals for the most part must move with the season's grass. Elephant herds acknowledge no territorial bond, but move like fleets of old gray galleons across the measureless African space. The gorilla, too, is a wanderer within a limited range who every night must build a new nest wherever his search for food may take him. [9]

In those countless species, however, which through long evolutionary trial and error have come to incorporate a territorial pattern into their whole behavior complex, we shall find a remarkable uniformity. Widely unrelated though the species may be, a few distinct patterns are endlessly repeated. For example, we shall examine arena behavior, in which solitary males defend mating stations to which females come solely for copulation. It makes little difference whether the species be antelope or sage grouse, the pattern will be almost the same. And after that we shall consider the pair territory, that portion of space occupied and defended by a breeding couple, as in robins and beavers and men. So we shall move along, surveying the territorial experience in our generation. [10]

It is information, all of it, which failed to enter your education and mine because it had not yet come to light. It is information, all of it, which yet fails to enter our children's textbooks or the processes of our own thought, through nothing but neglect. To me, this neglect seems a luxury which we cannot afford. Were we in a position to regard our knowledge of man as adequate in our negotiations with the human circumstance, and to look with satisfaction on our successful treatment of such human maladies as crime and war, racial antagonisms and social loneliness, then we might embrace the world of the animal simply to enjoy its intrinsic fascinations. But I find no evidence to support such self-satisfaction. And so this wealth of information concerning animal ways, placed before us by the new biology, must be regarded as a windfall in a time of human need. [11]

If, as I believe, man's innumerable territorial expressions are human responses to an imperative lying with equal force on mockingbirds and men, then human self-estimate is due for radical revision. We acknowledge a few such almighty forces, but very few: the will to survive, the sexual impulse, the tie, perhaps, between mother and infant. It has been our inadequate knowledge of the natural world, I suggest, that has led us to look no further. And it may come to us as the strangest of thoughts that the bond between a man and the soil he walks on should be more powerful than his bond with the woman he sleeps with. Even so, in a rough, preliminary way we may test the supposition with a single question: How many men have you known of, in your lifetime, who died for their country? And how many for a woman? [12]

Any force which may command us to act in opposition to the will to survive is a force to be inspected, at such a moment of history as ours, with the benefit of other than obsolete information. That I believe this force to be a portion of our evolutionary nature, a behavior pattern of such survival value to the emerging human being that it became fixed in our genetic endowment, just as the shape of our feet and the musculature of our buttocks became fixed, is the premise of this inquiry. Even as that behavior pattern called sex evolved in many organisms as nature's most effective answer to the problem of reproduction, so that behavior pattern called territory evolved in many organisms as a kind of defense mechanism, as nature's most effective answer to a variety of problems of survival. [13]

I regard the territorial imperative as no less essential to the existence of contemporary man than it was to those bands of small-brained proto-men on the high African savannah millions of years ago. I see it as a force shaping our lives in countless unexpected ways, threatening our existence only to the degree that we fail to understand it. We can neither accept nor reject my premise, however, or even begin to explore its consequence, on any basis other than science's new knowledge of the animal in a state of nature. And since that knowledge has been acquired at the same time that radical changes have come to our understanding of evolution itself, we shall do well to defer our entrance to the field and our first specific inspection of territory. Before we inspect the behavior of the animal, let us inspect the behavior of that equally intriguing being, the scientist. [14]

1700 words, 14 paragraphs

Diction

1. The title of the book from whence this chapter came is *The Territorial Imperative*. What does the *Imperative* in the title mean? What are the philosophical **connotations**?
2. Why does the author ask, "Are we sapient?" [4] instead of using a simpler word like "smart"?
3. The second most used **cliché** in the decade of the 1970s is "in terms of." (Mr. Ardrey uses it once in paragraph [4]—"in terms of present knowledge.") If you wish to be cured of the "in-terms-of **cliché**, rewrite paragraph [9], inserting "in terms of" wherever possible. The opening sentence could be aborted into "The value in terms of survival. . . ." What does the phrase really mean?
4. Paragraph [6] notes "prides" of lions, "packs" of wolves, "bands" of men. What are some of the other words we use to **denote** a group of animals? They are all collective nouns.

5. Words to look up in the dictionary: enhanced [3], inhibition [3], obsolete [13], paleolithic [5], radical [12], rigorously [4], sovereignty [7], species [1], territory (two meanings: the dictionary and the author's limitation) [1], windfall [11].

Rhetoric and Style

1. The author is introducing us to a topic that may arouse our hostility, so he prepares us for the **thesis** by asking some questions (a useful device). What are those questions? Look at paragraphs [3], [4], and [6] especially.
2. Do you find any striking **figures of speech**?
3. This chapter basically is explaining through use of **comparison;** what is the main comparison used?
4. If partial sentences are evil and are marked *Frag* by composition instructors, why does the author end paragraph [12] with a *Frag*?
5. Although this chapter is introductory to a longer book, the author offers **evidence** for his **conclusions.** What is some of it?
6. Does Mr. Ardrey's presentation make you want to get the book *The Territorial Imperative* from the library and read more?

Applications and Evaluation

1. What seems to be Mr. Ardrey's principal concern in inquiring into man and territory—scientific curiosity, need for useful knowledge, desire for gain?
2. Do men have innate behaviors? Instincts? What makes you believe we do or do not? Prepare a paper defending that belief.
3. The author states that the new material concerning the basic territoriality of many animals is not yet in our children's text [11]. Is that statement still valid? For college texts? High school texts?
4. If man is biologically territorial, then conflict between men seems unavoidable, does it not? (Question: Why do antelope not have wars?)
5. Is it demeaning to man's dignity and freedom for him to be equated with chipmunks and mockingbirds? Why? Question 3, 4, or 5 may be the basis for your next writing assignment.

Jim Murray (1919–) Jim Murray was educated at Trinity College (Hartford) and has been a reporter and writer since before his graduation. He has done cover stories for *Time*; worked on several newspapers; written for *Sports Illustrated*, which he helped found; and is now a sports columnist for the *Los Angeles Times*, where this essay first appeared. Mr. Murray has also won awards for his writing and has authored two books, *The Best of Jim Murray* and *The Sporting World of Jim Murray*.

The Enforcer

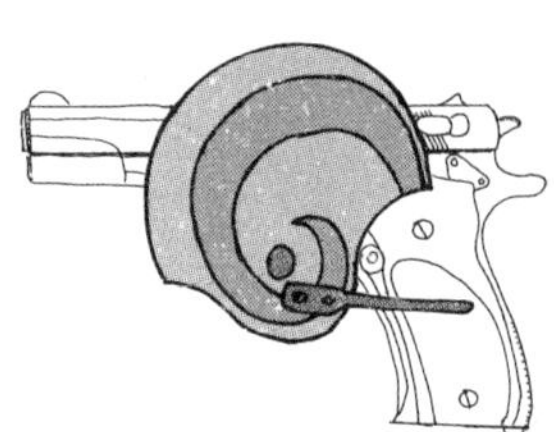

Fifteen years ago, if you asked even a season ticket holder what a "tight end" was, he would probably picture a football player weaving through a hotel lobby at 2 o'clock in the morning hiccuping. It wasn't a position, it was a condition. [1]

The prototype was Leon Hart of Notre Dame and the Detroit Lions, a mastodon in cleats who ambled down the field leaking tacklers who fell off his back like artichoke leaves. [2]

It was Clark Shaughnessy who invented the position and Vince Lombardi who institutionalized it. "The tight end calls for a guy who can knock down a building on his way across the line, catch a bullet with one hand, or a football in handcuffs, and run the 40 in under five seconds in leg chains," Shaughnessy explained. Lombardi put it simpler: "He's your enforcer out there. His job is to bust some heads." [3]

Tight ends run silent but they seldom run deep. They're supposed to run at somebody, not away from them. [4]

Robert O. Klein was born to be a tight end. They say when he was learning to walk, he bowled over three chairs and a sofa and knocked three bricks out of the fireplace. [5]

Bob has been in more Rose Bowls than Washington State. At USC, he thought it was part of the schedule. [6]

On the Rams, Bob Klein is on the field almost as often as the football. The Rams broke a 40-year-old rush-attempt record (set by the Detroit Lions in the days when the forward pass was considered a novelty) with 659 runs from scrimmage this year. On every one of them, Klein was knocking down a strong-side linebacker. [7]

The Rams kicked 30 field goals, a club record. On every one of them, Klein was sticking his helmet into somebody's numbers. On every point-after-touchdown, there he was, passing out headaches. He was also on other special kickoff and punt teams. [8]

They throw to him every time he's in a crowd of less than three opponents—which is not very often. You can always see Klein's patterns. They are littered by a trail of prone players. Some people drop scraps of paper to mark their trail. Klein drops players. [9]

The other day, against the Cleveland Browns, quarterback John Hadl noticed a curious thing in the final minutes of the first quarter: Bob Klein was standing there with only one player hanging off him. The player looked like a guy who wanted off on the third floor. [10]

Hadl thoughtfully delivered the ball to Klein who caught it, shook himself once like a dog who has just come out of the water with a mallard—and the tackler flew off and Klein charged into the end zone. Two other tacklers were there but stood like waiters pretending it wasn't their table. [11]

It was Klein's eighth touchdown catch as a Ram. He usually gets them in clusters of one a season because he is almost more valuable without the football. It was Klein's only reception of the game but his 22nd of the season. Twenty-two receptions wouldn't have been a particularly busy afternoon for Tom Fears or Elroy Hirsh but Klein must have thought it was raining footballs in his zone. Tight ends don't usually see that many footballs in a career. [12]

The hallmark of this Ram team is blocking. This team doesn't drop leaflets; it comes in the windows at you. It is a team of foot soldiers, the kind of infantrymen who would sleep on their helmets and would rather have two aspirin than the Purple Heart any day. This team lives or dies in the trenches, and calls for air support only when it's pinned down. [13]

This is why this team couldn't care less if Bob Klein knows what color the football is. They don't want to waste all that six feet five inches and 250 pounds of gristle just carrying a little old 15-ounce football. Not when it can carry as many as a half-ton of linebackers out of a play. [14]

Klein would be just as valuable to the Rams if he didn't have fingers. Two touchdowns a season from him is like finding oil under your gold mine. [15]

820 words, 15 paragraphs

Diction

1. The overall **analogy** of this selection is calling a football player an "enforcer"? What is an enforcer? (Clue: it is underworld **slang.**)
2. This essay is clearly understandable to most Americans and to all football fans, but what words would be not understood by, say, an Englishman? Find some **jargon.**
3. Paragraph [4] states that tight ends run silent but they seldom run deep. Why that particular phrasing?
4. The opening paragraph contains an example of **equivocation.** What is it, and what is a more common name for humorous equivocation?
5. The following words may not be in your vocabulary of precise meanings; look them up: gristle [14], hallmark [13], mastodon [1], prone [9], prototype [2], Purple Heart [13], scrimmage [7].

Rhetoric and Style

1. In spite of the highly **figurative** style, this essay does have some data. What are they?
2. Find and list both **similes** and **metaphors** used in this essay. Find at least three of each.
3. There is a **figure of speech** called "synechdoche," a type of **metaphor** in which a part is used to represent the whole; we say, "All *hands* on deck," where "hands" means "seamen." Find one or two examples in this essay.
4. The author also enlivens his writing by the use of **hyperbole;** find an example of it.

Applications and Evaluation

1. Do you find any benefits in this **style** of writing to praise a person that are not to be found in a more sober listing of achievements or records? Does this style present any distractions?

2. Mr. Murray describes the function of a tight end as well as praising one in particular. Try to write a brief essay in which you **define** the function of a job by using one person as a prototype or a "classic example." Pick a real job and a real person.
3. Two professional football teams are mentioned by name, the Lions and the Rams. What are some other names of professional athletic teams? What is the tendency in selecting such names? Could you develop an essay or paragraph with a title like "Sports Animals"?
4. The **analogy** between the Rams and an army is a switch on the usual **comparison** of any group effort to a team. Try to write an extended analogy in which you compare a specific job (or political effort) to a specific team. Topics might be "Supporting a strike is like playing hockey," or "Working in a restaurant is like playing on a baseball team," or "My Phrenology II class is like a football team with no quarterback."

John Holt (1923–   ) John Holt is primarily a teacher, having taught fifth grade in New York, English and mathematics in high school, education at Harvard, summer courses at Berkeley. He has been a prolific writer for reform in education, publishing in a great many journals and authoring three books, *How Children Fail, How Children Learn,* and *What Do I Do Monday?* A keen observer of children and their reactions to the educational system, he wrote this selection as an introduction to Herbert Kohl's book *Teaching the Unteachable.* Kohl's evidence showed that ghetto children, when allowed to write in their own dialect, about experiences and scenes real to them wrote freely and seemed truly to learn. Holt's introduction has a tone pleasing to most students and many teachers; he uses the occasion to present some of his own ideas about education and American society.

Is This Education?

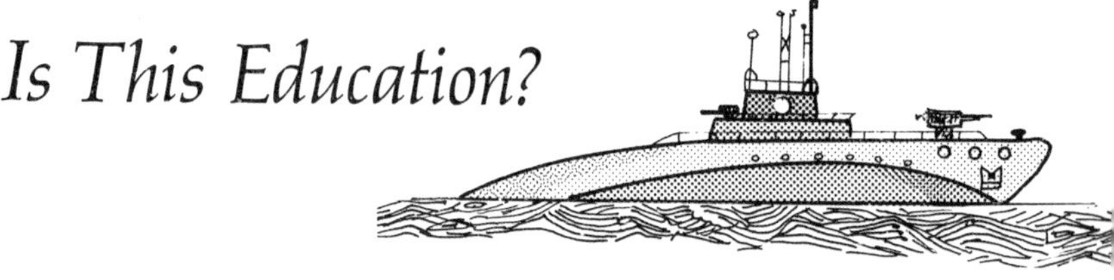

A few years ago, when the poverty program got under way, and we began to rediscover our poor, there was a rush of articles about the children growing up in our city slums. They proved to be strange, silent creatures indeed. We were told that they didn't know the names of things, didn't know that things had names, didn't even know their own names. We were told that, having never heard any real speech, they could hardly speak more than occasional monosyllables themselves. The people who reported these things were serious, and sympathetic, and sincerely believed every word they said—and I, like many other people, believed them. [1]

How do you find out, anyway, whether a child knows his own name? Smiling kindly at him, and speaking in a gentle and reassuring tone of voice, you ask him, "What's your name?" If he doesn't answer, it presumably shows that he doesn't know. Or perhaps, knowing his name, you call him by it. If, hearing his name, he makes no move or reply, again it shows that he doesn't know it. Simple. [2]

Only, as Mr. Kohl has shown, and by now some others as well, it may not be so simple. It makes a certain kind of sense to try to judge what a child knows by seeing what he can do, but it leaves out the possibility that he may choose not to show what he can do, that he may decide that at school the safest course is to say and do as little as possible—at least until he knows what and who this strange place and these strange people are. [3]

I am suddenly reminded of Submarine Officers Training School in New London in the fall of 1943. Here we sat, 270 student officers, and there up in front were our teachers, ex-sub skippers yanked away from the Pacific and their chances for heroism, fame, and advancement. "We want to know who you are," they told us. "If you see us in the bar at the Officer's Club come up, and introduce yourselves, and we'll have some talk." Some students took this advice. How friendly and welcoming was the submarine service! How pleasant and salty and exciting were these veteran skippers! Yes; but they were also, to a man, sore as hell about being in New London instead of the Pacific, and when, in class or on a training ship or wherever, their anger and impatience could not be contained, the students who got it in the neck were very likely to be the ones whose names they knew. They never knew mine; when I graduated, 13th in the class, the only officer who knew me by name was the school Exec, from whom I had had to get permission to leave on weekends. My caution paid off handsomely. It should not surprise us if slum children, finding themselves in a place where most of the grown-ups neither look nor sound like anyone they know, are equally cautious. [4]

There is no need to set forth here the many ways in which the schools of our city slums are in most cases an environment fiercely and unrelievedly hostile and destructive to the children who attend them. That story has been told in part by Mr. Kohl, and will be told many times again. I would like to stress here a somewhat different point. From Mr. Kohl's book we could easily get the impression that he is talking about a special problem—how to make disadvantaged children articulate and literate. In fact the problem is much wider. Our so-called best schools are turning out students most of whom, in any real and important sense, are as inarticulate as the most deprived children of the ghettos, as little able to speak or write simply and directly about things of importance to them, what they know, want, and care about. The training in writing that they get, unless they are very lucky, is largely training in bullslinging and snowjobbery. Every year students at all levels write millions of papers. It is a safe bet that most of the time—I would guess over 95 percent—the writers of these papers do not care about and in fact have no honest and genuine opinions about what they are writing, and would not write it if they were not made to. I once asked a very able high school senior, a straight A student in English, if she ever kept any of her old English papers. She looked at me amazed. "For heaven's sake," she said, "What for?" [5]

What for, indeed? And a senior, soon to graduate cum laude from one of the leading Ivy League colleges, told me not long ago—and I have to add that he was no radical or troublemaker—that he and everyone he knew were wholly convinced that their surest chance of getting an A on their papers and in their courses was to repeat the professor's ideas back to him, though of course in somewhat altered language. [6]

It would be easy to compile a bookful of horror stories about schools and classrooms where neatness, mechanical accuracy, and orthodoxy of opinion—i.e., agreeing with the teacher's spoken or even unspoken notions of what is right and proper for children to believe and say—count for far more than honest, independent, original expression. It is still common in a great many schools to fail papers that have more than a very few errors in grammar, punctuation, or spelling, regardless of any other merit they might have. Not long ago I talked to the mother of an eight- or nine-year-old whose most recent paper, entirely free of any mechanical errors and otherwise (as the teacher admitted) well written, was failed because he wrote it in three colors of ink. And this was in a "good" school system. But the real reason why our schools do not turn out people who can use language simply and strongly, let alone beautifully, lies deeper. It is that with very few exceptions the schools, from kindergarten through graduate school, do not give a damn what the students think. Think, care about, or want to know. What counts is what the system has decided they shall be made to learn. Teachers' manuals for the elementary and even secondary grades instruct teachers to have "discussions" in which they "bring out the following points." What kind of a discussion is that? And at my alma mater, Yale, when the sensible and overdue suggestion was recently made that the resident colleges institute non-credit seminars on matters of current interest and concern to the students, there was a howl of protest from many leading members of the faculty. They insisted that all courses must be instituted and controlled by the departments. One man spoke of the danger of "academic bull-sessions." Another said, hard as it may be to believe, that such issues as the war in Vietnam were too recent to be discussed "in depth" or "dispassionately," and that to try to discuss it would only lead to "sloppy and disorganized thinking." A shameful business; but probably all too typical. Easy to see why Paul Goodman speaks of "academic monks." [7]

If we are to make real progress in improving student writing, the first lesson we have to learn is this. A student will only be concerned with his own use of language, will only care about its effectiveness, and therefore try to judge its effectiveness—and therefore be able to improve its effectiveness—when he is talking to an audience, not just one that allows him to say what he wants as he wants, but one that takes him and his ideas seriously. This does not mean letting him take a shot at expressing his thoughts so that we teachers can then demolish them or show how much better are our own. In this respect the so-called and perhaps misnamed Socratic method is not only dishonest but destructive. It is easy for even half-smart adults to win arguments with children who are unskilled at arguing, or to lead them into logical traps and pitfalls. Children so outplayed at the word game will after a while simply stop playing it, or will concentrate on playing it our way. What we have to recognize is something quite different, that it is the effort to use words well, to say what he wants to say, to people whom he trusts, and wants to reach and move, that alone will teach a young person to use words better. No doubt, given this starting point, some technical advice and help may at times be useful; but we must begin from here or we will make no progress at all. [8]

A final question. What difference does it make? Above all, what difference does it make whether the children of our poor, and notably our Negro poor, learn to speak and write well or not? Should we not bend all our efforts to giving them the kind of training that will enable them to get jobs and do work that will lift them, at least a little, out of their poverty? The answer is that this is nowhere near enough. It is of the greatest importance to our society that the children of our poor, particularly if they are Negroes, shall be skillful in the use of words. Not just skillful enough to be able to read signs and instructions, but skillful enough to be able to reach, instruct, and move other men. For our society faces a choice. Either we become a genuinely integrated society, in which the color of a man's skin has no more to do with the way other men treat him and feel about him than, say, the color of his eyes or his hair, or we will become a genuinely, wholeheartedly, unashamedly racist society, like that of Nazi Germany or present South Africa—with perhaps our own Final Solution waiting at the end. In short, either we whites get cured of our racism, and fairly soon, or it will kill all of whatever decent is left in our society. One thing that might help cure us is a Negro population articulate enough to make us feel what racism is like for those who suffer under it. No doubt we have some Negro spokesmen today, but they are so few—too few, and too remote. What a few Baldwins, Kings, and Carmichaels now tell us, we need to be told by thousands, hundreds of thousands. Enough Negroes, with enough words, might break down our often unspoken and even unconscious feeling that they are different, inferior, despicable, even terrifying, and awaken instead in us an awareness of our common humanity, and their pain, and our responsibility for it. And while they are doing that, they might at the same time organize and educate themselves, and their allies among the other poor and dispossessed, into a political force strong and effective enough to make some of the changes we need to make our society, in Paul Goodman's words, not Great but only decent, a society in which all men can live without hate, fear, or guilt. [9]

1660 words, 9 paragraphs

Diction

1. The author uses two kinds of **jargon,** naval (skipper, salty, Exec) and collegiate (bullslinging, snowjobbery). What is the effect of this kind of language?
2. This short essay bristles with **clichés**: sore as hell [4], to a man [4], paid off handsomely [4], a safe bet [5], give a damn [7], howl of protest [7], a shameful business [7], to list a few. What might the reader assume about the author from so many unoriginal phrases?
3. Does the author's use of **slang** such as "got it in the neck," as well as **jargon,** give any strength to his essay? Is it a weakness?
4. The author discusses "our so-called best schools" [5] and the "so-called Socratic method" [8]. Why does he say "so-called"? Aren't our best schools really best? Isn't the method Socratic?
5. The author uses a great many **connotative** words in this short essay. List at least three that are especially strong emotionally.
6. Look up the main meaning of the following words (notice whether or not the author uses them in the same way in his

essay): articulate [5], compile [7], cum laude [6], despicable [9], ghetto [5], Ivy League [6], literate [5], orthodoxy [7], racist [9], slum [1].

Rhetoric and Style

1. The author refers to Paul Goodman twice. Who is Paul Goodman, and why would John Holt refer to him?
2. The author seeks to explain the refusal of slum children to talk in schools by use of an **analogy.** Is it a valid analogy?
3. What is the author's **attitude** toward his subject? Show how he lets that attitude be known.
4. Make a list of the striking **metaphors** and **similes** used by the author to enliven his essay.
5. By reading this essay, presumably about schools, we find out that John Holt is a teacher, went to Yale, was a submarine officer in World War I. Does the inclusion of such personal material aid or hinder his being persuasive?
6. Paragraph [8] contains the main part of the **thesis.** In the next to last sentence, "What we have to recognize . . ." the statement is made: "that alone will teach a young person to use words better." This seems to be a main point in the whole essay. To what referent does "that" point? State the sentence in as simple a fashion as possible. Comment?

Applications and Evaluation

1. This essay has many **generalizations.** Is there any evidence that:
   a. "Most slum schools are fiercely destructive to the children."
   b. "Our so-called best schools are turning out students most of whom are . . . inarticulate."
   c. Schools "do not give a damn what the students think."
   d. "Real progress in improving student writing" will come from "talking to an audience that takes him [the student] seriously."
2. John Holt uses **polar thinking** when he states that either our society must become "genuinely integrated" or "wholeheartedly racist." Is there any room for a workable society between these two extremes?
3. There are probably great areas of weakness in American school

systems. Can you note some weaknesses of the colleges, the high schools? Be as specific as possible. Are these weaknesses greater in ghetto schools than in suburban schools? What is your evidence?

4. Are there any areas of strength in American school systems? List a few, being as specific as possible. Your instructor may ask you to write an essay **comparing** the strengths and weaknesses in one specific segment of schools (college preparation, job training, mental health counseling, for example).
5. Does anybody in your school "give a damn" what you think? Why or why not?
6. Write a brief essay in which you **compare** school to a job (e.g., grades equal wages) or life in a school to life in a small society.

Paul Ralph Ehrlich (1932–   ) Paul Ehrlich was educated at the universities of Pennsylvania and Kansas. He has been a professor of biology at Stanford University as well as a member of many scientific organizations. He has written widely, contributing to many scientific journals and producing books ranging from *How to Know the Butterflies* to *How to be a Survivor*. This selection was taken from the frightening book *The Population Bomb*.

The Population Bomb

I have understood the population explosion intellectually for a long time. I came to understand it emotionally one stinking hot night in Delhi a couple of years ago. My wife and daughter and I were returning to our hotel in an ancient taxi. The seats were hopping with fleas. The only functional gear was third. As we crawled through the city, we entered a crowded slum area. The temperature was well over 100, and the air was a haze of dust and smoke. The streets seemed alive with people. People eating, people washing, people sleeping. People visiting, arguing, and screaming. People thrusting their hands through the taxi window, begging. People defecating and urinating. People clinging to buses. People herding animals. People, people, people, people. As we moved slowly through the mob, hand horn squawking, the dust, noise, heat, and cooking fires gave the scene a hellish aspect. Would we ever get to our hotel? All three of us were, frankly, frightened. It seemed that anything could happen—but, of course, nothing did. Old India hands will laugh at our reaction. We were just some overprivileged tourists, unaccustomed to the sights and sounds of India. Perhaps, but since that night I've known the *feel* of overpopulation. [1]

Americans are beginning to realize that the undeveloped countries of the world face an inevitable population-food crisis. Each year food production in undeveloped countries falls a bit further behind burgeoning population growth, and people go to bed a little bit hungrier. While there are temporary or local reversals of this trend, it now seems inevitable that it will continue to its logical conclusion: mass starvation. The rich are going to get richer, but the more numerous poor are going to get poorer. Of these poor, a minimum of three and one-half million will starve to death this year, mostly children. But this is a mere handful compared to the numbers that will be starving in a decade or so. And it is now too late to take action to save many of those people. [2] . . .

It has been estimated that the human population of 6000 B.C. was about five million people, taking perhaps one million years to get there from two and a half million. The population did not reach 500 million until almost 8,000 years later—about 1650 A.D. This means it doubled roughly once every thousand years or so. It reached a billion people around 1850, doubling in some 200 years. It took only 80 years or so for the next doubling, as the population reached two billion around 1930. We have not completed the next doubling to four billion yet, but we now have well over three billion people. The doubling time at present seems to be about 37 years. Quite a reduction in doubling times: 1,000,000 years, 1,000 years, 200 years, 80 years, 37 years. [3] . . .

One of the most ominous facts of the current situation is that roughly 40% of the population of the undeveloped world is made up of people *under 15 years old*. As that mass of young people moves into its reproductive years during the next decade, we're going to see the greatest baby boom of all time. Those youngsters are the reason for all the ominous predictions for the year 2000. They are the gunpowder for the population explosion. [4]

How did we get into this bind? It all happened a long time ago, and the story involves the process of natural selection, the development of culture, and man's swollen head. The essence of success in evolution is reproduction, . . . for reproduction is the key to winning the evolutionary game. Any structure, physiological process, or pattern of behavior that leads to greater reproductive success will tend to be perpetuated. The entire process by which man developed involves thousands of millenia of our ancestors being more successful breeders than their relatives. Facet number one of our bind—the urge to reproduce has been fixed in us by billions of years of evolution. [5]

Of course through all those years of evolution, our ancestors were fighting a continual battle to keep the birth rate ahead of the death rate. That they were successful is attested to by our very existence, for, if the death rate had overtaken the birth rate for any substantial period of time, the evolutionary line leading to man would have gone extinct. Among our apelike ancestors, a few million years ago, it was still very difficult for a mother to rear her children successfully. Most of the offspring died before they reached reproductive age. The death rate was near the birth rate. Then another factor entered the picture—cultural evolution was added to biological evolution. [6] . . .

Of course, in the early days the whole system did not prevent a very high mortality among the young, as well as among the older members of the group. Hunting and food-gathering is a risky business. Cavemen had to throw very impressive cave bears out of their caves before the men could move in. Witch doctors and shamans had a less than perfect record at treating wounds and curing disease. Life was short, if not sweet. Man's total population size doubtless increased slowly but steadily as human populations expanded out of the African cradle of our species. [7]

Then about 8,000 years ago a major change occurred—the agricultural revolution. People began to give up hunting food and settled down to grow it. Suddenly some of the risk was removed from life. The chances of dying of starvation diminished greatly in some human groups. Other threats associated with the nomadic life were also reduced, perhaps balanced by new threats of disease and large-scale warfare associated with the development of cities. But the overall result was a more secure existence than before, and the human population grew more rapidly. Around 1800, when the standard of living in what are today the developed countries was dramatically increasing due to industrialization, population growth really began to accelerate. The development of medical science was the straw that broke the camel's back. While lowering death rates in the developed countries was due in part to other factors, there is no question that "instant death control," exported by the developed countries has been responsible for the drastic lowering of death rates in the undeveloped countries. Medical science, with its efficient public health programs, has been able to depress the death rate with astonishing rapidity and at the same time drastically increase the birth rate; healthier people have more babies. [8]

Victory over malaria, yellow fever, smallpox, cholera, and other infectious diseases has been responsible for similar plunges in death rate throughout most of the UDCs. In the decade 1940–1950 the death rate declined 46% in Puerto Rico, 43% in Formosa, and 23% in Jamaica. In a sample of 18 undeveloped areas the average decline in death rate between 1945 and 1950 was 24%. [9]

It is, of course, socially very acceptable to reduce the death rate. Billions of years of evolution have given us all a powerful will to live. Intervening in the birth rate goes against our evolutionary values. During all those centuries of our evolutionary past, the individual who had the most children passed on their genetic endowment in greater quantities than those who reproduced less. Their genes dominate our heredity today. All our biological urges are for more reproduction, and they are all too often reinforced by our culture. In brief, death control goes with the grain, birth control against it. [10]

In summary, the world's population will continue to grow as long as the birth rate exceeds the death rate; it's as simple as that. When it stops growing or starts to shrink, it will mean that either the birth rate has gone down or the death rate has gone up or a combination of the two. Basically, then, there are only two kinds of solutions to the population problem. One is a "birth rate solution," in which we find ways to lower the birth rate. The other is a "death rate solution," in which ways to raise the death rate—war, famine, pestilence—*find us*. The problem could have been avoided by *population control*, in which mankind consciously adjusted the birth rate so that a "death rate solution" did not have to occur. [11]

1700 words 11 paragraphs

Diction

1. This essay is concerned with the population crisis. We have had a series of crises recently; are they really crises? What does "crisis" mean? Can you think of any other words we tend to overwork similarly?
2. The author asks, "How did we get into this bind?" [5]. At what **level of usage** would you place this sentence? Does it fit the rest of the essay?
3. Further in paragraph [5] the author says that one of the reasons for our problem is "man's swollen head." What does he mean?
4. The concept of birth control is familiar and understandable, but Dr. Ehrlich mentions "death control" in paragraph [8]. What does "death control" mean?

5. Check the exact meaning of these words in your dictionary: attested [6], drastic [8], endowment [10], essence [5], inevitable [2], millenia [5], nomadic [8], ominous [4], pestilence [11], shamans [7].

Rhetoric and Style

1. In paragraph [8] we find the phrase "the straw that broke the camel's back." What is the reference? Is it effective?
2. Paragraph [5] seems to have some confusing **metaphors** in it. Technically they are **mixed metaphors.** Can you spot them?
3. Do stock, almost **cliché**, phrases like mere handful [2], baby boom [4], risky business [7], short . . . but sweet [7], with the grain [11] aid communication? Did you even notice their use? Can you create better adjectives to link with "handful" or "business" for example?
4. In what way are youngsters "gunpowder"? [4] How does that image fit the main **analogy** of the essay?
5. In the prologue, paragraph [1], the author develops a feeling of being crushed by people. How does he do it?
6. What is the main method the author uses to get the essay to stick together? Look at the opening phrases of each paragraph; make a conclusion.

Applications and Evaluation

1. The first paragraph attempts to express a feeling. The author does so by stating vividly the impact on his senses—what he saw, heard, smelled, felt—in about two hundred words. Try a similar paragraph emphasizing one aspect of the scene such as loneliness; a sense of fear, anger, peace; noise; silence.
2. The problem of population seems to be in the UD or undeveloped nations. Is there a similar problem in this country? Explain.
3. Having offspring is necessary if a species is to survive, but having too many is countersurvival. Can you think of any other "natural" survival characteristics that can be detrimental if carried to an extreme? (Consider such simple elements as the need to eat.)
4. Does Dr. Ehrlich's use of statistics, **analogy, example** convince you that there really is a problem?

5. What might be some of the methods of population control mentioned in the last paragraph? What would be the reaction of the people if those methods were enforced? Any of the above questions could be answered in an essay.

Alvin Toffler (1928–   ) Educated at New York University, Alvin Toffler has been a Washington correspondent, an editor of both a national magazine, *Fortune*, and a prize-winning book, *The Schoolhouse in the City*. His interest in sociology and the impact of rapid technological change has led him to write and lecture widely and to an appointment as a visiting professor at Cornell University. He has written for many modern magazines and is now a visiting scholar at the Russell Sage Foundation. This selection is from his book *Future Shock*, which explains—by analogy—the impact of today upon tomorrow.

Future Shock

The 800th Lifetime

In the three short decades between now and the twenty-first century, millions of ordinary, psychologically normal people will face an abrupt collision with the future. Citizens of the world's richest and most technologically advanced nations, many of them will find it increasingly painful to keep up with the incessant demand for change that characterizes our time. For them, the future will have arrived too soon. [1] . . .

Western society for the past 300 years has been caught up in a fire storm of change. This storm, far from abating, now appears to be gathering force. Change sweeps through the highly industrialized countries with waves of ever accelerating speed and unprecedented impact. It spawns in its wake all sorts of curious social flora—from psychedelic churches and "free universities" to science cities in the Arctic and wife-swap clubs in California. [2]

It breeds odd personalities, too: children who at twelve are no longer childlike; adults who at fifty are children of twelve. There are rich men who playact poverty, computer programmers who turn on with LSD. There are anarchists who, beneath their dirty denim shirts, are outrageous conformists, and conformists who, beneath their button-down collars, are outrageous anarchists. There are married priests and atheist ministers and Jewish Zen Buddhists. We have pop . . . and op . . . and *art cinétique* . . . There are Playboy Clubs and homosexual movie theaters . . . amphetamines and tranquilizers . . . anger, affluence, and oblivion. Much oblivion. [3]

Is there some way to explain so strange a scene without recourse to the jargon of psychoanalysis or the murky clichés of existentialism? A strange new society is apparently erupting in our midst. Is there a way to understand it, to shape its development? How can we come to terms with it? [4]

Much that now strikes us as incomprehensible would be far less so if we took a fresh look at the racing rate of change that makes reality seem, sometimes, like a kaleidoscope run wild. For the acceleration of change does not merely buffet industries or nations. It is a concrete force that reaches deep into our personal lives, compels us to act out new roles, and confronts us with the danger of a new and powerfully upsetting psychological disease. This new disease can be called "future shock," and a knowledge of its sources and symptoms helps explain many things that otherwise defy rational analysis. [5]

THE UNPREPARED VISITOR

The parallel term "culture shock" has already begun to creep into the popular vocabulary. Culture shock is the effect that immersion in a strange culture has on the unprepared visitor. Peace Corps volunteers suffer from it in Borneo or Brazil. Marco Polo probably suffered from it in Cathay. Culture shock is what happens when a traveler suddenly finds himself in a place where yes may mean no, where a "fixed price" is negotiable, where to be kept waiting in an outer office is no cause for insult, where laughter may signify anger. It is what happens when the familiar psychological cues that help an individual to function in society are suddenly withdrawn and replaced by new ones that are strange or incomprehensible. [6]

The culture shock phenomenon accounts for much of the bewilderment, frustration, and disorientation that plagues Americans in their dealings with other societies. It causes a breakdown in communication, a misreading of reality, an inability to cope. Yet culture shock is relatively mild in comparison with the much more serious malady, future shock. Future shock is the dizzying disorientation brought on by the premature arrival of the future. It may well be the most important disease of tomorrow. [7]

Future shock will not be found in *Index Medicus* or in any listing of psychological abnormalities. Yet, unless intelligent steps are taken to combat it, millions of human beings will find themselves increasingly disoriented, progressively incompetent to deal rationally with their environments. The malaise, mass neurosis, irrationality, and free-floating violence already apparent in contemporary life are merely a foretaste of what may lie ahead unless we come to understand and treat this disease. [8]

Future shock is a time phenomenon, a product of the greatly accelerated rate of change in society. It arises from the superimposition of a new culture on an old one. It is culture shock in one's own society. But its impact is far worse. For most Peace Corps men, in fact most travelers, have the comforting knowledge that the culture they left behind will be there to return to. The victim of future shock does not. [9]

Take an individual out of his own culture and set him down suddenly in an environment sharply different from his own, with a different set of cues to react to—different conceptions of time, space, work, love, religion, sex, and everything else—then cut him off from any hope of retreat to a more familiar social landscape, and the dislocation he suffers is doubly severe. Moreover, if this new culture is itself in constant turmoil, and if—worse yet—its values are incessantly changing, the sense of disorientation will be still further intensified. Given few clues as to what kind of behavior is rational under the radically new circumstances, the victim may well become a hazard to himself and others. [10]

Now imagine not merely an individual but an entire society, an entire generation—including its weakest, least intelligent, and most irrational members—suddenly transported into this new world. The result is mass disorientation, future shock on a grand scale. [11]

This is the prospect that man now faces. Change is avalanching upon our heads and most people are grotesquely unprepared to cope with it. [12]

BREAK WITH THE PAST

Is all this exaggerated? I think not. It has become a cliché to say that what we are now living through is a "second industrial revolution." This phrase is supposed to impress us with the speed and profundity of the change around us. But in addition to being platitudinous, it is misleading. For what is occurring now is, in all likelihood, bigger, deeper, and more important than the industrial revolution. Indeed, a growing body of reputable opinion asserts that the present movement represents nothing less than the second great divide in human history, comparable in magnitude only with that first great break in historic continuity, the shift from barbarism to civilization. [13]

This idea crops up with increasing frequency in the writings of scientists and technologists. Sir George Thomson, the British physicist and Nobel prizewinner, suggests in *The Foreseeable Future* that the nearest historic parallel with today is not the industrial revolution but rather the "invention of agriculture in the neolithic age." John Diebold, the American automation expert, warns that "the effects of the technological revolution we are now living through will be deeper than any social change we have experienced before." Sir Leon Bagrit, the British computer manufacturer, insists that automation by itself represents "the greatest change in the whole history of mankind." [14]

Nor are the men of science and technology alone in these views. Sir Herbert Read, the philosopher of art, tells us that we are living through "a revolution so fundamental that we must search many past centuries for a parallel. Possibly the only comparable change is the one that took place between the Old and the New Stone Age . . ." And Kurt W. Marek, who under the name C. W. Ceram is best-known as the author of *Gods, Graves and Scholars,* observes that "we, in the twentieth century, are concluding an era of mankind five thousand years in length . . . We are not, as Spengler supposed, in the situation of Rome at the beginning of the Christian West, but in that of the year 3000 B.C. We open our eyes like prehistoric man, we see a world totally new." [15]

One of the most striking statements of this theme has come from Kenneth Boulding, an eminent economist and imaginative social thinker. In justifying his view that the present moment represents a crucial turning point in human history, Boulding observes that "as far as many statistical series related to activities of mankind are concerned, the date that divides human history into two equal parts is well within living memory." In effect, our century represents The Great Median Strip running down the center of human history. Thus he asserts, "The world of today . . . is as different from the world in which I was born as that world was from Julius Caesar's. I was born in the middle of human history, to date, roughly. Almost as much has happened since I was born as happened before." [16]

This startling statement can be illustrated in a number of ways. It has been observed, for example, that if the last 50,000 years of man's existence were divided into lifetimes of approximately sixty-two years each, there have been about 800 such lifetimes. Of these 800, fully 650 were spent in caves. [17]

Only during the last seventy lifetimes has it been possible to communicate effectively from one lifetime to another—as writing made it possible to do. Only during the last six lifetimes did masses of men ever see a printed word. Only during the last four has it been possible to measure time with any precision. Only in the last two has anyone anywhere used an electric motor. And the overwhelming majority of all the material goods we use in daily life today have been developed within the present, the 800th, lifetime. [18]

This 800th lifetime marks a sharp break with all past human experience because during this lifetime man's relationship to resources has reversed itself. This is most evident in the field of economic development. Within a single lifetime, agriculture, the original basis of civilization, has lost its dominance in nation after nation. Today in a dozen major countries agriculture employs fewer than 15 percent of the economically active population. In the United States, whose farms feed 200,000,000 Americans plus the equivalent of another 160,000,000 people around the world, this figure is already below 6 percent and it is still shrinking rapidly. [19]

Moreover, if agriculture is the first stage of economic development and industrialism the second, we can now see that still another stage—the third—has suddenly been reached. In about 1956 the United States became the first major power in which more than 50 percent of the non-farm labor force ceased to wear the blue collar of factory or manual labor. Blue collar workers were outnumbered by those in the so-called white-collar occupations—in retail trade, administration, communications, research, education, and other service categories. Within the same lifetime a society for the first time in human history not only threw off the yoke of agriculture, but managed within a few brief decades to throw off the yoke of manual labor as well. The world's first service economy had been born. [20]

Since then, one after another of the technologically advanced countries have moved in the same direction. Today, in those nations in which agriculture is down to the 15 percent level or below, white collars already outnumber blue in Sweden, Britain, Belgium, Canada, and the Netherlands. Ten thousand years for agriculture. A century or two for industrialism. And now, opening before us—super-industrialism. [21]

Jean Fourastié, the French planner and social philosopher, has declared that "Nothing will be less industrial than the civilization born of the industrial revolution." The significance of this staggering fact has yet to be digested. Perhaps U Thant, Secretary General of the United Nations, came closest to summarizing the meaning of the shift to super-industrialism when he declared that "The central stupendous truth about developed economies today is that they can have—in anything but the shortest run—the kind and scale of resources they decide to have. . . . It is no longer resources that limit decisions. It is the decision that makes the resources. This is the fundamental revolutionary change—perhaps the most revolutionary man has ever known." This monumental reversal has taken place in the 800th lifetime. [22]

This lifetime is also different from all others because of the astonishing expansion of the scale and scope of change. Clearly, there have been other lifetimes in which epochal upheavals occurred. Wars, plagues, earthquakes, and famine rocked many an earlier social order. But these shocks and upheavals were contained within the borders of one or a group of adjacent societies. It took generations, even centuries, for their impact to spread beyond these borders. [23]

In our lifetime the boundaries have burst. Today the network of social ties is so tightly woven that the consequences of contemporary events radiate instantaneously around the world. A war in Vietnam alters basic political alignments in Peking, Moscow, and Washington, touches off protests in Stockholm, affect financial transactions in Zurich, triggers secret diplomatic moves in Algiers. [24]

Indeed, not only do *contemporary* events radiate instantaneously—now we can be said to be feeling the impact of all *past* events in a new way. For the past is doubling back on us. We are caught in what might be called a "time skip." [25]

An event that affected only a handful of people at the time of its occurrence in the past can have large-scale consequences today. The Peloponnesian War, for example, was little more than a skirmish by modern standards. While Athens, Sparta and several nearby city-states battled, the population of the rest of the globe remained largely unaware of and undisturbed by the war. The Zapotec Indians living in Mexico at the time were wholly untouched by it. The ancient Japanese felt none of its impact. [26]

Yet the Peloponnesian War deeply altered the future course of Greek history. By changing the movement of men, the geographical distribution of genes, value, and ideas, it affected later events in

Rome, and, through Rome, all Europe. Today's Europeans are to some small degree different people because that conflict occurred. [27]

In turn, in the tightly wired world of today, these Europeans influence Mexicans and Japanese alike. Whatever trace of impact the Peloponnesian War left on the genetic structure, the ideas, and the values of today's Europeans is now exported by them to all parts of the world. Thus today's Mexicans and Japanese feel the distant, twice-removed impact of that war even though their ancestors, alive during its occurrence, did not. In this way, the events of the past, skipping as it were over generations and centuries, rise up to haunt and change us today. [28]

When we think not merely of the Peloponnesian War but of the building of the Great Wall of China, the Black Plague, the battle of the Bantu against the Hamites—indeed, of all the events of the past—the cumulative implications of the time-skip principle take on weight. Whatever happened to some men in the past affects virtually all men today. This was not always true. In short, all history is catching up with us, and this very difference, paradoxically, underscores our break with the past. Thus the scope of change is fundamentally altered. Across space and through time, change has a power and reach in this, the 800th lifetime, that it never did before. [29]

But the final, qualitative difference between this and all previous lifetimes is the one most easily overlooked. For we have not merely extended the scope and scale of change, we have radically altered its pace. We have in our time released a totally new social force—a stream of change so accelerated that it influences our sense of time, revolutionizes the tempo of daily life, and affects the very way we "feel" the world around us. We no longer "feel" life as men did in the past. And this is the ultimate difference, the distinction that separates the truly contemporary man from all others. For this acceleration lies behind the impermanence—the transience—that penetrates and tinctures our consciousness, radically affecting the way we relate to other people, to things, to the entire universe of ideas, art and values. [30]

To understand what is happening to us as we move into the age of super-industrialism, we must analyze the processes of acceleration and confront the concept of transience. If acceleration is a new social force, transience is its psychological counterpart, and without an understanding of the role it plays in contemporary human behavior, all our theories of personality, all our psychology, must remain premodern. Psychology without the concept of transience cannot take account of precisely those phenomena that are peculiarly contemporary. [31]

By changing our relationship to the resources that surround us, by violently expanding the scope of change, and, most crucially, by accelerating its pace, we have broken irretrievably with the past. We have cut ourselves off from the old ways of thinking, of feeling, of adapting. We have set the stage for a completely new society and we are now racing toward it. This is the crux of the 800th lifetime. And it is this that calls into question man's capacity for adaptation—how will he fare in this new society? Can he adapt to its imperatives? And if not, can he alter these imperatives? [32]

2960 words, 32 paragraphs

Plato (427 B.C.–347 B.C.) One of the world's greatest philosophers, Plato was born and educated in Athens, Greece and was one of Socrates' students. (His original name was Aristocles; the name Plato is from the Greek word *platus,* meaning "broad.") After Socrates' death in 399 B.C. he spent thirteen years traveling. Returning to Athens, he founded the Academy, finished his writings, and taught in Athens until his death. Among his extant works are *The Republic,* a picture of the ideal state, and some two dozen other dialogues. Among the early dialogues are the three dealing with the death of Socrates, *The Apology*, *The Crito*, and *The Phaedo*. The following selection is from *The Crito* and is a clear defense of the state against the whim of the individual to ignore the law. This translation is by James W. Davenport and somewhat modernized.

The Duty of a Citizen

INTRODUCTION

Socrates, part-time sculptor, full-time philosopher had been condemned to death for corrupting the youth. His indictment read, "Socrates is guilty of crime: first for not worshiping the gods whom the city worships, but introducing new divinities of his own; next for corrupting the youth. The penalty due is—death." It was posted by Anytus, a leather merchant whose son Socrates had "corrupted" from tanning to philosophy. The Law offered Socrates a choice of exile or death; he chose death. Here, Crito tries to persuade Socrates to escape.

CRITO: I know some people who can rescue you from here and get you out of the country for a modest sum. Wherever you go, you will find friends and a welcome.

Translation by James W. Davenport, revised by Charles M. Cobb. Reprinted by permission of the translators.

SOCRATES: I appreciate your feelings and your advice; but first we must decide whether to follow your advice or not, agreed?

CRITO: Why, yes.

SOCRATES: . . . Should a man fulfill his agreements, if he admits them to be right, or should he break them?

CRITO: He should fulfill them.

SOCRATES: Then consider. If we leave prison without the consent of the State, do we not do an injury where we least ought to injure? Are we or are we not fulfilling our agreements?

CRITO: I cannot answer, Socrates, for I am not sure.

SOCRATES: Then, look at it this way. Imagine we are going to run away (however you choose to call it) and the Laws and State of Athens stand before us and ask, "What are you about to do? Do you not see that this action you plan has the intention of overturning us—the laws and the state—as much as any act of yours can? Do you imagine that a state can exist and not be overthrown if its legal decisions are not obeyed but are set aside and destroyed by individuals?" What will we answer, Crito, to these and similar questions? There is much that can be said, especially by a rhetorician, to show that the law requiring a sentence to be carried out should be binding, once it has been enacted. He will argue that the Law should not be set aside and we shall say, "Yes, but the state has wronged us and given us an unjust sentence." Should we say that?

CRITO: Right, that is our answer, Socrates.

SOCRATES: And the Law would answer, "Where was such a provision in our agreement with you, Socrates, or did you agree to abide by the judgments of the Law? If we express surprise at this language, the Law would probably say, "Answer the question, Socrates—you who use the method of asking and answering questions—instead of showing surprise. What charge do you bring against the state that justifies your trying to destroy us? Did we not give you life in the first place? Did not your father marry your mother and beget you through our aid? Do you have an objection to the laws that regulate marriage?" No, none, I should reply. "Do you have objections to those laws which regulate children's upbringing and education, from which you benefitted yourself, Are you not grateful for the laws which commanded your father to train you in culture and physical education?" Yes, I should reply. "Well, then, since you have been born, reared, and trained by us, can you deny that you are our child and servant as were your fathers?

If this is true, you are not on equal terms with the Law. You have no equality with your father or your employer—had you one—to allow you to retaliate and answer back when you are scolded or to strike back when you are hit or beaten. You are no more justified in retaliating against the Law. Do you believe that if we have the right to put you to death that you have an equal right to destroy us as far as it is in your power to do so? Will you, the professor of true goodness, claim that you are justified in doing so? Do you not realize that you are bound to honor and respect your country, even more than father, mother, or ancestor; it is more precious, higher, and holier; it is held more sacred in the eyes of the gods and of all reasonable men. It is to be soothed when angry, obeyed when it commands—if you cannot persuade it otherwise—even if it orders you to be flogged or punished. If it leads you to battle and to death, you must follow; you must not yield or give way, but you must do whatever your country and its laws command both in battle and in the courts of law. Of course, you are at liberty to persuade them to change in accordance with the laws of universal justice, but failing to do so, you must obey, for as violence against one's parents is a sin, violence against one's country is a far greater sin." What shall we say to the Laws Crito? Is not what the Laws say true?

CRITO: Yes, I think so.

SOCRATES: The Laws would probably continue, "Consider, Socrates, whether or not it is true that your present attempt will do us an injury. For having brought you into the world, nurtured you, educated you, given you and every other citizen a share of all the good we have to offer we have further proclaimed that any Athenian, when he reaches manhood and has seen the political organization, the laws and the way they operate, may leave if he is not satisfied. He may take his property and go to a colony, emigrate to another country; not one of us Laws will stop him or penalize him. But he who has grown and has seen our ways and chooses to stay has entered into an implied contract with us and will do as we command him. He who stays and disobeys us is three times wrong: first because we are his parents, second because we are his mentors, and third because he has promised to obey us—and is neither obeying us nor persuading us that our commands are unjust. Our commands are even in the form or proposals which he can obey or show to be wrong; he is doing neither."

"These are the charges, Socrates, to which you will be exposed if you do what you plan, you above all others." Now, suppose I ask, 'Why me above all others?' The Laws would hotly and justly retort, "You above other men have acknowledged this agreement! We have clear evidence that you are satisfied with the state and the Laws. Of all citizens of Athens you have been the most constant resident; you have never left the city except for military service; you have never traveled as other men have done; you have never shown any curiosity to learn about other countries or laws; you have been contented with us. As final proof, you have had your children here. Moreover, you might have, in the course of the trial, fixed the penalty at banishment. That is, you could have done then, with our agreement, what you plan to do now without our agreement. But at that time you made a noble show and pretended to prefer death to exile. Now you show no regard for those earlier sentiments, for us the Laws, for the compact and agreement you made, but like the meanest of wretches plan to destroy us and run away. Answer first this question: 'Are we right in stating that you have agreed to be governed by us in deed, not in word only, and you agreed to live your life as a citizen in obedience to us?' " How shall we answer, Crito? Are we not bound to agree?

CRITO: We cannot help but agree, Socrates.

SOCRATES: "The fact is," they would say, "that you are breaking the covenants and agreements you have made, not at haste, not under compulsion, not in error, but leisurely over a period of seventy years. During that time you had freedom to leave the city if our agreements seemed unfair. You could have gone to Sparta or Crete—both praised by you for good government—or any Greek or foreign state. Obviously, you stand above other Athenians in your affection for the city and for us, its Laws. (and who would care for a state without laws?) After all this are you going to make yourself ridiculous by escaping? Take our advice and abide by your agreements."

Consider what will befall if you escape, if you commit this breach, if you stain your conscience. Your friends who might help will run the risk of banishment, loss of citizenship, or confiscation of property. Wherever you go, you will be regarded as a destroyer of law and order by all good patriots. Further, you will have confirmed the judgment of the jury, for a destroyer of the Law is likely to be a corrupter of the young and foolish. Will you avoid, then, these well-ordered cities and men or will you approach them without shame? What will you say to them, Socrates? Will you argue that goodness and integrity, institutions and laws are the most precious possessions of mankind—as you have argued here? Or will you flee to Crito's friends in wild, disordered Thessaly? They will be amused at the story of your flight clad in a shepherd's goatskin and in disguise. Probably no one will comment that a man so old would cling to a little more life at the cost of violating the most sacred of laws. . . . Or you may wish to live for the sake of your children, to educate them. Will you take them to Thessaly and make them foreigners? Will not your friends, if they are true friends, look after them as well if you are in the next world?

"No, Socrates, be advised by us your guardians. Do not think first of life, of children, of any other thing and of justice afterward, but think first of justice. As it is, you leave this place, as an innocent sufferer not as a doer of evil, a victim of a wrong done by other men, not by us, the Laws. But if you dishonorably escape, returning evil for evil and wrong for wrong, breaking your covenant with us, injuring those whom you want least to injure—yourself, your friends, your country and us—then you will have to face our anger in your lifetime; and our brothers, the laws of that world below, will not receive you kindly knowing that you have tried to destroy us. Listen to us and not to Crito."

"That, my dear friend Crito, is the voice I seem to hear as a mystic hears music, and their arguments sound so loudly in my ears that I cannot hear any other. Yet, if you think that it would do any good to urge a different view, say what you will, although it will be in vain.

CRITO: No, Socrates, I have nothing to say.

SOCRATES: Then permit me, Crito, to follow the will of God and go whither he leads.

1975 words

Writing Suggestions for Exposition

Each of the following suggestions emphasizes one method of exposition. As has been noted before, these methods may be mixed, they may overlap. It is for understanding and practice that one method is stressed in each suggestion. Similarly, the **stance** of the writer may vary from familiar to very formal.

A. **ANALYSIS**

1. **Technical analysis** answers the question, "How is it put together?" Try a technical analysis of one of the following:
    a. A rotary engine (or any other kind of engine).

b. A simple mechanical contrivance such as a ball point pen or a mechanical pencil.

2. **Functional analysis** answers the question, "How does it work?" Functional analyses are usually combined with technical analysis, which rarely occurs by itself. Show how:
   a. An organ, like the heart, works.
   b. One of the items in technical analysis works.
3. **Process analysis** answers the question. "How it is made?" It is the "How to" ______ paper. Show how to:
   a. Make something (sandals, macramé, a chair, a pot).
   b. Grow something (a plant, a fish, crystals, pigs).
   c. Put something together (a stew, a house, a term paper).
4. **Causal analysis** answers the question, "What caused it?" Write a paper showing the cause of:
   a. Your attending college.
   b. The lowest grade you ever received.
   c. Any conflict (from a war to a riot to an argument).

B. **COMPARISON AND CONTRAST**

These techniques show the similarities (**comparison**) or the differences (**contrast**).

1. Compare or contrast secondary school and college. Limit your discussion to one element such as the discipline, the instruction, athletics, or students.
2. Compare or contrast two forms of government. Using historical examples, limit the paper to one aspect of the governments such as lawmaking, individual freedoms, effectiveness in times of stress.
3. Compare or contrast two people. Again, so that you can write effectively, limit yourself to one aspect such as physical description, accomplishments, or moral stands.

C. **DEFINITION**

A **definition** is a request to share experience. It can be a brief **classification** as in a dictionary, or it can be **extended** by the use of many examples and details or by the use of detailed **directions** (see Tolkien, Holt, Forster). Define one of the following in a paragraph:

1. A specific tool (wrench, haemostat, drill, adze).
2. A complex abstraction (love, tyranny, fun, communism).
3. A type of person, such as a good doctor, a bad citizen, an effective politician, a nonconformist.

D. **ILLUSTRATION.** To **illustrate** is to use one typical example to explain an entire group. Some writers use two or three illustrations to support or explain an idea. Develop one of the following topics using illustration:

1. Effective use of colloquial language.
2. The destructiveness of progress.
3. Self-improvement through reading.
4. The steady shift in moral values.
5. The pendulum of fashion.

Note again that these categories are not absolute. It is possible to explain by use of **description,** of **narration,** of **analogy,** or of any of the other methods developed in this text. The careful writer, though, is sure what he is doing and deliberately finds a method that best suits his purpose, his **stance,** and his audience.

argumentation

When most people use the words "argue" or "argument" they refer to a quarrel, contention, or wrangling. The rhetorical mode called **argument** requires a more accurate and precise definition; it does not mean mere altercation! **Argument,** as we shall use it, means *a form of logical discourse in which a person tries to gain agreement by an appeal to reason.* Although argument might start in conflict, it should—ideally—end in truth. The art of persuasion is included by some in a broader definition of argumentation, but it differs both in appeal and in goal. **Persuasion** is *an attempt to gain either assent or* *action through an appeal to the emotions.* Rhetoricians in general consider persuasion an honorable art, for there are other less honest methods of urging people to agree, assent, or act: threats of force, fear of violence, lies, blackmail, and deceit in general.

There are several effective methods of shaping an argument; these methods can be used individually or in various combinations. One method is basically **inductive,** built around the amassing of evidence—examples and data—to convince or to establish truth. The essays by Stafford, Maddox, and Packard use this method. An equally fine method is the general use of a **deductive** pattern to apply general **premises** to specific problems. "Alternatives to Drugs," "Beyond Freedom and Dignity," and "The Declaration of Independence" are primarily deductive. The third is the **cause and effect** pattern. Cause and effect may be used in an **implied** argument (be careful what you name your child), as in Ralph Ellison's essay; it may be used to indicate a need for change, as in Jessica Mitford's essay; or it may be used to present an argument for social change, as in Gloria Steinem's essay. A useful method of presenting an argument is the debater's method. The basic **argumentative paragraph** is easy to use. When it is expanded into the **argumentative essay,** it is effective for most of the papers written by college students. A highly complex but effective method is the classical oration shown in Swift's "A Modest Proposal."

Note that "Alternatives to Drugs" and "Business Minorities" argue that something exists or has certain characteristics. "What It Will Be Like If Women Win" and "Beyond Freedom and Dignity" envision what will happen if certain practices are followed and what ought to be done. All arguments may be placed in one of two **classes,** *factual* or *ethical.* The *factual,* or declarative, argument states that something exists, has certain characteristics, or has a certain relationship with something else.

God exists.
Women have fewer business opportunities than men.
This is volcanic glass, not a Coke bottle.
The world is round.
Smoking cigarettes causes lung cancer.

The factual argument usually needs a mass of data or **evidence** or solid **examples** to support it. Clearly, the proof can be arranged according to any one of the methods noted above or a combination of them. The *ethical,* or conditional, argument places a value of good or bad on an idea, a plan, an action or states that this good or bad result will follow a given plan or action.

The government should limit barbiturate production.
Capital punishment should be abolished.
Pornography ought to be stopped.
Marijuana ought to be legalized.

Clearly, the ethical argument must appeal more to rules and principles than to sheer facts. When effective, it also appeals to the consequences, either moral or practical, of the plan or idea. "*If* we limit the production of barbiturates *then* there will be fewer pills on the illegal market." This type of argument often makes use of religious tenets and philosophical convictions as appeals. In both types of argument, though, the proposition must be clearly stated. It ought to be absolutely clear so both the argurer and the hearer will know precisely what is meant.

There are four types of fun and games for foolish folk that the seasoned rhetorician never indulges in—except for sport.

1. Never debate a matter of record; look it up. (Do not let your ego lure you into bets.)
   a. Babe Ruth hit 714 homers.
   b. The world's high-jump record is 7′7″.
2. Do not argue matters of absolute taste; each of us is entitled to personal preference.
   a. Square dancing is better than waltzing.
   b. Brunettes are lovelier than blondes.
3. Avoid fantasy, except for fun and speculation.
   a. Jack Dempsey in his prime could have beaten Joe Louis in his prime.
   b. The South could have won the Civil War if Stuart's cavalry had scouted Gettysburg more accurately.
4. Clarify matters of judgment; do not debate without defining.
   a. Ty Cobb played better baseball than Joe DiMaggio. (Define "better"; then get the data.)
   b. Chess is more stimulating than basketball. (This verges into matters of taste.)

A final caution for anyone who hears an argument or presents one: be wary of the facts. Check the evidence if possible. The following delightful story shows how a pun became glorified into an historical fact. It first appeared in Jerome Beatty, Jr.'s, "Trade Winds" column in the old *Saturday Review*. Copyright © by Jerome Beatty, Jr. Reprinted with his permission.

> I can tell you how history is made, or I should say, "made up." Back in 1961 I repeated here what I thought was a joke about Alexander the Great and his invention of the first wristwatch. It

consisted of a chemically treated cloth worn on the left forearm. Under the heat of the sun, the cloth changed colors each hour. It was known as "Alexander's Rag Timeband."

Since then my anecdote has become an integral part of a fairly new science known as "photochromism." Last year, an issue of *Product Engineering* defined it as "the reversible change in the color of a substance when it is exposed to radiant energy such as light." That magazine seriously told how Alexander had started it all, but the article carefully left out the punch line of the joke. It was irrelevant, apparently.

In the *Journal of the Canadian Ceramic Society* a treatise on "Photochromic Silver Halide Glasses" gave full credit to the Macedonian conqueror: "It is recorded that Alexander the Great discovered a substance . . . [etc.]. This became known as Alexander's rag timeband.[2]" That footnote adds class to it, as does the judicious use of the phrase, "It is recorded," which was also the wording in a piece on photochromism in a journal called *Spectrum*. Here we not only find Alexander's claim to scientific fame cemented more firmly but we are witness to how history can be improved. An authentic homey touch has been added. The cloth was "torn from the edge of his tunic."

The most recent reference to the subject was in a February 1967 issue of *Chemical and Engineering News*. . . . Volume I of a textbook, *Advances in Photochemistry*, by R. Dessauer and J. P. Paris published in 1963 goes into the matter in scientific depth:

"Early observations of photochromic systems include ter Meer's potassium salt of dinotroethane[9] and Phipson's gate post painted with lithopone pigment[10]. Application of photochromic materials was first exploited by Alexander the Great . . . [etc.]. Among historians it is known as Alexander's Rag Timeband[8]."

And footnote No. 8 refers to our original paragraph here in the August 5, 1961, Trade Winds. As I said, we make up history here!

Jean Stafford (19 –) Jean Stafford is a well-known author who was educated at the University of Colorado and did graduate work at Heidelberg. She has written essays and stories for many magazines such as *The New Yorker*, *Vogue*, and *Harper's*, and has written novels as well as stories for children. In 1970 she was honored by a Pulitzer Prize for *Collected Stories*. This selection, which argues by offering a multitude of data and examples, was developed from a lecture given at Barnard College.

The Decline and Fall of the American Language

In the April 1806 issue of *The Monthly Anthology and Boston Review*, republished by Nancy Hale in 1963 in her anthology *New England Discovery*, there appeared an article entitled "A New Language Proposed" by William Smith Shaw, which read in part: Since the liberation of our countrymen from the tuition of a cruel stepdame, who fondly hoped that in the decrepitude of age she should be nourished and sustained by our labour and love, our citizens, while engaged in lawful commerce, have been exposed to violence and impressment. The licensed buccaneers and royal robbers of the ocean have divorced our citizens from their friends and families and compelled them to exert, in the service of a king, every muscle not palsied by fear of the thong and scourge. Remonstrance only admonishes them of their power of inflicting still greater injuries, and the specious plea of justification is that *similarity of language prevents discrimination between Englishmen and Americans*. It is now proposed to strike at the root of the evil and to construct a language entirely novel. [The ingredients of Shaw's concoction will consist of indigenous Indian, Negro, and Irish dialects.] When this language shall have become . . . universal in our country, we shall be in a world by ourselves, and will surround our territory by an impregnable wall of brass, and all sit down, each in his whirligig chair, and philosophize. [1]

In 1806 Shaw was writing with his adder's tongue in his cheek. Today he would be persuaded that his proposition has been adopted, that the roots of our language have been infused with a bane more deadly than the nightshade. He would be gloomy. Besides the neologisms that are splashed all over the body of the American language like the daubings of a chimpanzee turned loose with finger paints, the poor thing has had its parts of speech broken to smithereens: Setting the fractures and dislocations has been undertaken by tinkers with tin ears they have fashioned for themselves out of old applesauce cans; and now verbs are used as nouns and nouns are used as verbs ("This course is structured for students interested in the overall construct of existentialism," says the college catalogue); and upon its stooped and aching back it carries an astounding burden of lumber piled on by the sociologists and the psychologists and the sociopsychologists and the psychosociologists, the Pentagon, the admen, and, lately, the alleged robbers and bug planters of Watergate. The prognosis for the ailing language is not good. I predict that it will not die in my lifetime, but I fear that it will be assailed by countless cerebral accidents and massive strokes and gross insults to the brain and finally will no longer be able to sit up in bed and take nourishment by mouth. [2]

Radio, television, the press, and all those other agencies that are dedicated to lulling and hoodwinking the public into talking falderal have so gummed up our language with solecisms and mongoloid bastards ("Vietnamize," "bodifier," "commonality") and knock-kneed metaphors (in *The New York Times Book Review* on September 2, 1973, I read in the review of a new novel that one of the characters was "haloed with clout"; my only comment is "Faugh!") and gibberish that a new kind of censorship should be in order; the board should be made up only of persons demonstrably literate, precise, immune to the viruses of jargon and whimsey, and severe in their quarantine of carriers of the aforesaid. [3]

At the same time that we have relaxed the prohibition of obscenities in the press and on the air and in the movies, we have clamped down on straightforward speech, and euphemisms teem; they do so with such a thunderous racket that it is next to impossible to tell what anybody is talking about. Once when I was listening to a detective describing on television the defusing of a bomb in the $2 million TWA ransom plot in 1970, I thought how bewildered I would have been if I had not tuned in at the beginning but had only picked up, ". . . we continued to render the suspected object inert." The fuzz are ever so keen on genteel pidgin: "The intoxicated individual exited the vehicle." You know full well that if the *drunk man who got out of the car* said, "*Exited* is not a transitive verb; it must be followed by a preposition," the arresting officer would relinquish his white gloves and, saying, "Up yours, mother," would clap on the handcuffs. As liars are called "pathological" and on these grounds are excused because they are "sick" and are treated with a lenity that would not be accorded plain garden-variety liars, so sinners and boors and bores are said to suffer from an inability to "relate." *Relate,* except when used in the sense of "to recount," requires the preposition *to* just as *exit* must be accompanied by *from.* My friend Laurence Lafore, the historian . . . puts the matter thus in a pamphlet of rules he gives all his students: "To say, 'He does not relate,' is not more sensible than to say, 'He does not.' " These sad sacks who can't relate are often further described as having "nothing going for them." What should be going for them? Should an agency supply them with tops and windup toys and free tickets to a carrousel? There's one thing that's going for just about everybody, whether he relates or not, and that is television, which spreads new plagues with the speed of light. [4]

Countless useful, onetime-respectable words have been so defaced and debased and deformed that those of us who look upon ourselves as the custodians of the mother tongue find our vocabularies diminished. We hesitate to use a word lest it be misconstrued in the incorrect but faddish sense. One functional word I miss is *irrelevant. Irrelevance* has come to denote the condition of "not being with it" or "not making the scene," of not being involved in a cause, whether it is the legalization of marijuana, the right to substitute the peace symbol for the stars in Old Glory, the renunciation of celibacy by the clergy, the decapitation of all policemen and all members of the standing army, or the movement to unman sexists. [5]

Lately the word *ethnic* has taken a fearful trouncing and for all practical purposes has, I'm afraid, been kayoed for keeps. I was invited once to an "ethnic" dinner party. The eight guests were American-born Caucasians: One was a Jew, one was of German descent, one of Hungarian, one of Norwegian, the other four of Scotch-Irish-English. Our first course was sashimi, a Japanese dish of raw pickled fish; the entrée was couscous, the staple of Tunisia; our salad was Maste khiar, a Pakistani concoction of cucumbers and yoghurt (I found it rather nasty); and for dessert we had gingered kumquats. The whisky beforehand was from Tennessee, and the wines were French. In the original sense of the word, our menu (save for the vinous and spiritous matters) was indeed ethnic, but we were not an ethnic gathering. Nor would we have been if we had consisted of a Puerto Rican, a non-naturalized immigrant Pole, a black from Mississippi, a Copt, an Israeli, a Sardinian newly arrived from Cagliari, a Ukrainian, and a Presbyterian patchouli oil merchant from the Seychelles. For, when the word first came into English in 1470 (my authority is the OED), it meant, "Pertaining to nations not Christian or Jewish; heathen, pagan." If our dinner party had been held any time between that date and 1851, we would have been securely within the ethnic pale. After 1851 the word took on a larger meaning and one closer to its root; it came to be synonymous with *ethnological,* the adjective deriving from "ethnology, the science which treats of races and people, their relations, their distinctive characteristics, etc." The etymon is *ethnos,* which means simply *nation* and is to be distinguished from the largest social order, *demos.* [6]

In 1972, therefore, our group was, according to the new meaning, no more and no less ethnic than if we had been a Bengali, a Berber, a Hopi, an aboriginal Australian of the Gurindji tribe, a practitioner of voodoo from Port-au-Prince, a Shintoist from southern California, and a Gabonese pygmy with a pantheon made up of animal, vegetable, and mineral deities. By the same token, our menu was no more and no less ethnic than if it had begun with pâté de foie gras and gone on to haggis and turnips, followed by a Mexican avocado salad and topped off with baklava. (We'd all have been so sick we wouldn't have given a hang about our ancestry.) [7]

Although the terminal letter of the word is, so far, still *c,* I cannot help feeling that in time it will be replaced with *k,* and then *ethnik* will have something in common with *beatnik* and *nudnik.* The fact is that everybody on earth is ethnic, just as everybody is *foreign* except within the limits of his own territorial imperative. [8]

Other words have been kidnaped, so to speak, from their rightful dwelling places, and the ransom asked for the return to their homes is too high ever to be paid. Such a word is *charisma.* I am not sure, but I believe it became fashionable during the Kennedy administration, and at the start it was used more or less correctly to describe one of the President's assets, which was—and I quote again from the

OED—"a rare quality or power attributed to those persons who have demonstrated an exceptional ability for leadership and for securing the devotion of large numbers of people." Unfortunately the admen and the gossip columnists got their grubby hands on the word, and now it is used by furriers to tout autumn-haze mink jackets and by perfumers (by the way, there is a perfume on the market said to be made of "strawberry musk"; since when does a strawberry have a glandular sac beneath the skin of the abdomen of the male that excretes *musk*?), and by the press agents of Hollywood starlets. It has come to be vaguely synonymous with *charming*, and it has acquired a worldly aura. It derives, in fact, from the Greek word meaning "grace," and when it was used anciently by theologians, it meant "a gift of God." What a beautiful word! How rare and subtle an essence it defines, and, therefore, how carefully and seldom it should be used! [9]

We are scarcely a nation now at all; we are, rather, a conglomeration of very nearly countless incoherent splinter groups. It seems to me that, paradoxically, it is our very conformity of speech and passing passions that have exploded the integer to which the founding fathers pledged their lives, their fortunes, and their sacred honor. And it seems to me, further, that this conformity has come about—a great part of it at any rate—through the reliance on platitudinous invectives, lifeless abstractions, and generalizations. News now travels instantly, and so does the language in which it is couched: Let someone of importance in Washington misuse *hopefully*, and before the hour is out, a cesspool repairman in Waukegan is saying to a customer, "Hopefully the pipe ain't broke too bad," and a hostess in Newport is saying, "Hopefully the sun will shine on the day of my *fête champêtre*," and college professors in Massachusetts and wheat farmers in Wyoming and editorial writers in Virginia are all eagerly saying and writing down this nice, shiny, new boo-boo. Within a week the unwholesome gobbet has been assimilated into the language and has settled permanently. [10]

But the official language of the United States is now cant. As I said at the beginning, the condition of the *real* language is critical. Many of the neoplasms are malign and may be inoperable (e.g., *escalate, Vietnamize, input*), and about all we can do is pray. If H. W. Fowler, whose *Modern English Usage* is the most dazzling record of a temper tantrum ever written, were alive today, he would die. [11]

1800 words, 11 paragraphs

Diction

1. The author shows hostility toward certain **classes** of words. She mentions, in particular, neologisms [2], solecisms [3], euphemisms [4], and neoplasms [11]; what are they?
2. Among her more vivid phrases is the one "tinkers with tin ears" [2]. Explain the **connotations** and **denotation.**
3. What is the OED the author mentions twice as a reference book?
4. Ms. Stafford claims the language carries a "burden of lumber" piled there by "the sociologists and the psychologists and the sociopsychologists and the psychosociologists." What manner of scientist are these last two?
5. What is the more standard term for "knock-kneed **metaphors**" such as "haloed with clout" [3]?
6. Among a great many sprightly terms used by Ms. Stafford are the following; look them up: cant [11], conglomeration [10], gibberish [3], gobbet [10], integer [10], lenity [4], malign [11], obscenities [3], pale (as in "beyond the pale") [6], pidgin [4].

Rhetoric and Style

1. The author's **tone** is clear. What is it, and how is it maintained?
2. Ms. Stafford uses **personification** at least three times; find two of them? (Clue: the thing personified is language.)
3. What, in one sentence, is her main complaint about language?
4. How does she **validate** her **thesis**?
5. What is the point of using a portion of an 1806 essay as an introduction?

Applications and Evaluation

1. Is there any way to make a language stay relatively static? Check the Academia Leal of Spain, or the Académie Français of France, whose function was to keep the language "pure."
2. Are there any localisms or phrases used every day that *you* find annoying? If so, make a brief list, **classify** them and write a paragraph condemning their use.
3. The fact that language is always changing is attested to by the dictionaries. Find at least ten words that were not in use fifteen

years ago and use them as examples in a paragraph in which you comment on the changeability of language. (*The Webster's Pocket Dictionary* has a new-word section at the back and the *World Book Encyclopedia* Annuals have a new-word section for each year.)

4. The author mentions that she would be in favor of a new kind of censorship. How would it work? Do you approve of such an idea?
5. Every so often someone gets hostile to the misuse of the Standard English language. The essay "Politics and The English Language" in this text is one such, though it is more concerned with bad thinking than this one is. Here are some others:

   "Gobbledygook" from *The Power of Words,* Stuart Chase (1953).

   "Sociological Habit Patterns in Linguistic Transmogrification" from *The Reporter,* Vol. 15, No. 4, Malcolm Crowley (1956).

   "This is Our Goodest Hour," *Saturday Review,* Ralph Schoenstein (October 14, 1961).

   "Dirty Words," *Harper's Magazine,* Russell Lynes (July 1968).

   "The Age of the Wordfact," *Atlantic Monthly,* John Kenneth Galbraith (1960).

John Royden Maddox (1925–) John Maddox is one of England's most respected scientists. A graduate of Christ Church College, Oxford, he has been a lecturer on theoretical physics at Manchester University and an affiliate of the Rockefeller Institution of New York. He has also been science correspondent for *The Manchester Guardian* and the editor of *Nature* magazine since 1966. He has written *The Spread of Nuclear Weapons* and *Revolution in Biology* as well as *The Doomsday Syndrome*, from which the following essay is extracted. The book, subtitled "An Attack on Pessimism," uses specific examples and data to counter the widespread belief that mankind is doomed.

The Doomsday Syndrome

This is not a scholarly work but a complaint. In the past decade, since the publication of Miss Rachel Carson's *Silent Spring*, the people of North America and, to a lesser extent, Western Europe have been assailed by prophecies of calamity. To some, population growth is the most immediate threat. Others make more of pollution of particular kinds, the risk that the world will run out of food or natural resources or even the possibility that economic growth and the prosperity it brings spell danger for the human race. And there is talk of potentially horrific uses for genetic engineering and even of the possibility that the temper of modern science may undermine the structure of modern society. But, although these prophecies are founded in science, they are at best pseudo-science. Their most common error is to suppose that the worst will always happen. And, to the extent that they are based on assumptions as to how people will behave, they ignore the ways in which social institutions and humane aspirations can conspire to solve the most daunting problems. [1]

Prophets of doom have multiplied remarkably in the past few years. It used to be commonplace for men to parade city streets with sandwich boards proclaiming "The End of the World Is at Hand!" They have been replaced by a throng of sober people, scientists, philosophers and politicians, proclaiming that there are more subtle calamities just around the corner. The human race, they say, is in danger of strangling itself by overbreeding, of poisoning itself with pollution, of undermining its essential human character by tampering with heredity and of perverting the whole basis of society with too much prosperity. [2]

The questions which these latter-day doomsday men have raised are subtle and interesting; the spirit in which they are asked is usually too jaundiced for intellectual comfort. Too often, reality is oversimplified or even ignored, so that there is a danger that much of this gloomy foreboding about the immediate future will accomplish the opposite of what its authors intend. Instead of alerting people to important problems, it may seriously undermine the capacity of the human race to look out for its survival. The doomsday syndrome may in itself be as much a hazard as any of the conundrums which society has created for itself. [3]

The doomsday cause would be more telling if it were more securely grounded in facts, better informed by a sense of history and an awareness of economics and less cataclysmic in temper. [4]

The defect of the case for thinking that calamity is the more important menace is its imprecision. There are some who fear that the burning of fuel on the scale to which modern industry is accustomed will wreck the climate on the surface of the earth, but few meteorologists are able unambiguously to endorse such prophecies. Some fear that the use of pesticides will irrevocably damage the human race, but that is an overdramatic statement of the need carefully to regulate the way in which such chemicals are sprayed on crops. Some fear that modern biology, with its artificially fertilized eggs and its detailed understanding of genetic processes, will degrade humanity; by doing so, they fly in the face of the past five centuries of the history of medicine, a consistent record of human endeavor. In short, the weakness of the doomsday prophecies is that they are exaggerations Many of them are irresponsible. [5]

Implicit in the fears of the consequences of population growth which are now rife is an oversimple method of prediction. If the population of the world is at present doubling every thirty-five years, does it not follow that the population will multiply by four in the next seventy years, so as to reach 14,000 million by the year 2040? In his book *The Population Bomb,* Dr. Ehrlich is scornful about those whom he calls "professional optimists . . . who like to greet every sign of dropping birth rate with wild pronouncements about the end of the population explosion." In his more soberly written *Population, Resources, Environment,* he choose to base calculations of the future population of the earth on the most pessimistic calculation of the United Nations, which assumes that there will be no change in the fertility of women of childbearing age between now and the end of the century. But in reality, there are already signs that fertility is declining in developing communities in exactly the same way, but possibly more rapidly than fertility declined in Western Europe between fifty and a hundred years ago. And, strange as it may seem, the real economic cost of extracting metals such as lead and copper from the ground is still decreasing as exploration and techniques of mining and metallurgy become more efficient. In economic terms the earth's resources seem to be becoming more plentiful. [6]

Famine is only one of several hypothetical catastrophes supposed to flow from population growth. Dr. Ehrlich is one of those who have argued that crowding caused by population growth is a cause of individual disorientation and psychological disturbance and of social tension and upheaval. One common argument for supposing that crowding as such is bad for people starts from experiments which have been carried out with laboratory animals, principally rats and mice. The best-known experiments, due to Dr. R. Colhoun, showed that rats kept in conditions of crowding to which they were unused developed all kinds of psychological disturbances—mother rats took to infanticide, males became unnaturally aggressive and death was accelerated. So is it not reasonable to suppose that people living in cities will be more disturbed than those who live in rural areas? With growing population densities, will not social aberrations such as civil violence or international conflict become more prevalent? These are common suspicions. Dr. Ehrlich and his wife Anne, in their book *Population, Resources, Environment,* say that there are "very high correlations among rates of population growth . . . and involvement in wars." [7]

The trouble is that the analogy between rats and people is at best a tenuous analogy—gregariousness of the kind that led to the development of cities some thousands of years ago distinguishes the human race from rodents. And the belief that violence and war are accompaniments of crowding rests on the most shaky and disputed statistical basis. Who, after all, would think that the Netherlands, the most crowded of all the nations in Western Europe, is more given to violence than, say, the United States? [8]

One recipe for disaster, for example, is that pollution of the surface layers of the oceans by insecticides or chemicals may destroy the microscopic plants which turn the energy of sunlight into chemical form, thus helping to support marine life of all kinds and to replenish the oxygen in the atmosphere. Another is that the accumulation of carbon dioxide produced by the burning of fossil fuels may so increase the temperature on the surface of the earth as to transform the present pattern of weather and perhaps even to melt the Antarctic ice. Fortunately, these chains of events are by no means inescapable. For one thing, the processes which are supposed to lead to disaster are only imperfectly understood. Second, their scale is still puny compared with that of the envelope of the earth in which living things exist—the ecosphere as it is called. The fear that pesticides might so affect oceanic plant life that the world's supply of oxygen would be reduced, first introduced in 1969, was recognized by 1970 to be based on hopelessly gloomy calculations. [9]

In any event, fallout was eventually replaced by pesticides as a battleground, and the late Miss Rachel Carson became the champion. In 1962, *Silent Spring* provided a new platform for the public protests about the uses to which science and technology were being put. Miss Carson was concerned almost entirely with the way in which insecticides were being used in the United States. Many of her complaints were entirely well-founded—it is absurd that insecticides should have been used to clear insects from inland lakes with such abandon as to kill the fish as well as the insects. Among Miss Carson's many cautionary tales is that of how the use of dieldrin, an insecticide similar to DDT but more powerful, against the Japanese beetle in the cornfields of the Middle West made life easier for another and more dangerous pest, the corn borer, which normally provided food for the Japanese beetle. In this and other ways, she marshaled enough evidence to demonstrate that pesticides should be more carefully regulated and controlled. The most seriously misleading part of her narrative is the use of horror stories of the misuse of DDT to create an impression that there are no safe uses worth consideration. [10]

Dr. Barry Commoner also uses Miss Carson's technique. He says in his book *Science and Survival*, for example, that "as large a body of water as Lake Erie has already been overwhelmed by pollutants and has in effect died." The truth is now what it was in 1963 when the book was written, that Lake Erie has indeed been seriously afflicted by pollution, for such a shallow body of water could not be expected to remain unchanged under the assault of such a vast amount of sewage and industrial effluent as the surrounding cities had come to discharge into it. But throughout the 1960s, the lake somehow managed to support a thriving fishing industry. In 1970, it yielded 25,000 tons of fish. Nobody can know for certain why the trout have been replaced by other species—is it the sewage or the influence of the Welland Canal, bypassing Niagara, connecting Lake Erie to Lake Ontario? At last it seems to have been agreed that something must be done to limit the discharge of effluents into Lake Erie, but the proclamation that the lake is already dead, whatever such a phrase may mean, has if anything given Lake Erie more prominence than it deserves. Fair play? In his more recent book, *The Closing Circle,* Dr. Commoner does not say the lake is dead but merely that "we have grossly, irreversibly changed the biological character of the lake and have greatly reduced, now and for the foreseeable future, its value to man." This is a more moderate statement of the position even if the dubious assertion of irreversibility is taken at its face value. [11]

The flaw in these protestations is that they label technology, and the science from which it sometimes springs, as a subversive force in society. It is true, of course, that most technical innovations will frequently have unexpected and even unpredictable consequences. This has always been the case. Who would have guessed that the motor car would create the suburbs of North America? [12]

Still more serious is the danger that the extreme wing of the environmental movement may inhibit communities of all kinds from making the fullest use of the technical means which exist for the improvement of the human condition. Insidiously, the suggestion has been advanced that science and technology are the sources of potential environmental hazard. The truth is that the blame, if any, attaches to the decisions that have been made about the uses to which technology should be put. And there is no doubt that as the striking of a comfortable balance between human communities and the environment becomes a more intricate task, science and technology between them have an increasingly important role to play. Worse still, the impression, quite falsely, has got about that prosperity as such is a danger. For is it not that the numbers of motor cars in city streets and the numbers of disposable bottles discarded in the countryside are measures of the amounts of money which people have to spend on these contraptions? To insist on this relationship will of course obscure the incontrovertible truth that prosperity in the sense now common in advanced societies is also the way in which communities of all kinds are able to afford health services, education and the other social benefits of amenities in advanced communities to which less fortunate people still aspire. [13]

The environmentalists are fond of using the eloquent metaphor of spaceship earth but this is not the most important point to make about the way in which living things have managed to survive for 3,000 million years and, so far, to evolve. Although everybody seems prepared now to accept that other planets elsewhere in the galaxy are likely to have living things on them, nobody makes light of the evolutionary barriers which the human race has had to surmount. After two million years of near extinction, is it any wonder that instinct should lead to temporary overfecundity? The truth is that the technology of survival has been more successful than could have been imagined in any previous century. It will be of immense importance to discover, in due course, the next important threat to survival, but the short list of doomsday talked of in the past few years contains nothing but paper tigers. Yet in the metaphor of spaceship earth, mere housekeeping needs courage. The most serious worry about the doomsday syndrome is that it will undermine our spirit. [14]

2000 words, 14 paragraphs

Diction

1. The author uses the phrase "men in sandwich boards" [2]. What are sandwich boards? What does he means to **connote** by the use of the phrase?
2. What does the phrase "genetic engineering" [1 and 5] **connote**?
3. The author states that "in economic terms, the earth's resources seem to be becoming more plentiful." Are more resources being found? What does that phrase really mean?
4. In paragraph [1] the author's **diction** shows his **attitude** toward the subject. For example, "*pseudo*-science," "*assailed* by prophets," "the *most common* error" tend to show his disdain for "prophets of doom." Pick another paragraph and find similar use of **diction** to show the author's attitude.
5. Is there any **evidence** in word choice that the author's dialect is not Standard American?
6. These words are merely a few of the many you might have to look up to thoroughly understand this abridgment: amenities [13], conundrums [3], doomsday [4], effluent [8], insidiously [13], jaundiced [3], pseudo- ________ [1], rife [6], syndrome (title), tenuous [8].

Rhetoric and Style

1. Although he is complaining, the author does mention the valid parts of the comments by Ehrlich, Carson, and Commoner. What does he admit is accurate? (Note how he uses a modification of the **argumentative paragraph**.)
2. In his response to the "doomsday syndrome" he uses three levels of data: generalities, checkable knowledge, and specific names, facts, figures. Find two examples of each.
3. See if you can find the pattern in the sentences in paragraph [5]. Why does the author not use it more often?
4. The author's use of **figures of speech** is sparing (see paragraphs [10], [13], and [14] for examples); list two or three and comment intelligently about this lack.
5. Paragraphs [1], [2], [3], and [4] seem to repeat the same thing; do they differ? If so, how?
6. The **topic sentence** in paragraph [7] starts out with "famine," but the paragraph is not about famine. Is the topic sentence weak? Write a **topic sentence** for the paragraph that is not so subtle but mentions the actual content of the paragraph.

Application and Evaluation

1. Do you accept the statement that it is not technology but the uses of it that cause hazards [13]? Develop an argument either proving that statement or showing that without technology there would be no pollution, pesticides, or hazards. (Stick to specifics as much as possible.)
2. Paragraph [12] claims that the automobile made possible the suburbs of North America. Has any other invention had a similar impact on the structure of society?
3. Prepare an outline showing the ethical responsibility of a scientist for the use of his discovery.
4. Who bears the responsibility for cleaning up the pollution that even Maddox admits chokes waterways and landscapes?
5. This author's stand is contrary to most articles on pollution; even though this is an abridgment, does he convince you of his **thesis?** How? What is the thesis?

Vance Packard (1914–) Vance Packard was educated at Pennsylvania State University and at Columbia. He has been a columnist, a writer, and an editor for the Associated Press; he has lectured on reporting and magazine writing at Columbia. His first book was *Animal I.Q.*, but he did not discover his forte until he wrote *The Hidden Persuaders* about advertising. Since then he has written seven more books examining American life. This particular selection is taken from one of his better-known works, *The Pyramid Climbers*. Note how effectively he uses specifics to validate his points.

Business Minorities

Application for Employment TM

1. Name__________
2. Parent's Name__________
3. Age__________ 4. Sex M F (circle)
5. Race__________
6. Religion__________
7. Nationality__________
8. Education__________

good
PRINTED IN U.S.A.

Prejco, Inc. I

The screening of candidates permitted to enter the competition on the pyramids of business power is considerably more intensive than the screening of gladiators for the arenas of ancient Rome. Our modern competitor must have a sound body, cool nerves, passable teeth, and a psyche that can survive the tapping of all manner of little rubber hammers. There are the official specifications for position (these may fill several pages). And then there are the unofficial specifications which may never be acknowledged or even realized. Such unwritten knockout factors often prevent a candidate from making even the so-called first list of serious prospects. [1]

Some years ago an admiring book, *America's Fifty Foremost Business Leaders,* edited by B. C. Forbes, made this remarkable statement: "Neither birth nor education, neither nationality nor religion, neither heredity nor environment are passports or obstacles to the highest success in this land of democracy." Only "worth," he said, counts. [2]

This happy bit of mythology has rarely fitted the situation that prevails in large business organizations as a whole and it has little relevance today. One accident of birth alone virtually eliminates from serious consideration half the human race residing within the U.S.—the elimination that occurs when an applicant for a management post is asked to check the appropriate box containing the letter *M* or *F*. A check in the *F* box is usually a knockout factor. [3]

I am uneasily aware that so far in this book I have used the pronoun *he* exclusively in referring to "the executive." Feminine readers might think me guilty of a male conceit. The word *he,* like the word *man,* can of course blanket both sexes in general usage. In the case of writing about the modern executive, however, I am being reasonably precise in using *he* in its specific gender sense. Although nearly four out of ten job-holders in the U.S.A. now are female, women rarely attain the executive suites of substantial corporations except in secretarial capacities. They are perhaps the most discriminated-against of all minority groups in industry. A Harvard doctoral dissertation by David Carson on executive-training programs for supermarket chains contains this sentence: "The selection process for the executive training program at [name of chain] was specifically designed for men only, and 'Manpower Inventory' in this company—and in the others included in this study—meant Male only." [4]

In the early fifties the Harvard Business School's division of research sent a research team into ninety-five business organizations to study executive opportunities for women. Its report said: "Very few women were found to be holding top executive jobs in the sense of corporate officers or senior executives. A number of women in a variety of fields, however, were found in positions of 'second in command.'" Several executives indicated that this was the highest level a woman could hope to attain in the near future. [5]

The shutout of women is gradually easing. Women who reach

the higher levels of sizable organizations, however, still tend to represent special situations or achieve their success within special fields more open to women than most. Many of the women heading corporations are the widows of former owners. A few others attained their eminence without family connections but started with the company when it was small. The best opportunities for women to rise to at least the department-head level appear to be in personnel, research, accounting, advertising, publishing, and design. General Foods had a woman as vice-president in early 1962; so did McGraw-Hill and a number of major advertising agencies. [6]

A second convenient and widespread way of screening out unlikely candidates among would-be executives is to throw out all applicants who write *None* where the candidate is asked to list his college degree or degrees. This will still eliminate nearly nine out of ten U.S. males. [7]

A college diploma is becoming an almost universal requirement for admission to the management group. Many companies tell clerical and production-line workers that there is room at the top for the best of them. But in recent years only one top manager in ten has come from such a background, and the number will decrease. [8]

In projecting what management will be like in the 1980s, Harold J. Leavitt, professor of industrial administration and psychology at Carnegie Tech, notes: "Apprenticeship as a basis for training managers will be used less and less, since movement up through the line will become increasingly unlikely. Top management training will be taken over increasingly by the universities." [9]

The most startling explanation for the insistence on a diploma was offered by an executive taking part in a round table on executive potential sponsored by the McKinsey Foundation for Management Research. He said: "We desperately need a means of screening. Education is one quick means of preliminary screening without having to think too much about it." [10]

A third general category of people who are often screened out in wholesale lots at an early stage of the selection process are the non-*WASPs*. The non-*WASPs* who survive the preliminary screening usually must have a lot more going for them in the way of qualifications than *WASP* candidates in order to be accepted and to make much headway up the sides of the typical modern business pyramid. [11]

A *WASP*—as originally defined by sociologist Digby Baltzell—is a White Anglo-Saxon Protestant. *WASPs* have traditionally been the in-group of the U.S. business world. They have been the gatekeepers to management of most large industries and financial institutions, notwithstanding the cheery assertion in *America's Fifty Foremost Business Leaders* that "neither nationality nor religion, neither heredity nor environment" have been obstacles to great success. To a large extent, the *WASPs* still are the in-group, although some moves have recently been made toward less flatly rejecting non-*WASPs*. [12]

One non-*WASP* who usually has difficulty getting a nod from the gatekeepers of larger enterprises is the Jew. Approximately 8 per cent of the college-trained population of the United States is Jewish. Against this, consider the fact that Jews constitute less than one half of 1 per cent of the total executive personnel in leading American industrial companies. [13]

This startling statistic can scarcely be due to any lack of interest or aptitude on the part of Jewish college graduates. The world's most famous—and perhaps most difficult—graduate school for business administration is at Harvard University. One graduate in seven who emerges from this school is Jewish. You get quite a different ratio, however, when you look at the middle-aged managers U.S. industry sends to Harvard each year to take part in the school's Advanced Management Program. These are men who are usually being groomed for important positions. Harvard has no control over the selection of the men who are sent. They are chosen by the participating companies. One person who has watched this program at close range for some years estimates that the proportion of Jewish managers sent to participate has been about one in two hundred! [14]

An official of the American Jewish Committee who tries to keep abreast of employment practices affecting executives has made a study of the management of many major companies. He reports: "We went over a directory containing the names of two thousand management people at U.S. Steel very thoroughly with knowledgeable people. Even making allowance for questionable cases, we could find only nine or ten Jewish managers there at that time." [15]

One curious fact is that several of the corporate giants that were pioneered by Jews or got much of their growth under Jewish leadership have gradually fallen into patterns pretty much like those of industry as a whole. The proportion of Jews among the younger executives at Sears, Roebuck and Radio Corporation of America is pretty much like that found in other giant companies. Those present —as in most of the industrial giants—are likely to be mainly clustered in advisory or creative "inside" staff jobs as in research. They are steered away from the main "line" of authority posts and from positions calling for a good deal of "outside contact." In short, the discriminatory pattern for Jewish executives is much what it is for that other minority group, women executives. [16]

In the past year or so, some slight increase in openmindedness about Jews has been noted in a number of the large industrial companies. And in a few, signs of a new liberalism have developed which officials of the American Jewish Committee consider most hopeful. American Motors (which has been headed by George Romney, a Mormon) has been showing a liberal viewpoint toward Jewish managers that is startling in an industry that has long had a closed mind on the subject. The leadership at International Business Machines has advanced a Jew to vice-presidency (research and development) and is taking other steps to shake up old, frozen attitudes. At Reynolds Aluminum the director of research is Jewish. [17]

The preference for *WASPs* in most of the major executive suites also affects Catholic candidates—particularly those of Italian or Slavic background—though less drastically. A good example of the difference was reported by Seymour Freedgood when he studied a hundred-odd auto executives living in the Bloomfield Hills area outside Detroit. He reported of these executives: "In one case out of ten he is a Roman Catholic of Irish or Italian ancestry. None of the hundred top auto executives is a Jew, and no Jewish families live in Bloomfield Hills proper." [18]

Sociologist Melville Dalton, in his study of informal factors influencing the careers of 226 people on one corporate pyramid, concluded that being Catholic was a real handicap. [19]

An interesting pattern of Protestant-Catholic division can be seen in the insurance companies in Manhattan. They tend to be either predominantly Protestant or predominantly Catholic. This separation is so drastic that the Catholic-dominated companies are clustered in parts of the financial district different from the Protestant-dominated companies. For example John Street is predominantly Protestant, Maiden Lane predominantly Catholic. William Street is split down the middle on the basis of religious dominance. [20]

A final large group that is eliminated by the *WASP* formula, of course, is the millions of people whose skin happens to be something other than pinkish-beige. The absence of dark-skinned people in the management ranks of major corporations is virtually absolute. [21]

Some of the graduate schools of business administration have had Negro students, but the impression is that virtually all have gone into business for themselves or into Negro-run businesses. Some banks have started hiring Negroes for clerical jobs. In 1961 the first Negro appeared on the floor of the New York Stock Exchange in a role other than that of runner or clerk. He was a customer's man, a difficult and responsible role. Early in 1962 Pepsi-Cola named a Negro, Harvey C. Russell, to a newly created vice-presidency. He has been directing the company's activities in reaching the Negro and Spanish market. As this is written, the New York State Commission against Discrimination has launched a campaign to create a climate in which it will be possible for Negroes to have a chance to become executives in business and industry. But that's about all that can be said for now. [22]

All of these categorical grounds for screening out candidates because of sex, education, religion, race, and ethnic background greatly narrow the field of executive possibilities. These limiting factors also help account for the close and restricted climate in which the candidates who *are* chosen will have to function. [23]

1980 words, 23 paragraphs

Diction

1. The author refers to a "knockout factor" in several places. What is a "knockout factor," and where do you suppose the term came from?
2. The **diction** clearly indicates the author's **level of usage.** Giving at least three examples, determine his level of usage.
3. Why does the author refer to business as a pyramid?
4. The use of "screening" and "screening out" of candidates seems strange; does not "to screen out" mean to keep out? Here it seems to mean "to let some in." Explain.
5. Is there any chance that someone might object to the use of "Jew" or "Negro" or "Slavic" in this essay?
6. The following are common words, but do you know their precise meanings? Look them up just for fun: conceit [4], eminence [6], factor [1+], forte (introduction), mythology [3], potential [10], psyche [1], relevance [3], Slavic [18], statistic [14].

Rhetoric and Style

1. What does the author **imply** when he **compares** the screening of businessmen to that of gladiators [1]?

2. There are twenty-three paragraphs in this essay; might some be combined? (See **Unity.**) Find at least one group (or pair) and write (if necessary) a new **topic sentence** for the combination.
3. Does any specific **tone** or attitude toward the subject seem clear? (For example, John Maddox is clearly hostile in his essay.) Give an example, if any.
4. What is the general pattern of this essay? (Clue: it is one of the logical processes.) Offer **evidence.**
5. What kinds of **evidence** does the author present. Do not list all items, but **classify** them by groups.
6. Which type of **argument** is this? (See the introduction to this section.)

Application and Evaluation

1. Why does the author not mention Chicanos or Indians as members of business minorities?
2. Write an argument showing a change in minority hiring since this book was written. The entertainment and advertising industries might furnish some specific **examples.**
3. This essay limits itself to the United States; might similar types of discrimination exist in other countries? (Perhaps anti-WASP?)
4. Write an essay, following Packard's pattern, pointing out valid reasons why women should not be in high executive positions in business.
5. In two lists jot down the strengths and weaknesses of this essay. Then write a brief evaluation of the effectiveness of the author's argument. Does he convince the reader of the **thesis**?

Consumers Union of the United States, Inc. (founded 1936) Consumers Union is a nationally respected, nonprofit, independent organization that tests all manner of products and services and reports to the public in its monthly publication, *Consumer Reports*. This selection is excerpted from Chapter 66, "Alternatives to the Drug Experience," of *Licit and Illicit Drugs,* one of the timely books the CU occasionally publishes. The text was written by Edward M. Brecher with assistance from the editors of the magazine. Mr. Brecher has won journalistic and medical awards for excellence in medical reporting and writing. He has also edited other books and has written *The Sex Researchers*. This essay not only makes use of much data but shapes the data into a logical pattern of thought.

Alternatives to Drugs

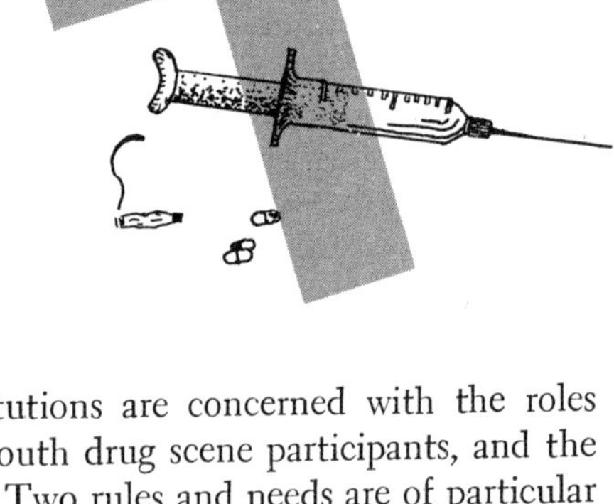

Staff members of various institutions are concerned with the roles that drugs play in the lives of youth drug scene participants, and the human needs that drugs satisfy. Two rules and needs are of particular significance. Drugs are used, on-the-scene observers quite generally report, for *mood-altering* and for *achieving altered states of consciousness*. As several chapters in this Report have demonstrated, *Homo*

sapiens over the centuries has employed drugs to attain those effects. Recently, some observers—and some drug users—have considered a provocative question: can other methods be found to alter moods and to achieve altered states of consciousness—methods not dependent upon drugs? [1]

Dr. Vincent Nowlis, psychologist at the University of Rochester, provides one thoughtful answer. A change in mood, he points out, is a "change in the way in which the individual is *disposed* to feel, to think, to evaluate, and to behave. . . . A drug which alters mood alters the self. . . . Man is frequently dissatisfied with his present self, with the current status of his mood, and seeks to change this mood—at least temporarily. [2]

This normal, natural, human desire to alter mood from time to time, Dr. Nowlis continues, is not limited to drug users. "A search through the literature shows that throughout history man has found many ways to change mood—through physical exercise, spiritual exercise, prayer, sex, diet, health nostrums, rest, recreation, bathing, massage, travel, rehabilitation, active and passive participation in all art forms, commercial entertainment, rituals, games, and drugs." Television is perhaps the mood-changing nostrum in most common use today. Much the same, Dr. Nowlis adds, is true of the common human desire—among abstainers as well as drug users—to achieve altered states of consciousness. [3]

The falling-in-love experience, the ecstasy of sexual fulfillment, and the mystical religious experience are familiar examples of such "altered states of consciousness." Dr. Andrew T. Weil adds that in his opinion this desire to alter consciousness is an innate psychological drive arising out of the neurological structure of the human brain. Strong evidence for this idea comes from observations of very young children, who regularly use techniques of consciousness alteration on themselves and each other when they think no adults are watching them. These methods include whirling until vertigo and collapse ensue, hyperventilating and . . . fainting. Such practices appear to be universal, irrespective of culture, and present at ages when social conditioning is unlikely to be an important influence (in two and three years olds, for example). Psychiatrists have paid little attention to these activities of all children. Freud noted them and called them "sexual equivalents," which they may be, although that formulation is not very useful. [4]

Adults offer children many mood-altering and consciousness-altering "trips," of course—ranging from the cradle, the merry-go-round, the swing, and the teeter-totter to the roller coaster and the ski slope. Anyone who has watched a four-year-old on a swing can see for himself the delight produced by consciousness alteration. The child is experiencing a "high." [5]

"Until a few years ago," Dr. Weil adds, "most children in our society who wanted to continue [in adolescence] to indulge in these states were content to use alcohol, the one intoxicant we make available legally. Now, large numbers of young people are seeking chemical alterations of consciousness by means of a variety of illegal and medically disapproved drugs." To understand this change, society must "listen to what many drug users, themselves, say: they say they choose illegal drugs over alcohol in order to get better highs." And, we might add, fewer fights, fewer accidents, less devastating hangovers. [6]

However, Dr. Weil continues: Most societies, like our own, are uncomfortable about having people go off into trances, mystic raptures, and hallucinatory intoxications. Indeed, the reason we have laws against possession of drugs in the first place is to discourage people from getting high. But innate, neuropsychological drives cannot be banned by legislation. They will be satisfied at any cost. And the cost in our country is very great: by trying to deny young people these important experiences, we maximize the probability that they will obtain them in negative ways—that is, in ways harmful to themselves and to society. [7]

At youth drug centers throughout Western civilization, the obvious moral of all this is being put to practical use. From San Francisco and Vancouver to London and Amsterdam, innovative institutions serving youthful drug users have begun to introduce nonchemical ways of "turning on" or "getting high"—nonchemical routes to altered states of consciousness. Here are a few:

Sensitivity training
Encounter therapy
Zen Buddhism
Yoga
Transcendental meditation
Massage
Hypnosis and self-hypnosis

One youth drug center is even contemplating the introduction of a program of parachute-jumping. [8]

Ordinary religious services appear to have little appeal in this connection. But special services stressing ritual, mystical insight, and the emotional aspects of religion—"religious highs"—attract large audiences in the youth drug centers. The Eastern religions at first appeared to have the greatest appeal; but recent reports suggest that esoteric and fundamentalist forms of Christianity such as Jehovah's Witnesses are also attracting some youthful drug users. In the Jewish tradition, a return to the Chassidic mode of "singing and dancing God's ecstasy" is enjoying a revival; and the Catholic Mass has on occasion been similarly adapted to the ecstatic goal. Long-haired denizens of the youth drug scene who have turned from drugs to Christianity became numerous enough by the early 1970s to earn a distinctive title—"Jesus freaks." These nonchemical routes to mood-altering and to altered states of consciousness, of course, may bring their own problems. [9]

These and other "alternatives to the drug experience" are gaining favor among young people primarily because they are superior to drugs, not because they are safer than drugs. An experienced drug user, Dr. Weil points out, "often finds that some form of meditation more effectively satisfies his desire to get high. *One sees a great many drug takers give up drugs for meditation, but one does not see any meditators give up meditation for drugs.*" (Italics supplied.) "Once you have learned from a drug what being high really is, you can begin to reproduce it without the drug; all persons who accomplish this feat testify that the non-drug high is superior." [10]

Several years ago, Dr. Herbert Benson of the Harvard Medical School and Thorndike Memorial Laboratory, Boston City Hospital, trained monkeys to control their own blood pressure, and wondered whether a technique known as transcendental meditation might not similarly lower the blood pressure of humans. He began with 1,862 practitioners of transcendental meditation, all of whom had meditated daily for three months or longer; the average length of time they had been practicing daily meditation was about twenty months. In this population, marijuana smoking declined from 78.3 percent before entering meditation to 26.9 percent after meditating from four to nine months, and to 12.2 percent after twenty-two or more months of meditation. Moreover, only one subject who had meditated for twenty-two or more months reported that he was still smoking marijuana daily, as compared with 417 (22.4 percent) who reported smoking marijuana daily *before* entering transcendental meditation. [11]

The LSD results were similar. In the sample as a whole, 48.3 percent reported having used LSD; among those who had meditated for twenty-two or more months only 3 percent were still using LSD. For the sample as a whole, 132 subjects (7.1 percent) reported having used LSD once a week or oftener before entering transcendental meditation; none of those who had meditated for more than twenty-two months was using LSD that frequently. Dr. Benson reported his findings in November 1970 at a University of Michigan International Symposium on Drug Abuse. [12]

These studies are subject to a number of qualifications. [13]

First, the participants in both the Winquist and Benson studies were mostly college students or ex-students; the effects on other groups have not been similarly studied. [14]

Second, the participants in both studies were *self-selected.* They were the students attracted to transcendental meditation. The remarkable results cannot be generalized to apply to drug users who are *not* voluntarily attracted to transcendental meditation. [15]

Third, applicants were expected to refrain from drug use for fifteen days *before* entering a transcendental meditation program; many confirmed drug users (and all or almost all addicts) are no doubt screened out of the program by this condition. [16]

Fourth, both studies were limited to participants who *continued* to practice transcendental meditation. How many dropped out of transcendental meditation instead of dropping out of drugs is not reported. [17]

Fifth, both studies lacked controls. As the Benson study itself points out, the number of similar college students who formerly used drugs and who dropped out of the drug scene during the same period *without* embracing transcendental meditation is not known. [18]

Finally, neither the Winquist nor the Benson study establishes the superiority of transcendental meditation as compared with *other* alternatives to drug use. Transcendental meditation happens to be the only alternative for which such statistics are available. Perhaps sensitivity training, or Yoga, or Zen, or other alternatives are even more effective; no one knows. [19]

It should further be noted that young people use drugs—just as their elders use drugs—in order to achieve such specific effects as relief from anxiety, or from boredom, or from depression, or, in many cases, just for fun or for "kicks." An alternative to the drug experience is most likely to be effective if it fulfills the same need for which the drug was previously used. [20]

Despite their limitations, the Winquist and Benson studies are still landmarks in consideration of the youth drug scene. They indicate how fragile is the tie that binds many marijuana smokers to their joints and many LSD users to their acid. [21]

At youth drug centers across the country, and especially in comprehensive centers, these and other alternatives to the chemical high and to the chemical induction of altered states of consciousness are currently being offered, and accepted. In the course of research for this Report, young people were encountered in drug centers from Vancouver's Fourth Avenue to Amsterdam's Paradiso who sat "stoned on life" while those around them sat stoned on marijuana or LSD. They looked and dressed like drug users and spent their time in drug centers with drug users—but their highs came neither from a pharmacy nor from a "pusher." [22]

Meanwhile, in a few high schools and other agencies, especially in California, educators and others who have seen the results achieved by alternatives to the drug experience have begun to ask what is obviously the next question:

Why should illicit drug use be required as a ticket of admission to the achievement of nondrug "highs" and to nondrug approaches to altered states of consciousness? Why should not schools and other agencies make sensitivity training, encounter therapy, nature study, transcendental meditation, skiing, enjoyment of music, enjoyment of art, and other nonchemical highs available *before* students migrate, physically or internally, to the country's Haight-Ashburys? [23]

In a growing number of schools, churches, and other agencies, such programs have been instituted. It is too early to evaluate them. But they are surely more promising than traditional approaches to prevention—the imprisonment of drug users, dire (and incredible) warnings against the hazards of drug use, and the other futile and counterproductive measures described at length throughout the earlier chapters of this Report. [24]

Many thoughtful observers within the youth drug scene, however, view alternatives to the drug experience, like the drug experience itself, as at best mere palliatives. The alternatives can no doubt prove enormously helpful in particular cases. They may be necessary in many communities. But the ultimate goal, perhaps, should be a way of life free of dependence on alternatives to the drug experience as well as free of dependence on drugs. [25]

A satisfying way of life is thus the ultimate prescription, and the immediate goal should be improvements in the *quality of life*—a topic that falls outside the scope of this Consumers Union Report. [26]

1950 words, 26 paragraphs

Diction

1. This argument is written in the **style** of a report (see Section III, Exposition"); can you find, nevertheless, any **slang, jargon,** or stereotyped language?

2. What is the reference to "the country's Haight-Ashburys"? Note both **connotation** and **denotation.**
3. The author distinguishes between "mood-altering" and "consciousness-altering"; so do many of the authorities he quotes. What is the difference? (**Definition** is needed.)
4. Paragraph [9] mentions Chassidic Jews and Jehovah's Witnesses as enjoying a revival. What have they in common? (More **definition** is needed.)
5. Paragraph [8] starts out, "At youth drug centers throughout Western civilization, the obvious moral of all this is being put to practical use." What is the "obvious moral"; what is "all this"?
6. Although there are other interesting words in the essay, here are some that students should know; look up the meanings: abstainer [4], dire [24], ecstasy [4], esoteric [9], illicit [23], innate [4], nostrums [3], palliatives [25], provocative [1], rapture [7].

Rhetoric and Style

1. What is the effect of listing—paragraphs [14] through [20]—the qualifications on the experiments referred to?
2. Paragraph [10] notes "italics supplied." What kind of stylistic device is that? Why does the author tell us that he supplied the italics?
3. Does the author make use of any of the **figurative language** devices to heighten communication? What are they?
4. How successfully does the author **validate** his various general statements? What kinds of validation does he use?
5. Can you discern the general logical pattern of development?
6. A **major premise,** proven in paragraphs [3] through [7], is that *getting high satisfies an innate desire.* If we add a **minor premise** that *it is illegal to use most drugs to get high,* what is the **conclusion?** (Another minor premise might be: *society discourages most ways of getting high.*) Working backwards from the author's conclusion [25], show his reasoning.

Applications and Evaluation

1. Does our society condone any type of getting high? Is the pattern changing? Do we distinguish between public and private experiences?

2. Write a paragraph or essay developing the author's statement: [3] "Television is perhaps the mood-changing nostrum in most common use today."
3. What objections does society (however you wish to define the term) have to people getting high? What grounds are there for such disapproval?
4. Do you think it is the function of "high schools and other agencies" to teach young people to turn on? (A course description or two would be fun to write; example: Turning On 1-A, 3 units, MW ?)
5. The last paragraph urges an immediate improvement of the *quality of life* as a step toward a *satisfying way of life.* Write an essay stating your **definition** of either and presenting an argument for your choice of definition. (Convince the reader that X is a satisfying way of life, for example.)

Burrhus Frederic Skinner (1904–   ) B. F. Skinner is America's foremost proponent of the behavioral school of psychology. He was educated at Hamilton College and at Harvard, where he is now a professor of psychology. He has published a great many papers in the professional journals as well as a novel, *Walden Two*. A recipient of many awards and honorary degrees, Dr. Skinner has also helped to develop the concept of the teaching machine, which has found wide acceptance among both educators and industry. The following selection is from his controversial bestseller *Beyond Freedom and Dignity* (1971).

Beyond Freedom and Dignity

In trying to solve the terrifying problems that face us in the world today, we naturally turn to the things we do best. We play from strength, and our strength is science and technology. To contain a population explosion we look for better methods of birth control. Threatened by a nuclear holocaust, we build bigger deterrent forces and anti-ballistic-missile systems. We try to stave off world famine with new foods and better ways of growing them. Improved sanitation and medicine will, we hope, control disease, better housing and transportation will solve the problems of the ghettos, and new ways of reducing or disposing of waste will stop the pollution of the environment. We can point to remarkable achievements in all these fields, and it is not surprising that we should try to extend them. But things grow steadily worse and it is disheartening to find that technology itself is increasingly at fault. Sanitation and medicine have made the problems of population more acute, war has acquired a new horror with the invention of nuclear weapons, and the affluent pursuit of happiness is largely responsible for pollution. As Darlington[1] has said, "Every new source from which man has increased his power on the earth has been used to diminish the prospects of his successors. All his progress has been made at the expense of damage to his environment which he cannot repair and could not foresee." [1]

Whether or not he could have foreseen the damage, man must repair it or all is lost. And he can do so if he will recognize the nature of the difficulty. The application of the physical and biological sciences alone will not solve our problems because the solutions lie in another field. Better contraceptives will control population only if people use them. New weapons may offset new defenses and vice versa, but a nuclear holocaust can be prevented only if the conditions under which nations make war can be changed. New methods of agriculture and medicine will not help if they are not practiced, and housing is a matter not only of buildings and cities but of how people live. Overcrowding can be corrected only by inducing people not to crowd, and the environment will continue to deteriorate until polluting practices are abandoned. [2]

In short, we need to make vast changes in human behavior, and we cannot make them with the help of nothing more than physics or biology, no matter how hard we try. (And there are other problems, such as the breakdown of our educational system and the disaffection and revolt of the young, to which physical and biological technologies are so obviously irrelevant that they have never been applied.) It is not enough to "use technology with a deeper understanding of human issues," or to "dedicate technology to man's spiritual needs," or to "encourage technologists to look at human problems." Such expressions imply that where human behavior begins, technology stops, and that we must carry on, as we have in the past, with what we have learned from personal experience or from those collections of personal experiences called history, or with the distillations of experience to be found in folk wisdom and practical rules of thumb. These have been available for centuries, and all we have to show for them is the state of the world today. [3]

What we need is a technology of behavior. We could solve our problems quickly enough if we could adjust the growth of the world's population as precisely as we adjust the course of a spaceship, or improve agriculture and industry with some of the confidence with which we accelerate high-energy particles, or move toward a peaceful

[1] C. D. Darlington, *The Evolution of Man and Society*. Quoted in *Science*, 1970, 168, 1332.

world with something like the steady progress with which physics has approached absolute zero (even though both remain presumably out of reach). But a behavioral technology comparable in power and precision to physical and biological technology is lacking, and those who do not find the very possibility ridiculous are more likely to be frightened by it than reassured. That is how far we are from "understanding human issues" in the sense in which physics and biology understand their fields, and how far we are from preventing the catastrophe toward which the world seems to be inexorably moving. . . . [4]

Such a technology is ethically neutral. It can be used by villain or saint. There is nothing in a methodology which determines the values of governing its use. We are concerned here, however, not merely with practices, but with the design of a whole culture, and the survival of a culture then emerges as a special kind of value. A person may design a better way of raising children primarily to escape from children who do not behave well. He may solve his problem, for example, by being a martinet. Or his new method may promote the good of the children or of parents in general. It may demand time and effort and the sacrifice of personal reinforcers, but he will propose and use it if he has been sufficiently induced to work for the good of others. If he is strongly reinforced when he sees other people enjoying themselves, for example, he will design an environment in which children are happy. If his culture has induced him to take an interest in its survival, however, he may study the contribution which people make to their culture as a result of their early history, and he may design a better method in order to increase that contribution. . . . [5]

Science has probably never demanded a more sweeping change in a traditional way of thinking about a subject, nor has there ever been a more important subject. In the traditional picture a person perceives the world around him, selects features to be perceived, discriminates among them, judges them good or bad, changes them to make them better (or, if he is careless, worse), and may be held responsible for his action and justly rewarded or punished for its consequences. [6] . . .

An experimental analysis shifts the determination of behavior from autonomous man to the environment—an environment responsible both for the evolution of the species and for the repertoire acquired by each member. Early versions of environmentalism were inadequate because they could not explain how the environment worked, and much seemed to be left for autonomous man to do. But environmental contingencies now take over functions once attributed to autonomous man, and certain questions arise. Is man then "abolished"? Certainly not as a species or as an individual achiever. It is the autonomous inner man who is abolished, and that is a step forward. But does man not then become merely a victim or passive observer of what is happening to him? He is indeed controlled by his environment, but we must remember that it is an environment largely of his own making. . . . [7]

Gilbert Seldes wrote, "that man is a creature of circumstance, that if you changed the environments of thirty little Hottentots and thirty little aristocratic English children, the aristocrats would become Hottentots, for all practical purposes, and the Hottentots little conservatives." [2] [8]

The evidence for a crude environmentalism is clear enough. People are extraordinarily different in different places, and possibly just because of the places. The nomad on horseback in Outer Mongolia and the astronaut in outer space are different people, but, as far as we know, if they had been exchanged at birth, they would have taken each other's place. (The expression "change places" shows how closely we identify a person's behavior with the environment in which it occurs.) But we need to know a great deal more before that fact becomes useful. What is it about the environment that produces a Hottentot? And what would need to be changed to produce an English conservative instead? [9] . . .

The evolution of a culture is a gigantic exercise in self-control. It is often said that a scientific view of man leads to wounded vanity, a sense of hopelessness, and nostalgia. But no theory changes what it is a theory about; man remains what he has always been. And a new theory may change what can be done with its subject matter. A scientific view of man offers exciting possibilities. We have not yet seen what man can make of man. [10]

1600 words, 10 paragraphs

Diction

1. Dr. Skinner writes of "the sacrifice of personal reinforcers" to promote the good of others [5]. What does he mean?
2. What are the **connotations** of "pursuit of happiness" [1]?
3. Another phrase that may have special meaning is "autonomous inner man" [7]. What seems to be the meaning?
4. The author, scientifically, often refrains from making absolute

[2] Gilbert Seldes, *The Stammering Century* (New York: Day 1928).

statements; that is, he qualifies what he says. Find one or two of these qualifying phrases (paragraphs [8] and [9] have several).

5. It would be beneficial to know the exact meaning of the following words; look them up: autonomous [7], catastrophe [4], disaffection [3], ethically [5], holocaust [2], Hottentots [8], inexorably [4], martinet [5], nostalgia [10], technology [1].

Rhetoric and Style

1. One of Dr. Skinner's **rhetorical** devices is to show the benefits of technology and couple them with the detriments. List, from paragraph [1], the benefits and in the next column list the flaws of each. Next, look at paragraph [2] and list *why* he feels technology has failed in each case. His pattern should be apparent.
2. In paragraph [3] the author uses some seldom seen scientific **irony.** Can you pinpoint it?
3. In several places the author makes use of **analogy** either to clarify a point or as argument. Find at least one good instance of analogy used to clarify.
4. What is the author's **thesis?** Try to state it in one sentence.
5. Dr. Skinner points out that most of our problems are caused by technology, and technology cannot solve them. Then he says that human behavior prevents possible technical solutions from working. How does he finish his logical sequence, and what is his **conclusion?**

Applications and Evaluation

1. The final statement: "what man can make of man" leads one to ponder. Should we use the controlled genetics on man that we have found so effective on livestock? Prepare an outline for an essay either pro or con.
2. The author states that autonomous inner man will perish but the culture will survive. Which is more important? **Define** your terms!
3. Is the concept that man is not responsible for his responses really an excuse or a "cop out" for behavior problems? Can people be held responsible if the environment is at fault? (Trick question; reread paragraph [7] once.)
4. How much of the environment that shapes your behavior is of

your own creating? How much of it can you change? How much of it can a mass effort—say, of a whole nation—change?

5. Is the argument that a truly effective behavioral technology could be used by evil people to control the rest of us a valid argument?

Thomas Jefferson (1742–1826) Born in Virginia, Thomas Jefferson was educated at William and Mary College and was both a lawyer and a member of the Virginia House of Burgesses. He served as the third President of the new United States. The Continental Congress appointed him, Benjamin Franklin, John Adams, Robert Livingston, and Roger Sherman to prepare this declaration. It is notable for the forthright polemic as well as for the fine combination of inductive and deductive logic. Although a few changes were made by Franklin and Adams and a few more by the Congress, it is essentially the work of Jefferson.

The Declaration of Independence

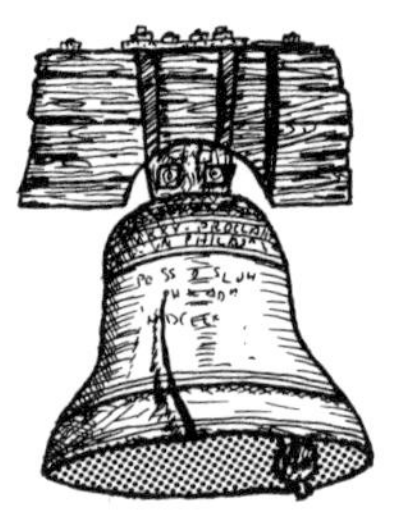

When, in the Course of human events, it becomes necessary for one people to dissolve the political bands which have connected them with another, and to assume, among the Powers of the earth, the separate and equal station to which the Laws of Nature and of Nature's God entitle them, a decent respect to the opinions of mankind requires that they should declare the causes which impel them to the separation. [1]

We hold these truths to be self-evident, that all men are created equal, that they are endowed by their Creator with certain unalienable Rights, that among these, are Life, Liberty, and the pursuit of Happiness. That, to secure these rights, Governments are instituted among Men, deriving their just Powers from the consent of the governed. That, whenever any form of Government becomes destructive of these ends, it is the Right of the People to alter or to abolish it, and to institute new Government, laying its foundation on such Principles, and organizing its Powers in such form, as to them shall seem most likely to effect their Safety and Happiness. Prudence, indeed, will dictate that Governments long established should not be changed for light and transient causes; and, accordingly, all experience hath shewn, that mankind are more disposed to suffer, while evils are sufferable, than to right themselves by abolishing the forms to which they are accustomed. But, when a long train of abuses and usurpations, pursuing invariably the same Object, evinces a design to reduce them under absolute Despotism, it is their right, it is their duty, to throw off such Government, and to provide new Guards for their future Security. Such has been the patient sufferance of these Colonies; and such is now the necessity which constrains them to alter their former Systems of Government. The history of the present King of Great Britain is a history of repeated injuries and usurpations, all having in direct object the establishment of an absolute Tyranny over these States. To prove this, let Facts be submitted to a candid world. [2]

He has refused his Assent to Laws the most wholesome and necessary for the public good. [3]

He has forbidden his Governors to pass Laws of immediate and pressing importance, unless suspended in their operation till his Assent should be obtained; and when so suspended, he has utterly neglected to attend to them. [4]

He has refused to pass other Laws for the accommodation of large districts of People, unless those People would relinquish the right of Representation in the legislature; a right inestimable to them and formidable to tyrants only. [5]

He has called together legislative bodies at places unusual, uncomfortable, and distant from the depository of their Public Records, for the sole Purpose of fatiguing them into compliance with his measures. [6]

He has dissolved Representative Houses repeatedly, for opposing, with manly firmness, his invasions on the rights of the People. [7]

He has refused for a long time, after such dissolutions, to cause others to be elected; whereby the Legislative Powers, incapable of Annihilation, have returned to the People at large for their exercise; the State remaining in the mean time exposed to all the dangers of invasion from without, and convulsions within. [8]

He has endeavoured to prevent the Population of these States; for that purpose obstructing the Laws of Naturalization of Foreigners; refusing to pass others to encourage their migrations hither, and raising the conditions of new Appropriations of Lands. [9]

He has obstructed the Administration of Justice, by refusing his Assent to Laws for establishing Judiciary Powers. [10]

He has made Judges dependent on his Will alone, for the tenure of their offices, and the amount and payment of their salaries. [11]

He has erected a multitude of New Offices, and sent hither swarms of Officers to harrass our People, and eat out their substance. [12]

He has kept among us, in times of Peace, Standing Armies, without the Consent of our legislatures. [13]

He has affected to render the Military independent of and superior to the Civil Power. [14]

He has combined with others to subject us to a jurisdiction foreign to our constitution, and unacknowledged by our laws; giving his Assent to their Acts of pretended Legislation: [15]

For quartering large bodies of armed troops among us: [16]

For protecting them, by a mock Trial, from Punishment for any Murders which they should commit on the Inhabitants of these States: [17]

For cutting off our Trade with all parts of the world: [18]

For imposing Taxes on us without our Consent: [19]

For depriving us, in many cases, of the benefits of Trial by Jury: [20]

For transporting us beyond Seas to be tried for pretended offences: [21]

For abolishing the free System of English Laws in a neighbouring province, establishing therein an Arbitrary government, and enlarging its Boundaries, so as to render it at once an example and fit instrument for introducing the same absolute rule into these Colonies: [22]

For taking away our Charters, abolishing our most valuable Laws, and altering fundamentally the Forms of our Governments: [23]

For suspending our own Legislatures, and declaring themselves invested with Power to legislate for us in all cases whatsoever. [24]

He has abdicated Government here, by declaring us out of his protection, and waging War against us. [25]

He has plundered our seas, ravaged our Coasts, burnt our towns, and destroyed the Lives of our People. [26]

He is at this time transporting large Armies of foreign Mercenaries to compleat the works of death, desolation and tyranny, already begun with circumstances of Cruelty and perfidy scarcely paralleled in the most barbarous ages, and totally unworthy the Head of a civilized nation. [27]

He has constrained our fellow Citizens, taken Captive on the high Seas, to bear Arms against their Country, to become the executioners of their friends and Brethren, or to fall themselves by their Hands. [28]

He has excited domestic insurrections amongst us, and has endeavoured to bring on the inhabitants of our frontiers, the merciless Indian Savages, whose known rule of warfare, is an undistinguished destruction of all ages, sexes and conditions. [29]

In every stage of these Oppressions, We have Petitioned for Redress, in the most humble terms: Our repeated Petitions, have been answered only by repeated injury. A Prince, whose character is thus marked by every act which may define a Tyrant, is unfit to be the ruler of a free People. [30]

Nor have We been wanting in attentions to our British brethren. We have warned them from time to time of attempts by their legislature to extend an unwarrantable jurisdiction over us. We have reminded them of the circumstances of our emigration and settlement here. We have appealed to their native justice and magnanimity, and we have conjured them by the ties of our common kindred, to disavow these usurpations, which, would inevitably interrupt our connexions and correspondence. They too have been deaf to the voice of justice and consanguinity. We must, therefore, acquiesce in the necessity, which denounces our Separation, and hold them, as we hold the rest of mankind, Enemies in war, in Peace Friends. [31]

WE, THEREFORE, the Representatives of the UNITED STATES OF AMERICA, in GENERAL CONGRESS assembled, appealing to the Supreme Judge of the World for the rectitude of our intentions, DO, in the Name, and by Authority of the good People of these Colonies, solemnly PUBLISH and DECLARE, That these United Colonies are, and of Right, ought to be FREE AND INDEPENDENT STATES; that they are Absolved from all Allegiance to the British Crown, and that all political connexion between them and the State of Great Britain, is and ought to be totally dissolved; and that, as FREE and INDEPENDENT STATES, they have full Power to levy War, conclude Peace, contract Alliances, establish Commerce, and to do all other Acts and Things which INDEPENDENT STATES may of right do. AND for the support of this Declaration, with a firm reliance on the protection of divine Providence, we mutually pledge to each other our Lives, our Fortunes, and our sacred Honour. [32]

1323 words, 32 paragraphs

Diction

1. Some versions use the word "inalienable" [1] while the original uses "unalienable." What is the difference?
2. What can you **infer** about the writer(s) of these words, "all experience hath shewn, that mankind are more disposed to suffer" [2]? Clearly it is not written in Standard American.
3. Find the entire sentence from which Question 2 is taken and rewrite it in contemporary American.
4. Although this document is primarily intellectual, find some **connotative language.** List three or four specifically connotative words (see paragraph [12] for an example of some).
5. The "self-evident truth" that "all men are created equal" has many meanings to many people; it is an **abstraction.** What could it mean, and what did it probably mean to the writers?
6. Make use of your dictionary to find the meanings of the following words: absolved [32], consanguinity [31], constrains [2], evinces [2], magnanimity [31], perfidy [27], polemic (introduction), redress [30], transient [2], usurpations [2].

Rhetoric and Style

1. What was the purpose of writing the Declaration of Independence? How do you know?
2. Primarily a rational document, the Declaration of Independence uses both **inductive** and **deductive** logic. Find an instance of clear and obvious induction; write the hypothesis developed. (Look for a list of data and a conclusion.)
3. The major **premise** for the deductive argument may be stated: *When a government is tyrannical, then the people have a right and duty to change it.* What is the minor premise? What is the **conclusion**? Write the whole syllogism.
4. There is another **syllogism** based upon the primary certitude or axiom, stated in paragraph [2], that the Creator endows. It is also mentioned in paragraph [1] as the Laws of Nature. Given the statements that Nature's Law (God) is opposed to disorder and that despotism or tyranny is disorder, develop the basic syllogism.
5. The evils that are listed seem to be **abstractions.** Why did the Founding Fathers list such vague charges?
6. There is extant the rough draft of "The Unanimous Declaration

of the thirteen united States of America." It was revised! Even so felicitous a writer as Jefferson had to revise. Check the following improvement and revise your prose forever more!

self-evident
We hold these truths to be^ *~~sacred & undeniable;~~ that all men are*
they are endowed by their creator with
created equal ~~& independent;~~ that^ *~~from that equal creation they de-~~*
~~equal rights some of which are~~ rights; that these
~~rive in rights~~^ *inherent & inalienable*^ *among ~~which~~*^ *are ~~the preservation~~*
~~of~~ life, ~~&~~ liberty, & the pursuit of happiness.

Applications and Evaluation

1. While you are admiring the use of **parallel structure** in the list of abuses in paragraphs [3] to [29], comment on their effectiveness. Is the device overdone? In the original document they were not written as separate paragraphs but simply separated by dashes.
2. These men pledged "our Lives, our Fortunes, and our sacred Honour" in the cause of liberty and freedom. Write an argument using current political data on the general topic of honor in politics.
3. Using either **induction** or **deduction** as your main pattern, develop a "Declaration of Independence" or "Freedom" for some particular group. (For example: children; parents; women; the gay gang; dedicated, overworked English instructors; an ethnic group.)
4. The Colonies dissolved their bonds with England; the South tried to dissolve its bonds with the North and failed; Thoreau claimed he rejected—all by himself—"the government of the slave" (*Civil Disobedience*). Would it still be possible for a group to disassociate from its nominal government? How many people would it take?
5. According to paragraph [2] governments are instituted to secure rights for individual men; some people maintain that individuals are supposed to serve the government. Which do you think more necessary? Should there be a balance between the two? Make a list showing duties of citizen and duties of government. Develop a strong **thesis** from the data.

Ralph Waldo Ellison (1914–) Ralph W. Ellison was educated at the Tuskegee Institute in Alabama. He has been an instructor at many schools including the University of Chicago, Rutgers, and Yale. He has been an editor—*The Negro Quarterly*—and has won many awards for his writing. Perhaps his best known work is *The Invisible Man*. The following selection is taken from a collection of essays and addresses entitled *Shadow and Act*. Mr. Ellison is currently working on a new novel.

Hidden Names and Complex Fates

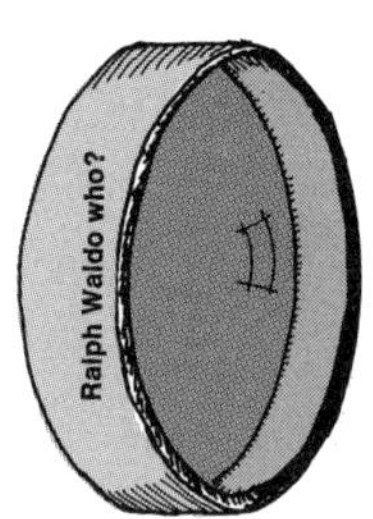

Once while listening to the play of a two-year-old girl who did not know she was under observation, I heard her saying over and over again, at first with questioning and then with sounds of growing satisfaction, "I am Mimi Livisay? . . . *I* am Mimi Livisay. I *am* Mimi Livisay . . . I am *Mimi* Li-vi-say! I am Mimi . . ." [1]

And in deed and in fact she was—or became so soon thereafter, by working playfully to establish the unity between herself and her name. [2]

For many of us this is far from easy. We must learn to wear our names within all the noise and confusion of the environment in which we find ourselves; make them the center of all of our associations with the world, with man and with nature. We must charge them with all our emotions, our hopes, hates, loves, aspirations. They must become our masks and our shields and the containers of all those values and traditions which we learn and/or imagine as being the meaning of our familial past. [3]

And when we are reminded so constantly that we bear, as Negroes, names originally possessed by those who owned our enslaved grandparents, we are apt, especially if we are potential writers, to be more than ordinarily concerned with the veiled and mysterious events, the fusions of blood, the furtive couplings, the business transactions, the violations of faith and loyalty, the assaults; yes, and the unrecognized and unrecognizable loves through which our names were handed down unto us. [4]

So charged with emotion does this concern become for some of us, that we have, earlier, the example of the followers of Father Divine and, now, the Black Muslims, discarding their original names in rejection of the bloodstained, the brutal, the sinful images of the past. Thus they would declare new identities, would clarify a new program of intention and destroy the verbal evidence of a willed and ritualized discontinuity of blood and human intercourse. [5]

Not all of us, actually only a few, seek to deal with our names in this manner. We take what we have and make of them what we can. And there are even those who know where the old broken connections lie, who recognize their relatives across the chasm of historical denial and the artificial barriers of society, and who see themselves as bearers of many of the qualities which were admirable in the original sources of their common line (Faulkner has made much of this); and I speak here not of mere forgiveness, nor of obsequious insensitivity to the outrages symbolized by the denial and the division, but of the conscious acceptance of the harsh realities of the human condition, of the ambiguities and hypocrisies of human history as they have played themselves out in the United States. [6]

Perhaps, taken in aggregate, these European names which (sometimes with irony, sometimes with pride, but always with personal investment) represent a certain triumph of the spirit, speaking to us of those who rallied, reassembled and transformed themselves and who under dismembering pressures refused to die. "Brothers and sisters," I once heard a Negro preacher exhort, "let us make up our faces before the world, and our names shall sound throughout the land with honor! For we ourselves are our *true* names, not their epithets! So let us, I say, Make Up Our Faces and Our Minds!" [7]

Perhaps my preacher had read T. S. Eliot, although I doubt it. And in actuality, it was unnecessary that he do so, for a concern with names and naming was very much a part of that special area of American culture from which I come, and it is precisely for this reason that this example should come to mind in a discussion of my own experience as a writer. [8]

Undoubtedly, writers begin their *conditioning* as manipulators of words long before they become aware of literature—certain Freudians would say at the breast. Perhaps. But if so, that is far too early to be of use at this moment. Of this, though, I am certain: that despite the misconceptions of those educators who trace the reading difficulties experienced by large numbers of Negro children in Northern schools to their Southern background, these children are, in *their* familiar South, facile manipulators of words. I know, too, that the Negro community is deadly in its ability to create nicknames and to spot all that is ludicrous in an unlikely name or that which is incongruous in conduct. Names are not qualities; nor are words, in this particular sense, actions. To assume that they are could cost one his life many times a day. Language skills depend to a large extent upon a knowledge of the details, the manners, the objects, the folkways, the psychological patterns, of a given environment. Humor and wit depend upon much the same awareness, and so does the suggestive power of names. [9]

"A small brown bowlegged Negro with the name 'Franklin D. Roosevelt Jones' might sound like a clown to someone who looks at him from the outside," said my friend Albert Murray, "but on the other hand he just might turn out to be a hell of a fireside operator. He might just lie back in all of that comic juxtaposition of names and manipulate you deaf, dumb and blind—and you not even suspecting it, because you're thrown out of stance by his name! There you are, so dazzled by the F.D.R. image—which you *know* you can't see—and so delighted with your own superior position that you don't realize that its *Jones* who must be confronted." [10]

Well, as you must suspect, all of this speculation on the matter of names has a purpose, and now, because it is tied up so ironically with my own experience as a writer, I must turn to my own name. [11]

For in the dim beginnings, before I ever thought consciously of writing, there was my own name, and there was, doubtless, a certain magic in it. From the start I was uncomfortable with it, and in my earliest years it caused me much puzzlement. Neither could I understand what a poet was, nor why, exactly, my father had chosen to name me after one. Perhaps I could have understood it perfectly well had he named me after his own father, but that name had been given to an older brother who died and thus was out of the question. But why hadn't he named me after a hero, such as Jack Johnson, or a soldier like Colonel Charles Young, or a great seaman like Admiral Dewey, or an educator like Booker T. Washington, or a great orator and abolitionist like Frederick Douglass? Or again, why hadn't he named me (as so many Negro parents had done) after President Teddy Roosevelt? [12]

Instead, he named me after someone called Ralph Waldo Emerson, and then, when I was three, he died. It was too early for me to have understood his choice, although I'm sure he must have explained it many times, and it was also too soon for me to have made the connection between my name and my father's love for reading. Much later, after I began to write and work with words, I came to suspect that he was aware of the suggestive powers of names and of the magic involved in naming. [13]

I recall an odd conversation with my mother during my early teens in which she mentioned their interest in, of all things, prenatal culture! But for a long time I actually knew only that my father read a lot, and that he admired this remote Mr. Emerson, who was something called a "poet and philosopher"—so much so that he named his second son after *him.* [14]

I knew, also, that whatever his motives, the combination of names he'd given me caused me no end of trouble from the moment when I could talk well enough to respond to the ritualized question which grownups put to very young children. Emerson's name was quite familiar to Negroes in Oklahoma during those days when World War I was brewing, and adults, eager to show off their knowledge of literary figures, and obviously amused by the joke implicit in such a small brown nubbin of a boy carrying around such a heavy moniker, would invariably repeat my first two names and then to my great annoyance, they'd add "Emerson." [15]

And I, in my confusion, would reply, "No, *no, I'm* not Emerson; he's the little boy who lives next door." Which only made them laugh all the louder. "Oh no," they'd say, "*you're* Ralph Waldo Emerson," while I had fantasies of blue murder. [16]

For a while the presence next door of my little friend, Emerson, made it unnecessary for me to puzzle too often over this peculiar adult confusion. And since there were other Negro boys named Ralph in the city, I came to suspect that there was something about the combination of names which produced their laughter. Even today I know of only one other Ralph who had as much comedy made out of his name, a campus politician and deep-voiced orator whom I knew at Tuskegee, who was called in friendly ribbing, *Ralph Waldo Emerson Edgar Allan Poe,* spelled Powe. This must have been quite a trial for him, but I had been initiated much earlier. [17]

During my early school years the name continued to puzzle me, for it constantly evoked in the faces of others some secret. It was as thought I possessed some treasure or some defect, which was invisible to my own eyes and ears; something which I had but did not *possess*, like a piece of property in South Carolina, which was mine but which I could not have until some future time. I recall finding, about this time, while seeking adventure in back alleys—which possess for boys a superiority over playgrounds like that which kitchen utensils possess over toys designed for infants—a large photographic lens. I remember nothing of its optical qualities, of its speed or color correction, but it gleamed with crystal mystery and it was beautiful. [18]

Mounted handsomely in a tube of shiny brass, it spoke to me of distant worlds of possibility. I played with it, looking through it was squinted eyes, holding it in shafts of sunlight, and tried to use it for a magic lantern. But most of this was as unrewarding as my attempts to make the music come from a phonograph record by holding the needle in my fingers. [19]

I could burn holes through newspapers with it, or I could pretend that it was a telescope, the barrel of a cannon, or the third eye of a monster—*I* being the monster—but I could do nothing at all about its proper function of making images; nothing to make it yield its secret. But I could not discard it. [20]

Older boys sought to get it away from me by offering knives or tops, agate marbles or whole zoos of grass snakes and horned toads in trade, but I held on to it. No one, not even the white boys I knew, had such a lens, and it was my own good luck to have found it. Thus I would hold on to it until such time as I could acquire the parts needed to make it function. Finally I put it aside and it remained buried in my box of treasures, dusty and dull, to be lost and forgotten as I grew older and became interested in music. [21]

I had reached by now the grades where it was necessary to learn something about Mr. Emerson and what he had written, such as the "Concord Hymn" and the essay "Self-Reliance," and in following his advice, I reduced the "Waldo" to a simple and, I hoped, mysterious "W," and in my own reading I avoided his works like the plague. I could no more deal with my name—I shall never really master it—than I could find a creative use for my lens. Fortunately there were other problems to occupy my mind. [22]

I could suppress the name of my namesake out of respect for the achievements of its original bearer but I cannot escape the obligation of attempting to achieve some of the things which he asked of the American writer. As Henry James suggested, being an American is an arduous task, and for most of us, I suspect, the difficulty begins with the name. [23]

2100 words, 23 paragraphs

Diction

1. The author uses the word "Negro" to refer to himself and his particular subset of mankind; what word is more often used today, and why?
2. He mentions Tuskegee [17], seeming assured that his readers will understand. What is Tuskegee?
3. What do Father Divine and the Black Muslims have to do with names [5]?
4. It is possible to tell that E. M. Forster is from England by his writing. Is it possible to tell Mr. Ellison's place of origin (e.g., which state) from his writing?
5. What is a name besides a label?
6. Here are some words to look up: ambiguities [6], arduous [23], exhort [7], facile [9], furtive [4], implicit [15], incongruous [9], juxtaposition [10], obsequious [6], prenatal [14].

Rhetoric and Style

1. This essay is rich in **metaphor** and **imagery.** In particular, the extended metaphor comparing the lens and the name needs explaining.
2. What is the main manner in which the author links the paragraphs together?
3. What are the references to the Nobel Laureates T. S. Eliot [8] and William Faulkner [6]?
4. Does the author seem to be angry about his strange name? What is the **tone** of the essay?
5. Please explain the meaning of the last line of the essay.
6. The "Negro community is deadly in its ability to create nicknames" and also to spot incongruities. Can you think of any particularly apt nicknames? Do you have a nickname?

Applications and Evaluation

1. Write an essay using **cause and effect** as the main method of development; use as a topic this sentence, "Being an American is an arduous task, and the difficulty begins with the name."
2. Find the meaning of your name—first, last, or both. Most names have a meaning, some may have two or more. Write your name,

its meaning, your source of information, and a brief summary about your name.

3. Has your name (or other label you might carry) been an influence in your life? Give a specific example.
4. Mr. Ellison says he hides the Waldo behind a mysterious W. Are you hiding anything behind an initial? Could you change your name if you wished? Has anyone you know changed his name? Why?
5. Ponder the **symbolic** function of names (check the third paragraph for some ideas). Does primitive name magic have any carryover in modern America?

Jessica Mitford (19 –) Jessica Mitford was born and educated in England. She tells about her early life in her first book, called *Daughters and Rebels.* She gained wide renown in the United States when she published *The American Way of Death,* which took a penetrating look at the strange patterns and rituals of American burials and funerals. She has also written *The Trial of Dr. Spock* and *Kind and Usual Punishments.*

The American Way of Death

O death, where is thy sting? O grave, where is thy victory? Where, indeed. Many a badly stung survivor, faced with the aftermath of some relative's funeral, has ruefully concluded that the victory had been won hands down by a funeral establishment—in disastrously unequal battle. [1]

Much has been written of late about the affluent society in which we live, and much fun poked at some of the irrational "status symbols" set out like golden snares to trap the unwary consumer at every turn. Until recently, little has been said about the most irrational and weirdest of the lot, lying in ambush for all of us at the end of the road—the modern American funeral. [2]

If the Dismal Traders (as an eighteenth-century English writer calls them) have traditionally been cast in a comic role in literature, a universally recognized symbol of humor from Shakespeare to Dickens to Evelyn Waugh, they have successfully turned the tables in recent years to perpetrate a huge, macabre and expensive practical joke on the American public. It is not consciously conceived of as a joke, of course; on the contrary, it is hedged with admirably contrived rationalizations. [3]

Gradually, almost imperceptibly, over the years the funeral men have constructed their own grotesque cloud-cuckoo-land where the trappings of Gracious Living are transformed, as in a nightmore, into the trappings of Gracious Dying. The same familiar Madison Avenue language, with its peculiar adjectival range designed to anesthetize sales resistance to all sorts of products, has seeped into the funeral industry in a new and bizarre guise. The emphasis is on the same desirable qualities that we have all been schooled to look for in our daily search for excellence: comfort, durability, beauty, craftsmanship. The attuned ear will recognize too the convincing quasi-scientific language, so reassuring even if unintelligible. [4]

So that this too, too solid flesh might not melt, we are offered "solid copper—a quality casket which offers superb value to the client seeking long-lasting protection," or "the Colonial Classic Beauty—18 gauge lead coated steel, seamless top, lap-jointed welded body construction." Some are equipped with foam rubber, some with innerspring mattresses. Elgin offers "the revolutionary 'Perfect-Posture' bed." Not every casket need have a silver lining, for one may choose between "more than 60 color matched shades, magnificent and unique masterpieces" by the Cheney casket-lining people. Shrouds no longer exist. Instead, you may patronize a grave-wear couturière who promises "handmade original fashions—styles from the best in life for the last memory—dresses, men's suits, negligees, accessories." For the final, perfect grooming: "Nature-Glo—the ultimate in cosmetic embalming." And, where have we heard that phrase "peace of mind protection" before? No matter. In funeral advertising, it is applied to the Wilbert Burial Vault, with its ⅜-inch precast asphalt inner liner plus extra-thick, reinforced concrete—all this "guaranteed by Good Housekeeping." Here again the Cadillac, status symbol par excellence, appears in all its gleaming glory, this time transformed into a pastel-colored funeral hearse. [5]

You, the potential customer for all this luxury, are unlikely to read the lyrical descriptions quoted above, for they are culled from *Mortuary Management* and *Casket and Sunnyside,* two of the industry's eleven trade magazines. For you there are ads in your daily newspaper, generally found on the obituary page, stressing dignity, refinement, high-caliber professional service and that intangible quality, *sincerity*. The trade advertisements are, however, instructive, because they furnish an important clue to the frame of mind into which the funeral industry has hypnotized itself. [6]

A new mythology, essential to the twentieth-century American funeral rite, has grown up—or rather has been built up step by step—to justify the peculiar customs surrounding the disposal of our dead. And, just as the witch doctor must be convinced of his own infallibility in order to maintains a hold over his clientele, so the funeral industry has had to "sell itself" on its articles of faith in the course of passing them along to the public. [7]

The first of these is the tenet that today's funeral procedures are founded in "American tradition." The story comes to mind of a sign on the freshly sown lawn of a brand-new Midwest college: "There is a tradition on this campus that students never walk on this strip of grass. This tradition goes into effect next Tuesday." The most cursory look at American funerals of past times will establish the parallel. Simplicity to the point of starkness, the plain pine box, the laying out of the dead by friends and family who also bore the coffin to the grave—these were the hallmarks of the traditional funeral until the end of the nineteenth century. [8]

Secondly, there is the myth that the American public is only being given what it wants—an opportunity to keep up with the Joneses to the end. "In keeping with our high standard of living, there should be an equally high standard of dying," says the past president of the Funeral Directors of San Francisco. "The cost of a funeral varies according to individual taste and the niceties of living the family has been accustomed to." Actually, choice doesn't enter the picture for the average individual, faced, generally for the first time, with the necessity of buying a product of which he is totally ignorant, at a moment when he is least in a position to quibble. In point of fact the cost of a funeral almost always varies, not "according to individual taste" but according to what the traffic will bear. [9]

Thirdly, there is an assortment of myths based on half-digested psychiatric theories. The importance of the "memory picture" is stressed—meaning the last glimpse of the deceased in open casket, done up with the latest in embalming techniques and finished off with a dusting of makeup. A newer one, impressively authentic-sounding, is the need for "grief therapy," which is beginning to go over big in mortuary circles. A historian of American funeral directing hints at the grief-therapist idea when speaking of the new role of the undertaker—"the dramaturgic role, in which the undertaker becomes a stage manager to create an appropriate atmosphere and to move the funeral party through a drama in which social relationships are stressed and an emotional catharsis or release is provided through ceremony." [10]

Lastly, a whole new terminology, as ornately shoddy as the satin rayon casket liner, has been invented by the funeral industry to replace the direct and serviceable vocabulary of former times. Undertaker has been supplanted by "funeral director" or "mortician." (Even the classified section of the telephone directory gives recognition to this; in its pages you will find "Undertakers—see Funeral Directors.") Coffins are "caskets"; hearses are "coaches," or "professional cars"; flowers are "floral tributes"; corpses generally are "loved ones," but mortuary etiquette dictates that a specific corpse be referred to by name only—as, "Mr. Jones"; cremated ashes are "cremains." Euphemisms such as "slumber room," "reposing room," and "calcination—the *kindlier* heat" abound in the funeral business. [11]

If the undertaker is the stage manager of the fabulous production that is the modern American funeral, the stellar role is reserved for the occupant of the open casket. The decor, the stagehands, the supporting cast are all arranged for the most advantageous display of the deceased, without which the rest of the paraphernalia would lose its point—*Hamlet* without the Prince of Denmark. It is to this end that a fantastic array of costly merchandise and services is pyramided to dazzle the mourners and facilitate the plunder of the next of kin. [12]

Grief therapy, anyone? But it's going to come high. According to the funeral industry's own figures, the *average* undertaker's bill in 1961 was $708 for casket and "services," to which must be added the cost of a burial vault, flowers, clothing, clergy and musician's honorarium, and cemetery charges. When these costs are added to the undertaker's bill, the total average cost for an adult's funeral is, as we shall see, closer to $1,450. [13]

The question naturally arises, *is* this what most people want for themselves and their families? For several reasons, this has been a hard one to answer until recently. It is a subject seldom discussed. Those who have never had to arrange for a funeral frequently shy away from its implications, preferring to take comfort in the thought that sufficient unto the day is the evil thereof. Those who have acquired personal and painful knowledge of the subject would often rather forget about it. Pioneering "Funeral Societies" or "Memorial Associations," dedicated to the principle of dignified funerals at reasonable cost, have existed in a number of communities throughout the country, but their membership has been limited for the most part to the more sophisticated element in the population—university people, liberal intellectuals—and those who, like doctors and lawyers, come up against problems in arranging funerals for their clients. [14]

Some indication of the pent-up resentment felt by vast numbers of people against the funeral interests was furnished by the astonishing response to an article by Roul Tunley, titled "Can You Afford to Die?" in *The Saturday Evening Post* of June 17, 1961. As though a dike had burst, letters poured in from every part of the country to the *Post*, to the funeral societies, to local newspapers. They came from clergymen, professional people, old-age pensioners, trade unionists. Three months after the article appeared, an estimated six thousand had taken pen in hand to comment on some phase of the high cost of dying. Many recounted their own bitter experiences at the hands of funeral directors; hundreds asked for advice on how to establish a consumer organization in communities where none exists; others sought information about pre-need plans. The membership of the funeral societies skyrocketed. The funeral industry, finding itself in the glare of public spotlight, has begun to engage in serious debate about its own future course—as well it might. [15]

Is the funeral inflation bubble ripe for bursting? A few years ago, the United States public suddenly rebelled against the trend in the auto industry towards ever more showy cars, with their ostentatious and nonfunctional fins, and a demand was created for compact cars patterned after European models. The all-powerful auto industry, accustomed to *telling* the customer what sort of car he wanted, was suddenly forced to *listen* for a change. Overnight, the little cars became for millions a new kind of status symbol. Could it be that the same cycle is working itself out in the attitude towards the final return of dust to dust, that the American public is becoming sickened by ever more ornate and costly funerals, and that a status symbol of the future may indeed be the simplest kind of "funeral without fins"? [16]

1860 words, 16 paragraphs

Diction

1. The author mentions **euphemisms.** What are some used by the funeral industry?
2. The author uses a highly **colloquial** style. Check the last three paragraphs for any phrases that might be a bit overworked. Are they effectively used?

3. Most people know who Shakespeare and Dickens are, but why is the name *Evelyn Waugh* used with them?
4. The opening lines of paragraph [1] and [5] are taken from other works. Do you recognize them?
5. In addition to **euphemisms,** the funeral industry invents words and odd spellings of standard words. What are some of these *neologisms?*
6. The following words are standard words, neither euphemisms nor neologisms; what do they mean? Affluent [2], couturière [5], hallmark [8], intangible [6], macabre [3], ostentation [16], paraphernalia [12], par excellence [5], rationalization [3], tenet [8].

Rhetoric and Style

1. The author effectively uses **comparisons** to emphasize her points; the last line mentions a "funeral without fins." Explain the comparison. Is it effective?
2. What **examples** taken from outside the field of undertaking does the author use to clarify her points? Find one.
3. Find two or three **metaphors** that work to heighten communication.
4. In what way does the author link paragraphs [7] through [11] into a kind of "mini-essay"?
5. The main point of this essay is that there is a **cause and effect** relationship in operation in the undertaking industry. What is the cause and what the effect?
6. What kinds of **evidence** does the author use to validate some of her **coordinate points**? Give an example or two.

Applications and Evaluation

1. Does an ornate, expensive funeral benefit anyone other than the funeral parlor?
2. What are some other areas of American life where we tend to use **euphemisms** or neologisms?
3. Do we use conspicuous display in any other part of life than in our leaving of it?
4. Is there any other segment of our commercial life that has "hypnotized itself" into thinking that the services it performs

for the public are beneficial when they really are not? (Consider real estate, all the media, sales, some religions, perhaps, or education.)

5. Select any one of the four questions above. Find at least three specific **examples** to support your answer and write a **paragraph.**

Gloria Steinem was educated at Smith College, the University of Delhi, and the University of Calcutta. She has been a writer of wide-ranging interests, contributing to *Esquire, Vogue, Life, McCall's*; writing television scripts; producing a book, *The Thousand Indias*; and serving as a contributing editor to *New Yorker* Magazine. She considers herself both a critic of and an adherent to the Women's Liberation movement. She is now the editor of *Ms. Magazine*.

What It Would Be Like If Women Win

Any change is fearful, especially one affecting both politics and sex roles, so let me begin these utopian speculations with a fact. To break the ice. [1]

Women don't want to exchange places with men. Male chauvinists, science-fiction writers and comedians may favor that idea for its shock value, but psychologists say it is a fantasy based on ruling-class ego and guilt. Men assume that women want to imitate them, which is just what white people assumed about blacks. An assumption so strong that it may convince the second-class group of the need to imitate, but for both women and blacks that stage has passed. Guilt produces the question: What if they could treat us as we have treated them? [2]

That is not our goal. But we do want to change the economic system to one more based on merit. In Women's Lib Utopia, there will be free access to good jobs—and decent pay for the bad ones women have been performing all along, including housework. Increased skilled labor might lead to a four-hour workday, and higher wages would encourage further mechanization of repetitive jobs now kept alive by cheap labor. [3]

With women as half the country's elected representatives, and a woman President once in a while, the country's *machismo* problems would be greatly reduced. The old-fashioned idea that manhood depends on violence and victory is, after all, an important part of our troubles in the streets. I'm not saying that women leaders would eliminate violence. We are not more moral than men; we are only uncorrupted by power so far. When we do acquire power, we might turn out to have an equal impulse toward aggression. Even now, Margaret Mead believes that women fight less often but more fiercely than men, because women are not taught the rules of the war game and fight only when cornered. But for the next 50 years or so, women in politics will be very valuable by tempering the idea of manhood into something less aggressive and better suited to this crowded, post-atomic planet. Consumer protection and children's rights, for instance, might get more legislative attention. [4]

Men will have to give up ruling-class privileges, but in return they will no longer be the only ones to support the family, get drafted, bear the strain of power and responsibility. Freud to the contrary, anatomy is not destiny, at least not for more than nine months at a time. In Israel, women are drafted, and some have gone to war. In England, more men type and run switchboards. In India and Israel, a woman rules. In Sweden, both parents take care of the children. In this country, come Utopia, men and women won't reverse roles; they will be free to choose according to individual talents and preferences. [5]

If role reform sounds sexually unsettling, think how it will change the sexual hypocrisy we have now. No more sex arranged on the barter system, with women pretending interest, and men never sure whether they are loved for themselves or for the security few women can get any other way. (Married or not, for sexual reasons or social ones, most women still find it second nature to Uncle-Tom.) No more men who are encouraged to spend a lifetime living with inferiors; with housekeepers, or dependent creatures who are still children. No more domineering wives, emasculating women, and "Jewish mothers," all of whom are simply human beings with all their normal ambition and drive confined to the home. No more unequal partnerships that eventually doom love and sex. [6]

In order to produce that kind of confidence and individuality, child rearing will train according to talent. Little girls will no longer be surrounded by air-tight, self-fulfilling prophecies of natural passivity, lack of ambition and objectivity, inability to exercise power, and dexterity (so long as special aptitude for jobs requiring patience and dexterity is confined to poorly paid jobs; brain surgery is for males). [7]

Schools and universities will help to break down traditional sex roles, even when parents will not. Half the teachers will be men, a rarity now at preschool and elementary levels; girls will not necessarily serve cookies or boys hoist up the flag. Athletic teams will be picked only by strength and skill. Sexually segregated courses like auto mechanics and home economics will be taken by boys and girls together. New courses in sexual politics will explore female subjugation as the model for political oppression, and women's history will be an academic staple, along with black history, at least until the white-male-oriented textbooks are integrated and rewritten. [8]

As for the American child's classic problem—too much mother, too little father—that would be cured by an equalization of parental responsibility. Free nurseries, school lunches, family cafeterias built into every housing complex, service companies that will do household cleaning chores in a regular, businesslike way, and more responsibility by the entire community for the children: all these will make it possible for both mother and father to work, and to have equal leisure time with the children at home. For parents of very young children, however, a special job category, created by Government and unions, would allow such parents a shorter work day. [9]

The revolution would not take away the option of being a housewife. A woman who prefers to be her husband's housekeeper and/or hostess would receive a percentage of his pay determined by the domestic relations courts. If divorced, she might be eligible for a pension fund, and for a job-training allowance. Or a divorce could be treated the same way that the dissolution of a business partnership is now. [10]

If these proposals seem farfetched, consider Sweden, where most of them are already in effect. Sweden is not yet a working Women's Lib model; most of the role-reform programs began less than a decade ago, and are just beginning to take hold. But that country is so far ahead of us in recognizing the problem that Swedish statements on sex and equality sound like bulletins from the moon. [11]

Our marriage laws, for instance, are so reactionary that Women's

Lib groups want couples to take a compulsory written exam on the law, as for a driver's license, before going through with the wedding. A man has alimony and wifely debts to worry about, but a woman may lose so many of her civil rights that in the U.S. now, in important legal ways, she becomes a child again. In some states, she cannot sign credit agreements, use her maiden name, incorporate a business, or establish a legal residence of her own. Being a wife, according to most social and legal definitions, is still a 19th century thing. [12]

Assuming, however, that these blatantly sexist laws are abolished or reformed, that job discrimination is forbidden, that parents share financial responsibility for each other and the children, and that sexual relationships become partnerships of equal adults (some pretty big assumptions), then marriage will probably go right on. Men and women are, after all, physically complementary. When society stops encouraging men to be exploiters and women to be parasites, they may turn out to be more complementary in emotion as well. Women's Lib is not trying to destroy the American family. A look at the statistics on divorce—plus the way in which old people are farmed out with strangers and young people flee the home—shows the destruction that has already been done. Liberated women are just trying to point out the disaster, and build compassionate and practical alternatives from the ruins. [13]

What will exist is a variety of alternative life-styles. Since the population explosion dictates that childbearing be kept to a minimum, parents-and-children will be only of many families": couples, age groups, working groups, mixed communes, blood-related clans, class groups, creative groups. Single women will have the right to stay single without ridicule, without the attitudes now betrayed by "spinster" and "bachelor." Lesbians or homosexuals will no longer be denied legally binding marriages, complete with mutual-support agreements and inheritance rights. Paradoxically, the number of homosexuals may get smaller. With fewer overpossessive mothers and fewer fathers who hold up an impossibly cruel or perfectionist idea of manhood, boys will be less likely to be denied or reject their identity as males. [14]

Changes that now seem small may get bigger:

MEN'S LIB

Men now suffer from more diseases due to stress, heart attacks, ulcers, a higher suicide rate, greater difficulty living alone, less adaptability to change and, in general, a shorter life span than women. There is some scientific evidence that what produces physical problems is not work itself, but the inability to choose which work, and how much. With women bearing half the financial responsibility, and with the idea of "masculine" jobs gone, men might well feel freer and live longer. [15]

RELIGION

Protestant women are already becoming ordained ministers; radical nuns are carrying out liturgical functions that were once the exclusive property of priests; Jewish women are rewriting prayers—particularly those that Orthodox Jews recite every morning thanking God they are not female. In the future, the church will become an area of equal participation by women. This means, of course, that organized reliigon will have to give up one of its great historical weapons: sexual repression. In most structured faiths, from Hinduism through Roman Catholicism, the status of women went down as the position of priests ascended. Male clergy implied, if they did not teach, that women were unclean, unworthy and sources of ungodly temptation, in order to remove them as rivals for the emotional forces of men. Full participation of women in ecclesiastical life might involve certain changes in theology, such as, for instance, a radical redefinition of sin. [16]

LITERARY PROBLEMS

Revised sex roles will outdate more children's books than civil rights ever did. Only a few children had the problem of a *Little Black Sambo,* but most have the male-female stereotypes of "Dick and Jane." A boomlet of children's books about mothers who work has already begun, and liberated parents and editors are beginning to pressure for change in the textbook industry. Fiction writing will change more gradually, but romantic novels with wilting heroines and swashbuckling heroes will be reduced to historical value. Or perhaps to the sado-masochist trade. (*Marjorie Morningstar,* a romantic novel that took the '50s by storm, has already begun to seem as unreal as its '20s predecessor, *The Sheik.*) As far the literary plots that turn on forced marriages or horrific abortions, they will seem as dated as Prohibition stories. Free legal abortions and free birth control will force writers to give up pregnancy as the *deus ex machina.* [17]

MANNERS AND FASHION

Dress will be more androgynous, with class symbols becoming more important than sexual ones. Pro or anti-Establishment styles may already be more vital than who is wearing them. Hardhats are just as likely to rough up antiwar girls as antiwar men in the street, and police understand that women are just as likely to be pushers or bombers. Dances haven't required that one partner lead the other for years, anyway. Chivalry will transfer itself to those who need it, or deserve respect: old people, admired people, anyone with an armload of packages. Women with normal work identities will be less likely to attach their whole sense of self to youth and appearance; thus there will be fewer nervous breakdowns when the first wrinkles appear. Lighting cigarettes and other treasured niceties will become gestures of mutual affection. "I like to be helped on with my coat," says one Women's Lib worker, "but not if it costs me $2,000 a year in salary." [18]

For those with nostalgia for a simpler past, here is a word of comfort. Anthropologist Geoffrey Gorer studied the few peaceful human tribes and discovered one common characteristic: sex roles were not polarized. Differences of dress and occupation were at a minimum. Society, in other words, was not using sexual blackmail as a way of getting women to do cheap labor, or men to be aggressive. [19]

Thus Women's Lib may achieve a more peaceful society on the way toward its other goals. That is why the Swedish government considers reform to bring about greater equality in the sex roles one of its most important concerns. As Prime Minister Olof Palme explained in a widely ignored speech delivered in Washington in 1970. "It is *human beings* we shall emancipate in Sweden today, if a politician should declare that the woman ought to have a different role from man's he would be regarded as something from the Stone Age." In other words, the most radical goal of the movement is egalitarianism. [20]

If Women's Lib wins, perhaps we all do. [21]

2164 words, 21 paragraphs

Diction

1. What is the meaning of the phrase in parenthesis [6] that most women "find it second nature to Uncle-Tom"?
2. Any revolution or new movement inevitably develops its own

special vocabulary. Can you note any newly coined or special words in this essay?
3. Explain the phrase [5] "anatomy is not destiny." It is a clever aphorism.
4. Is there really such a word as "boomlet" [17]? What does it mean? What process is used to develop such a word?
5. Here are some vocabulary words to look up: androgynous [18], blatantly [13], chauvinist [2], dexterity [7], egalitarianism [20], emasculating [6], *machismo* [4], polarized [19], subjugation [8], utopian [1].

Rhetoric and Style

1. What is the general pattern of this essay? The first part defines Women's Lib; what do the next four parts do? Where do paragraphs [11] and [12] fit into the general scheme? (Make an outline if it will help.)
2. What is the author's **thesis**? Where does she place the thesis?
3. Can you find any indications of biased writing in this essay? (Suggestion: look at the use of adjectives.)
4. Paragraph [4] starts to discuss women as elected representatives. Is that paragraph linked to the rest of the essay in any way at all, or is it off the **topic**?
5. Why is it permissible for Ms. Steinem to use fragments in her essay when English students are forbidden to use them?
6. Is this essay marked by effective use of **figurative language**?

Application and Evaluation

1. In what way do *Dick and Jane* and similar books designed for primary readers maintain the divided sex roles? Are such books unrealistic in any other way?
2. Compare recent women leaders of contemporary countries with women in American elective offices.
3. Is it possible that certain sex roles are biologically determined? Consider both primitive and contemporary societies before you outline the essay.
4. This essay was written in 1970. Evaluate the accuracy of Ms. Steinem as a prophet by comparing the elements listed in para-

graphs [15] through [18] with the way those same things are today.

5. Do men need liberating from their roles in society too? How about other groups that might be in need of some kind of "liberation" such as teen-agers, old people, or bald folk? Develop one of these ideas into an essay patterned on Ms. Steinem's.

Gene Lees (1928–   ) Gene Lees was born and educated in Canada, where he worked as a reporter for various Canadian newspapers. He has been editor of *Down Beat* magazine and a contributing editor to *Hi Fi and Stereo Review*. In addition to publishing numerous stories and articles, he has written a novel, *And Sleep Until Noon*. Mr. Lees also writes songs and lyrics. This selection, a modern version of Jonathan Swift's famous satire, appeared in *High Fidelity*, for which magazine Mr. Lees serves as popular music editor.

A Modern Proposal

Jonathan Swift once made what he called a Modest Proposal: since the Irish could not grow enough food to feed themselves but had no trouble producing babies, he suggested that babies should be made the prime Irish export (perhaps served as a table delicacy in England). There were those who thought he meant it. Perhaps, in a bitter and angry way, he did. [1]

I wish to make a Modest Proposal myself. It relates to two serious contemporary problems: narcotics addiction and overpopulation. I feel that it is incumbent upon me as a man who makes his living from the record industry to offer this proposal. For the record industry is as responsible as any sector of our society for the growing number of deaths from the use of heroin and other drugs. [2]

Now don't be hasty in condemning them. They've done no more than other industries have. Detroit finds 40,000 deaths a year in crashworthy cars an acceptable price for profits. Why shouldn't the record industry too be allowed to kill its quota of people for profit? [3]

Ten years ago I devoted an issue of *Down Beat* to the drug problem. At the time only a few music-business people thought addiction was an important issue. A Negro singer I know said to me recently, "Nobody gave a damn about it when only black kids were

Published in *High Fidelity*, June 1970. Reprinted by permission of High Fidelity.

dying in the doorways of Harlem. Nobody gave a damn until the well-to-do middle-class white kids started dying." *Touché.* [4]

There is a great deal of criminal money invested in the music business, both in groups and in some record labels. Rock groups began pushing drug use. The kids bought it. The kids are dying. The underworld is making money on it. This is all coincidence, right? Oh sure. [5]

Drug education in the schools is only going to make the problem worse, I am convinced. It will increase fascination, or even cause it, among youngsters who had never even thought much about using drugs. Watch it happen in the next two years. [6]

And so I have come around to another view of the matter. I modestly propose that to all our other welfare programs we add free narcotics for the kids, including heroin. If you're a parent, this may shock you. But it shouldn't. You have been permitting your kids to take dope intellectually for years—from Bob Dylan, the Jefferson Airplane, the Lovin' Spoonful, the Beatles. When your five-year-old was wandering around the house singing, "I get by with a little help from my friends, I get high with a little help from my friends," didn't you say, "Isn't that cute? He's singing a Beatles song." All right, so now he's a few years older, and you're startled at the circulation of drugs in his school, and fearful that he'll start using them. (Maybe he's already started.) Why? You permitted it. [7]

Now the main thing wrong with junkies is that they steal. Sometimes they go farther than that: in desperation for money, they *kill* and steal. This is a great social inconvenience, tying up the time of all kinds of policemen whom we need for such things as messing up traffic. [8]

If I get my way, and the government subsidizes addiction the way it now subsidizes lethargy, all this will stop. It is useless to tell young people that the Beatles and heroin are bad for them. It simply is not so: the kids have told us this. And they are the wisest and most honest and idealistic and decent and loving and unprejudiced and well-informed generation of Americans in history. We know it because they have told us this too. And the advertising industry and Marshall McLuhan have confirmed it. Who in his right mind would doubt the combined wisdom of Marshall McLuhan, the advertising industry, and our wonderful young people? [9]

Now, if we supply them with all the heroin they can use—and I am talking about the pure, uncut stuff, not the powdered sugar that's floating around in many places these days—it will have immediate and far-reaching social benefits. [10]

First, they'll stop rioting. Heroin makes you terribly passive. They'll start nodding out all over the place, and this will permit the police to catch up on *their* sleep in parked cruisers. [11]

Then a lot of them will start dropping out of school. This will reduce the overload on our schools and universities. It will stop the building program, thus braking the felling of trees which give us our oxygen. Our air will improve. [12]

Third, it will increase the food supply, since junkies don't eat much even when they can get it. [13]

Fourth (and here is the real genius of my plan), ultimately the program will end the population explosion. One junkie I know told me that he and his strung-out wife hadn't had sexual relations in two years. Heroin produces profound sexual indifference, and impotence. But that isn't the end of it. Junkies die. In the late 1940s and early 1950s, a great many jazz musicians were on heroin. None of them are now. They are either in their graves or they are off drugs. There is no middle road, apparently. [14]

Kids constitute nearly fifty per cent of the population. The population explosion, then, *is them*. Now since anyone forty years old is going to be around only for another thirty years or so tops, *they're* not going to be much of a problem. They're starting to die off now, from working too hard to make enough money for their kids to buy the Doors' records and acid and junk. But that eighteen-year-old over there—man, he's going to be around breathing air, using up food, making garbage for another forty or fifty years. Even a kid can grasp that he himself is the real enemy. [15]

Now when we begin the widespread free distribution of drugs, this group will start dying like flies. And still more benefits will accrue to society as a whole. [16]

Junk music will fade from the radio. There won't be so many cars on the highway, and those that are there won't be in such steady use. Air pollution will be further reduced. Since we won't need so many highways, the grass and trees will grow again, making more oxygen. Drug use, incidentally, including acid, is becoming as common a cause of traffic deaths as alcohol. So we get a bonus here too. [17]

I know there are those out there in Readerland who will write me letters telling me I've got it all wrong—like the people who wrote me letters telling me New York is not dying. They'll say my proposal is heartless and cruel. But it isn't, I assure you. We have given the young what they want until now. Why should we draw the line at death? [18]

To young people I would say this: don't believe old squares when they tell you that drugs, even grass, are damn dangerous. Don't believe the growing reports that the grass available now is often spiked with heroin to hook you on hard narcotics. Don't believe those who tell you that heroin is evil stuff. You know all those people are just trying to keep you from having a hip kind of good time. [19]

And don't think about death. Think instead how you will be reducing the pressures of population on the rest of us. Think what a noble deed you'll be doing. Think Zen thoughts about eternity and the continuum of consciousness and about astrology and how mortal existence is a mere passing cloud. Think not of going into a valley of blackness. Think instead how you are going to join the great All-Consciousness and rest forever in nirvana. As you sit there, listening to John and Yoko with a needle in your arm, reflect not on the dying you're about to do. Just think how high you're going to be as you go. [20]

And to the record industry I would say: keep up the good work, gentlemen. You've done a hell of a job thus far. [21]

1460 words, 21 paragraphs

Jonathan Swift (1667–1745) Jonathan Swift was born and educated in Ireland but was influenced by British men of letters he met when secretary for Sir William Temple. He became Dean of St. Patrick's in Dublin and worked to benefit the Irish. Best known for *Gulliver's Travels,* he attacked other kinds of human folly in a variety of works. This selection is satire after the biting manner of the Roman poet, Juvenal. It has been left in the original form so that students can get the flavor of eighteenth-century writing and spelling. The titles that show the seven parts of the Classical Oration were not included in the original but have been inserted to show modern students how closely Swift followed the ancient pattern.

A Modest Proposal for Preventing the Children of poor People in Ireland, from being a Burden to their Parents or Country; and for making them beneficial to the Publick

EXORDIUM

It is a melancholly Object to those, who walk through this great Town, or travel in the Country; when they see the *Streets*, the *Roads*, and *Cabbins-doors* crowded with *Beggars* of the Female Sex, followed by three, four, or six Children, *all in Rags*, and importuning every Passenger for an Alms. These *Mothers*, instead of being able to work for their honest Livelyhood, are forced to employ all their Time in stroling to beg Sustenance for their *helpless Infants*; who, as they grow up, either turn *Thieves* for want of Work; or leave their *dear Native Country, to fight for the Pretender in* Spain; or sell themselves to the *Barbadoes*. [1]

I think it is agreed by all Parties, that this prodigious Number of Children in the Arms, or on the Backs, or at the *Heels* of their *Mothers*, and frequently of their *Fathers*, is *in the present deplorable State of the Kingdom*, a very great additional Grievance; and therefore, whoever could find out a fair, cheap, and easy Method of making these Children sound and useful Members of the Commonwealth; would deserve so well of the Publick, as to have his Statue set up for a Preserver of the Nation. [2]

But my Intention is very far from being confined to provide only for the Children of *professed Beggars*: It is of a much greater Extent, and shall take in the whole Number of Infants at a certain Age, who are born of Parents, in effect as little able to support them, as those who demand our Charity in the Streets. [3]

NARRATION

As to my own Part, having turned my Thoughts for many Years, upon this important Subject; and maturely weighed the several *Schemes of other Projectors*, I have always found them grosly mistaken in their Computation. It is true, a Child *just dropt from its Dam*, may be supported by her Milk, for a Solar Year with little other Nourishment; at most not above the Value of two Shillings; which the Mother may certainly get, or the Value in *Scraps*, by her lawful Occupation of *Begging*: And, it is exactly at one Year old, that I propose to provide for them in such a Manner, as, instead of being a Charge upon their *Parents*, or the *Parish*, or *wanting Food and Raiment* for the rest of their Lives; they shall, on the contrary, contribute to the Feeding, and partly to the Cloathing, of many Thousands. [4]

There is likewise another great Advantage in my *Scheme*, that it will prevent those *voluntary Abortions,* and that horrid Practice of *Women murdering their Bastard Children;* alas! too frequent among us; sacrificing the *poor innocent Babes,* I doubt, more to avoid the Expence than the Shame; which would move Tears and Pity in the most Savage and inhuman Breast. [5]

The Number of Souls in *Ireland* being usually reckoned one Million and a half; of these I calculate there may be about Two Hundred Thousand Couples whose Wives are Breeders; from which Number I subtract thirty thousand Couples, who are able to maintain their own Children; although I apprehend there cannot be so many, under *the present Distresses of the Kingdom;* but this being granted, there will remain an Hundred and Seventy Thousand Breeders. I again subtract Fifty Thousand, for those Women who miscarry, or whose Children die by Accident, or Disease, within the Year. There only remain an Hundred and Twenty Thousand Children of poor Parents, annually born: The Question therefore is, How this Number shall be reared, and provided for? Which, as I have already said, under the present Situation of Affairs, is utterly impossible, by all the Methods hitherto proposed: For we can *neither employ them in Handicraft* or *Agriculture;* we neither build Houses, (I mean in the Country) nor cultivate Land: They can very seldom pick up a Livelyhood *by Stealing* until they arrive at six Years old; except where they are of towardly Parts; although, I confess, they learn the Rudiments much earlier; during which Time, they can, however, be properly looked upon only as *Probationers;* as I have been informed by a principal Gentleman in the County of *Cavan,* who protested to me, that he never knew above one or two Instances under the Age of six, even in a Part of the Kingdom *so renowned for the quickest Proficiency in that Art.* [6]

I am assured by our Merchants, that a Boy or a Girl before twelve Years old, is no saleable Commodity; and even when they come to this Age, they will not yield above Three Pounds, or Three Pounds and half a Crown at most, on the Exchange; which cannot turn to Account either to the Parents or Kingdom; the Charge of Nutriment and Rags, having been at least four Times that Value. [7]

PROPOSITION (THESIS)

I shall now therefore humbly propose my own Thoughts; which I hope will not be liable to the least Objection. [8]

I have been assured by a very knowing *American* of my Acquaintance in *London;* that a young healthy Child, well nursed, is, at a Year old, a most delicious, nourishing, and wholesome Food; whether *Stewed, Roasted, Baked,* or *Boiled;* and, I make no doubt, that it will equally serve in a *Fricasie,* or *Ragoust.* [9]

I do therefore humbly offer it to *publick Consideration,* that of the Hundred and Twenty thousand Children, already computed, Twenty thousand may be reserved for Breed; whereof only one Fourth Part to be Males; which is more than we allow to *Sheep, black Cattle,* or *Swine;* and my Reason is, that these Children are seldom the Fruits of Marriage, *a Circumstance not much regarded by our Savages;* therefore, *one Male* will be sufficient to serve *four Females.* That the remaining Hundred thousand, may, at a Year old, be offered in Sale to the *Persons of Quality* and *Fortune,* through the Kingdom; always advising the Mother to let them suck plentifully in the last Month, so as to render them plump, and fat for a good Table. A Child will make two Dishes at an Entertainment for Friends; and when the Family dines alone, the fore or hind Quarter will make a reasonable Dish; and seasoned with a little Pepper or Salt, will be very good Boiled on the fourth Day, especially in *Winter.* [10]

DIVISION

I have reckoned upon a Medium, that a Child just born will weigh Twelve Pounds; and in a solar Year, if tolerably nursed, encreaseth to twenty eight Pounds. [11]

I grant this Food will be somewhat dear, and therefore very *proper for Landlords;* who, as they have already devoured most of the Parents, seem to have the best Title to the Children. [12]

Infants Flesh will be in Season throughout the Year; but more plentiful in *March,* and a little before and after: For we are told by a grave Author, an eminent *French* Physician, that *Fish being a prolifick Dyet,* there are more Children born in *Roman Catholick Countries* about Nine Months after *Lent,* than at any other Season: Therefore reckoning a Year after *Lent,* the Markets will be more glutted than usual; because the Number of *Popish Infants,* is, at least, three to one in this Kingdom; and therefore it will have one other Collateral Advantage, by lessening the Number of *Papists* among us. [13]

I have already computed the Charge of nursing a Beggar's Child (in which List I reckon all *Cottagers, Labourers,* and Four fifths of the *Farmers*) to be about two Shillings *per Annum,* Rags included; and I believe, no Gentleman would repine to give Ten Shillings for the *Carcase of a good fat child;* which, as I have said, will make four

Dishes of excellent nutritive Meat, when he hath only some particular Friend, or his own Family, to dine with him. Thus the Squire will learn to be a good Landlord, and grow popular among his Tenants; the Mother will have Eight Shillings net Profit, and be fit for Work until she produceth another Child. [14]

Those who are more thrifty (*as I must confess the Times require*) may flay the Carcase; the Skin of which, artificially dressed, will make admirable *Gloves for Ladies*, and *Summer Boots for fine Gentlemen*. 15]

As to our City of *Dublin*; Shambles may be appointed for this Purpose, in the most convenient Parts of it; and Butchers we may be assured will not be wanting; although I rather recommend buying the Children alive, and dressing them hot from the Knife, as we do *roasting Pigs*. [16]

A very worthy Person, *a true Lover of his Country*, and whose Virtues I highly esteem, was lately pleased, in discoursing on this Matter, to offer a Refinement upon my Scheme. He said, that many Gentlemen of this Kingdom, having of late destroyed their Deer; he conceived, that the Want of Venison might be well supplied by the Bodies of young Lads and Maidens, not exceeding fourteen Years of Age, nor under twelve; so great a Number of both Sexes in every County being now ready to starve, for Want of Work and Service: And these to be disposed of by their Parents, if alive, or otherwise by their nearest Relations. But with due Deference to so excellent a Friend, and so deserving a Patriot, I cannot be altogether in his Sentiments. For as to the Males, my *American* Acquaintance assured me from frequent Experience, that their Flesh was generally tough and lean, like that of our School-boys, by continual Exercise; and their Taste disagreeable; and to fatten them would not answer the Charge. Then, as to the Females, it would, I think, with humble Submission, *be a Loss to the Publick*, because they soon would become Breeders themselves: And besides it is not improbable, that some scrupulous People might be apt to censure such a Practice (although indeed very unjustly) as a little bordering upon Cruelty; which, I confess, hath always been with me the strongest Objection against any Project, how well so-ever intended. [17]

But in order to justify my Friend; he confessed, that this Expedient was put into his Head by the famous *Salmanaazor*, a Native of the Island *Formosa*, who came from thence to *London*, above twenty Years ago, and in Conversation told my Friend, that in his Country, when any young Person happened to be put to Death, the

Executioner sold the Carcase to *Persons of Quality,* as a prime Dainty; and that, in his Time, the Body of a plump Girl of fifteen, who was crucified for an Attempt to poison the Emperor, was sold to his Imperial *Majesty's prime Minister of State,* and other great *Mandarines* of the Court, *in Joints from the Gibbet,* at Four hundred Crowns. Neither indeed can I deny, that if the same Use were made of several plump young Girls in this Town, who, without one single Groat to their Fortunes, cannot stir Abroad without a Chair, and appear at a *Play-house,* and *Assemblies* in foreign Fineries, which they never will pay for; the Kingdom would not be the worse. [18]

Some Persons of a desponding Spirit are in great Concern about that vast Number of poor People, who are Aged, Diseased, or Maimed; and I have been desired to employ my Thoughts what Course may be taken, to ease the Nation of so grievous an Incumbrance. But I am not in the least Pain upon that Matter; because it is very well known, that they are every Day *dying,* and *rotting,* by *Cold* and *Famine,* and *Filth,* and *Vermin,* as fast as can be reasonably expected. And as to the younger Labourers, they are now in almost as hopeful a Condition: They cannot get Work, and consequently pine away for Want of Nourishment, to a Degree, that if at any Time they are accidentally hired to common Labour, they have not Strength to perform it; and thus the Country, and themselves, are in a fair Way of being soon delivered from the Evils to come. [19]

CONFIRMATION

I have too long digressed; and therefore shall return to my Subject. I think the Advantages by the Proposal which I have made, are obvious, and many, as well as of the highest Importance. [20]

For, *First,* as I have already observed, it would greatly lessen *the Number of Papists,* with whom we are yearly over-run; being the principal Breeders of the Nation, as well as our most dangerous Enemies; and who stay at home on Purpose, with a Design *to deliver the Kingdom to the Pretender;* hoping to take their Advantage by the Absence *of so many good Protestants,* who have chosen rather to leave their Country, then stay at home, and pay Tithes against their Conscience, to an idolatrous *Episcopal Curate.* [21]

Secondly, The poorer Tenants will have something valuable of their own; which, by Law, may be made liable to Distress, and help to pay their Landlord's Rent; their Corn and Cattle being already seized, and *Money a Thing unknown.* [22]

Thirdly, Whereas the Maintenance of an Hundred Thousand Children, from two Years old, and upwards, cannot be computed at less than ten Shillings a Piece *per Annum,* the Nation's Stock will be thereby encreased Fifty Thousand Pounds *per Annum;* besides the Profit of a new Dish, introduced to the Tables of all *Gentlemen of Fortune* in the Kingdom, who have any Refinement in Taste; and the Money will circulate among ourselves, the Goods being entirely of our own Growth and Manufacture. [23]

Fourthly, The constant Breeders, besides the Gain of Eight Shillings *Sterling per Annum,* by the Sale of their Children, will be rid of the Charge of maintaining them after the first Year. [24]

Fifthly, This Food would likewise bring great *Custom to Taverns,* where the Vintners will certainly be so prudent, as to procure the best Receipts for dressing it to Perfection; and consequently, have their Houses frequented by all the *fine Gentlemen,* who justly value themselves upon their Knowledge in good Eating; and a skilful Cook, who understands how to oblige his Guests, will contrive to make it as expensive as they please. [25]

Sixthly, This would be a great Inducement to Marriage, which all wise Nations have either encouraged by Rewards, or enforced by Laws and Penalties. It would encrease the Care and Tenderness of Mothers towards their Children, when they were sure of a Settlement for Life, to the poor Babes, provided in some Sort by the Publick, to their annual Profit instead of Expence. We should soon see an honest Emulation among the married Women, *which of them could bring the fattest Child to the Market.* Men would become as *fond* of their Wives, during the Time of their Pregnancy, as they are now of their *Mares* in Foal, their *Cows* in Calf, or *Sows* when they are ready to farrow; nor offer to beat or kick them, (as it is too *frequent* a Practice) for fear of a Miscarriage. [26]

Many other Advantages might be enumerated. For Instance, the Addition of some Thousand Carcasses in our Exportation of barrelled Beef: The Propagation of *Swines Flesh,* and Improvement in the Art of making good *Bacon;* so much wanted among us by the great Destruction of *Pigs,* too frequent at our Tables, and are no way comparable in Taste, or Magnificence, to a well-grown fat yearly Child; which, roasted whole, will make a considerable Figure at a *Lord Mayor's Feast,* or any other publick Entertainment. But this, and many others, I omit; being studious of Brevity. [27]

Supposing that one Thousand Families in this City, would be constant Customers for Infants Flesh; besides others who might have it at *merry Meetings,* particularly at *Weddings* and *Christenings;* I compute that *Dublin* would take off, annually, about Twenty Thousand Carcasses; and the rest of the Kingdom (where probably they will be sold somewhat cheaper) the remaining Eighty Thousand. [28]

REFUTATION

I can think of no one Objection, that will possibly be raised against this Proposal; unless it should be urged, that the Number of People will be thereby much lessened in the Kingdom. This I freely own; and it was indeed one principal Design in offering it to the World. I desire the Reader will observe, that I calculate my Remedy *for this one individual Kingdom of* IRELAND, *and for no other that ever was, is, or I think ever can be upon Earth.* Therefore, let no Man talk to me of other Expedients: *Of taxing our Absentees at five shillings a Pound: Of using neither Cloaths, nor Houshold Furniture; except what is of our own Growth and Manufacture: Of utterly rejecting the Materials and Instruments that promote foreign Luxury: Of curing the Expensiveness of Pride, Vanity, Idleness, and Gaming in our Women: Of introducing a Vein of Parsimony, Prudence and Temperance: Of learning to love our Country; wherein we differ even from* LAPLANDERS, *and the Inhabitants of* TOPINAMBOO: *Of quitting our Animosities, and Factions; nor act any longer like the* JEWS, *who were murdering one another at the very Moment their City was taken: Of being a little cautious not to sell our Country and Consciences for nothing: Of teaching Landlord to have, at least, one Degree of Mercy towards their Tenants.* Lastly, *Of putting a Spirit of Honesty, Industry, and Skill into our Shop-keepers; who, if a Resolution could now be taken to buy only our native Goods, would immediately unite to cheat and exact upon us in the Price, the Measure, and the Goodness; nor could ever yet be brought to make one fair Proposal of just Dealing, though often and earnestly invited to it.* [29]

Therefore I repeat; let no Man talk to me of these and the like Expedients; till he hath, at least, a Glimpse of Hope, that there will ever be some hearty and sincere Attempt to put *them in Practice.* [30]

PERORATION

But, as to my self; having been wearied out for many Years with offering vain, idle, visionary Thoughts; and at length utterly despairing of Success, I fortunately fell upon this Proposal; which, as it is wholly new, so it hath something *solid* and *real*, of no Expence, and little Trouble, full in our own Power; and whereby we can incur no Danger in *disobliging* ENGLAND: For, this Kind of Commodity will not bear Exportation; the Flesh being of too tender a Consistence, to admit a long Continuance in Salt; *although, perhaps, I could name a Country, which would be glad to eat up our whole Nation without it.* [31]

After all, I am not so violently bent upon my own Opinion, as to reject any Offer proposed by wise Men, which shall be found equally innocent, cheap, easy, and effectual. But before something of that Kind shall be advanced, in Contradiction to my Scheme, and offering a better; I desire the Author, or Authors, will be pleased maturely to consider two Points. *First*, As Things now stand, how they will be able to find Food and Raiment, for a Hundred Thousand useless Mouths and Backs? And *secondly*, There being a round Million of Creatures in human Figure, throughout this Kingdom; whose whole Subsistence, put into a common Stock, would leave them in Debt two Millions of Pounds *Sterling*; adding those, who are Beggars by Profession, to the Bulk of Farmers, Cottagers, and Labourers, with their Wives and Children, who are Beggars in Effect; I desire those Politicians, who dislike my Overture, and may perhaps be so bold to attempt an Answer, that they will first ask the Parents of these Mortals, Whether they would not, at this Day, think it a great Happiness to have been sold for Food at a Year old, in the Manner I prescribe; and thereby have avoided such a perpetual Scene of Misfortunes, as they have since gone through; by the *Oppression of Landlords;* the Impossibility of paying Rent, without Money or Trade; the Want of common Sustenance, with neither House nor Cloaths, to cover them from the Inclemencies of the Weather; and the most inevitable Prospect of intailing the like, or greater Miseries upon their Breed for ever. [32]

I profess, in the Sincerity of my Heart, that I have not the least personal Interest, in endeavouring to promote this necessary Work; having no other Motive than the *publick Good of my Country, by advancing our Trade, providing for Infants, relieving the Poor, and giving some Pleasure to the Rich.* I have no Children, by which I can propose to get a single Penny; the youngest being nine Years old, and my Wife past Childbearing. [33]

3295 words, 33 paragraphs

Finif

Writing Suggestions for Argumentation

First review the introduction to Part 4, Argumentation, and the segments in the Glossary on the **argumentative paragraph** and **essay.**

The Factual and Ethical Argument

The following topics are in pairs or triplets. The first of each pair may be proven as a factual argument; the second requires the different proof of the ethical argument. It is possible to combine each pair into a longer, documented argument paper.

1-a. Moral standards have changed demonstrably in the last twenty-five years.

1-b. The recent change in moral standards is detrimental to the United States (or the world, or . . .)

1-c. The refreshing change in moral standards will benefit the United States.

2-a. America is becoming a country of spectators. (Limit the data to one area for a shorter paper, i.e., sports, *or* television, *or* motion pictures. Combine many areas for the longer paper.)

2-b. The increase in spectator events in America will surely prove to be beneficial/detrimental (pick *one*).

3-a. The more democratic a government becomes the less efficient it is, but the more fair and just.

3-b. Democratic governments are too inefficient to endure.

3-c. Democratic governments are the only ones for free men.

The Cause and Effect Pattern

1. Unethical business practices must lead inevitably to unethical practices in government.
2. Paying athletes (or entertainers) so much more than doctors (or scientists) will eventually elevate fun over necessity. (Define all terms in this one.)
3. Students who cheat in school will develop habits of cheating that will continue the rest of their lives.

The Prediction Pattern of Argument

These are open arguments; the final element may be inserted to suit your own prejudice, predeliction, or politics.

1. The continued liberation of women will lead to ________.
2. Pornography should be ________.
3. The practice of keeping animals as pets is ________.
4. Environmental pollution will ________.
5. Affluence and wealth of a country will lead to its subsequent ________.
6. If none of these topics appeals to you, try any of the suggestions that have been listed as examples under the explanations of *ethical argument* or *factual argument* on pages 228 and 229.

glossary

Throughout the text are words, phrases, rhetorical or grammatical terms that have an entry in the Glossary. They are distinguished by being in **boldface** type. Sometimes the boldface reference may **not** be identical to the Glossary entry. For example, **deductive** may be in boldface type; the nearest entry in the Glossary is **deduction,** so check there for information. Similarly, **connote** or **connotative** will be found under **connotation.**

Where to Find the Information

This Glossary is limited to general entries useful to the student writer. It is not intended to be a text on logic, on rhetoric, or on grammar and usage. There are readily available references for the student who wants more information or who is seeking answers to some of the questions in the text.

General

The Holt Guide to English (Irmscher) is a most comprehensive handbook. It contains sections on rhetoric, paragraph development, logic, and language history and has good material on style, grammar, usage, and punctuation.
The World Almanac and Book of Facts contains a remarkable collection of data on almost every subject.

Words and Phrases, General

The American Heritage Dictionary of the English Language is recommended for college students, for it still gives labels such as "colloquial" or "slang" that are useful.
Webster's Third New International Dictionary contains nearly half a million words. It is still *the* dictionary.
Dictionary of Slang and Unconventional English (Partridge) gives most of the slang and street terms.
A Dictionary of Foreign Words and Phrases (Bliss) will help the

student to get the meaning of the occasional foreign word in head-note or essay.

Words and Phrases, History and Usage

Oxford English Dictionary (12 vols.) shows the first use of the word in print and its subsequent changes in meaning and spelling as well as its origin.
Origins: A Short Etymological Dictionary of Modern English (Partridge) does exactly what the title states; it gives the origin of a great many modern words.
Current American Usage (Bryant) tells the way educated Americans use words and phrases. It includes a great many idioms.
American-English Usage (Nicholsen) and *Dictionary of Modern English Usage* (Fowler) are also good.

People

Who's Who (British); *Who's Who in America; Who's Who in the West;* and *Who's Who in Education* give brief biographies of prominent people.
Current Biography gives brief biographies of people who are in the news for various reasons.
Dictionary of American Biography covers deceased Americans.
Dictionary of National Biography does the same for England.

Literary References

A Glossary of Literary Terms (Abrams) has a full treatment of poetic, dramatic, and literary terminology.
Handbook to Literature (Thrall and Hibbard) is even more comprehensive than Abrams.
The Reader's Encyclopedia (Benet) is also a fine general reference for literary matters, but its two volumes make it bulkier than the paperback Abrams.

There are, of course, dozens more—Bartlett's *Quotations,* Beardsley's *Thinking Straight* on logic, and encyclopedias on every subject imaginable. When a subject is not covered fully enough in the following glossary, the student is urged to use one of these standard references to extend his knowledge.

Abstract words are words that refer to highly general ideas such as love, patriotism, democracy. The opposite of abstract is **concrete.** Students tend to be too abstract in their writing. "I am going to learn much and be a success" is too abstract to be meaningful. "I am planning to study mortuary science and earn $50,000.00 a year" is a bit more concrete.

Abstraction is the process of separating qualities from the physical entity to which they belong. We take a pig, a duck, a chicken, and from them we *abstract* the concept of "livestock." **An abstraction** is the name for such a general word. Some abstractions we use everyday are: GNP, the Establishment, love, the media. There is a sequence of abstraction (sometimes called *levels*) from very specific to very abstract; for example, my bungalow (specific, one single item) → bungalow → house → dwelling → shelter → property → asset. *Asset* is far more abstract than *house*. See also **Abstract** and **Concrete** for use in writing.

Ad hominem fallacy. See **Fallacy.**

Ad verecundiam fallacy. See **Fallacy.**

Allegory. See **Narration.**

Alliteration is the device, much used in poetry, of repeating the initial sounds of several successive words—for example, calm and collected, tried and true, seldom sought seldom seen. Sparingly done, it makes prose effective; overdone, it makes prose trite.

Allusion. See **Figures of speech.**

Analogy is an extended comparison of two persons, ideas, or items to clarify or illustrate. Usually a familiar thing is used to clarify an unfamiliar, though not always. Life may be compared to walking a road and taking various turnings. Springtime and youth may be compared. Analogy is often used as argument, but it should never be accepted as proof or evidence; it is only clarification. "A man gets old, fails and dies; a nation that is old is about to fail and die!" "The brain is a kind of organic computer" (or vice versa).

Analyzing essays is an efficient method of understanding what the author intended. **Analysis** means "taking apart." To analyze an essay, the reader must find the author's **thesis** and see how well it is substantiated. To determine whether or not the thesis is well supported, the reader will examine each **coordinate point** and the **details** used as specific examples. A convenient shape (or format) for an analysis is the *rhetorical outline*.

Bibliographical data: Author, title, date.
Thesis: State author's thesis in one sentence.
Coordinate point 1: State main support in one sentence.
(*Coordinate point n*: As many C.P.'s as necessary.)
Detail: Note the author's concrete examples.
Note: Comment on introduction or conclusion if outside the body of the essay. Explain placement of *thesis* if unusual, and mark any elements off the topic.

Analysis as development is a standard method of exposition. There are four kinds of analysis.

1. **Technical analysis** answers the question "How is it put together?" Often simply an objective description, it may be as complicated as an analysis of a machine, a computer, a living creature. The purpose of the analyzer often determines the kind of analysis. An advertisement offering a car for sale might differ greatly from an honest listing of the components.
2. **Functional analysis** answers the question "How does it work?" Often the parts are shown (**technical analysis**), and then their functions are described. It is possible to analyze the function of a part; for example, "The eccentric on a cam shaft lifts the valves in a pre-determined sequence."
3. **Process analysis** usually tells the reader how to perform an action, make an item, produce a result. A good process analysis carefully notes the sequence of each step and clearly details the procedure. This type of analysis answers the question "How is it made?" or "How is it done?"
4. **Causal analysis** answers the question "What caused it?" It works like **cause and effect** thinking but starts with the result and shows the various causes. Carefully used, causal analysis is logically precise enough to predict that for a given cause, a specific event must follow. Generally used, causal analysis means the taking apart of something to see what caused the malfunction or the effective functioning.

Anecdote is a brief story of an event. Anecdotes are used to illustrate and to clarify. Often a humorous anecdote is used as an introduction to gain the reader's good will.

Annotation means clarification or explanation of difficult material by the use of critical commentary or notes.

Appeal to authority fallacy. See **Fallacy, ad vericundiam.**

Argument is one of the four main modes of rhetoric. Argument begins in conflict and ends in resolution. The purpose of argument is to seek agreement through an appeal to reason

Argumentative essay can be constructed by following a simple procedure: *PREMISE* is clearly stated.

OPPOSITION's best argument is given, countered.

PREMISE is firmly stated, and the opposition's argument is destroyed.

This pattern is the same for the **argumentative paragraph.** Witness the outline below.

Kill The Killers?

THESIS PARAGRAPH: In spite of arguments to the contrary by well-meaning people, capital punishment should be abolished in every Christian, civilized country for five valid reasons.

PARAGRAPH ONE: (First reason)

PREMISE: It is no deterrent to crimes of passion.

DETAIL: Specific data; F.B.I. examples.

OPPOSITION: Those who kill in the heat of passion should pay the same penalty.

PREMISE: (and counter) A lifetime of prison is just as heavy a penalty without bloodshed.

DETAIL: Statement by "lifer."

PARAGRAPH TWO: (Second reason)

PREMISE: There is no evidence that capital punishment or its threat stops killers.

DETAIL: Statistics; statement of killer.

OPPOSITION: It is impossible to know how many people did not kill because of fear of the death penalty.

PREMISE: However, a comparison of states with and without capital punishment shows similar rates of crime.

PARAGRAPH THREE: It is no deterrent to political assassination. (Develop using the same pattern.)

PARAGRAPH FOUR: Capital punishment is incorrectable in case of error. (Develop using same pattern.)

PARAGRAPH FIVE: It is contrary to the word of God. (Develop using the same pattern.)

PARAGRAPH SIX: Conclusion.

The number of paragraphs will vary with the number of points to be made to support the argument.

Argumentative paragraph is designed for the student who needs to develop an argument and wants a standard format as a guide. Read the following sample paragraph and analysis.

Kill the Killers?

Capital punishment is a most immoral act (1). There are those who say it is necessary to execute a murderer, for then he will kill no more (2). If one man is to die for killing, should not his killer, also, be killed (3)? There would be no end to the sequence of "executions" until the lone surviving executioner stood before God (4). Capital punishment must be abolished; life imprisonment is as sound a way to isolate the murderer, and no blood is shed (5).

PREMISE is clearly stated in sentence (1).
OPPOSITION's best argument is given next in (2) and then it is countered in (3) and (4).
PREMISE is firmly restated and the opposition's argument destroyed.

This format will serve the novice as well as the skilled rhetorician. It will serve for a paragraph or for a long essay (see **Argumentative essay**). Just remember **POP!**
Premise—Opposition—Premise

Article is the term used for **essays** appearing in newspapers and magazines. Articles are usually impersonal, more factual than other types of essays.

Attacking the man fallacy. See **Fallacy, ad hominem.**

Attitude. See **Tonc.**

Balanced sentence is a sentence in which the thoughts are arranged in similar structure. For example, Caesar's "I came, I saw, I conquered." See **Parallel structure.**

Begging the question. See **Fallacy, petitio principii.**

Causal Analysis. See **Analysis as development.**

Cause and effect is both a method of development and a method for analysis in which the emphasis is placed on the causal relationship between two (or more) events. It is far trickier than it appears, for most events have a multitude of causes. There may be *immediate* causes (bombing Pearl Harbor made the United States enter World War II) and *ultimate* causes (the Japanese Empire was running out of raw materials and markets). A fairly safe method is to use a sequential or **inductive** procedure. Show, for example, that students who do not study get low marks and learn very little, that athletes who practice regularly tend to win more often than those who do not, or that drinking large amounts of beer results in headache and brownmouth. In spite of its tendency toward simplification and generalization, cause and effect is a fine method of organizing a paragraph or an essay.

Cause and Effect Shape

THESIS: April showers bring May flowers.

SENTENCE 1  Apparent primary cause.

SENTENCE 2 Seeming immediate result.

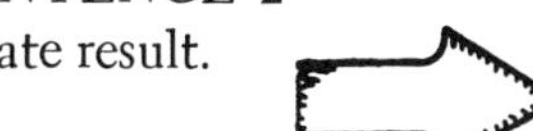

CONCLUSION (conditional statement): "Without the showers the flowers probably would not have bloomed."

Factors not considered; the necessary seeds, the intervening sunshine, condition of the soil.

Given the cause (showers) other possible results could be flooding (washing seeds away) or erosion.

Future results might be June drying of the foliage followed by July brush fires. Examine cause and effect statements very carefully!

Circular reasoning fallacy. See **Fallacy, Petitio principii.**

Classification or *taxonomy* is the science of *putting things into groups based upon similarities* so that we can understand the diversity of the world. All reasoning beings classify; the field mouse that fails to distinguish class *owl* from class *duck* is soon reclassified as prey. Classes may be huge (living or nonliving) or small (left-handed, red-headed), but (1) all members must be included, (2) subclasses must not overlap, and (3) the basis must not change or shift.

EXAMPLE FOR CLARIFICATION:

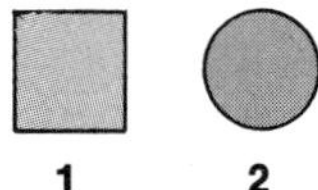

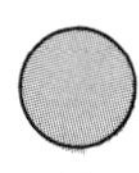

1 2 3 4 5 6

a. What class are all six items members of?
b. What subclass contains 2 and 5?
c. How many classes can item 4 be placed in?
d. Classify using two points of similarity instead of one.
e. Are there any other possible patterns of classification?

Answers:

a. Geometric shapes, or just shapes.
b. Circles or round shapes.
c. Squares; striped things; geometric shapes.
d. Angular and dark (1, 6); angular and striped (3, 4).
e. Dark or filled in (1, 5, 6); squares; triangles.

Cliché actually means a *stereotype plate* (French *clicher*) used to reproduce an illustration over and over again—hence, an overused phrase. Also called *trite* or *hackneyed*, examples are "tried and true," "heart of gold," and "In our modern age of today it is better than ever to be safe than sorry and save the wear and tear of working one's fingers to the bone." If you have heard a descriptive phrase often before, do not use it unless you deliberately wish to call up a standard response in your reader.

Coherence is sticking together, literally. In writing, the word refers to the clear relationship of sentence to sentence in a paragraph, or paragraph to paragraph in an essay. In addition to unity of content, coherence may be achieved by five techniques.

1. Putting the parts in a meaningful sequence.
   a. Chronological order (First, second, third . . .)
   b. Logical sequence
   c. Order of importance
2. Repetition of key words in subsequent parts of the paragraph or essay.
3. Use of pronouns like "it," "he," "this," or "those" to tie sentences together.
4. Deliberate use of **transitions.**
5. Use of **parallel structure.**

Colloquialisms are expressions (from colloquy, a "conversation") or written words that seek to imitate that style. Contractions, folksy expressions, slang words, and cute expressions are not used in standard or formal writing. Check a usage manual or dictionary when in doubt.

Comparison and **contrast** (compare *or* contrast). These methods are usually linked but may be used separately. A careful user of language distinguishes between them clearly: to **compare** means to show how things are alike; to **contrast** means to show how things differ. To show similarities or differences is a most effective way of developing an essay or a paragraph. Beware of a common problem: do not attempt to compare items that do not belong to the same class (see **Classification**). No one would compare "monarchy" and "aluminum," but some might try, wrongly, to compare "monarchy" and "capitalism." (The first is class *form of government* and the second is class *economic system.*) If we are careful users of our language we will compare monarchy only with other forms of government—democracy, oligarchy. We will compare capitalism only with other economic systems—socialism, communism.

There are two basic shapes for paragraphs that compare or contrast. Suppose we wish to compare (or contrast) *trucks* to *tractors* and have, for example, three elements.

Shape 1

THESIS: Tractors are similar to trucks in three important functions.

Sentence 1

Function One

Sentence 2

Function Two

Sentence 3

Function Three

CONCLUSION: . . .

Shape 2

THESIS: Tractors are similar to trucks in three important functions.

Sentence 1

Sentence 2

CONCLUSION: . . .

Shape 1 enables the reader to understand each point as the writer makes it; shape 2 emphasizes the part placed last. Either shape works well for both comparing and contrasting and, in a longer paper, could be combined. Naturally, in a longer essay the sentences would grow into paragraphs, but the basic shapes would remain the same.

Completeness is one of the elements of a well-written paragraph.

Completeness means that there is nothing introduced in the **topic sentence** that is not developed in the body of the paragraph. The same criterion applies to an **essay** and its **thesis.**

Conclusions are specific methods to end a paragraph or an essay without just trickling off.

A good conclusion is deliberately written; it is not a happy chance. Common ineffective conclusions may (a) introduce a new topic, (b) apologize, (c) tack on an afterthought, or (d) use an inappropriate moral. Here are nine effective concluding devices.

1. Repeat **thesis** or briefly summarize argument.
2. Close with a striking **example** or **illustration.**
3. Use a parting **inference.**
4. In **narration** end at the climax.
5. In **narration** use the dénouement.
6. Present the solution to the problem.
7. End with a forecast.
8. Close with a parting question.
9. Have a final call to action!

Be sure that the ending fits the content of the essay.

Concrete is the antonym of **abstract.** As used by writers it means specific **details,** actual names of places, true events, real people. The sentence "I have transportation" is not concrete. The sentence "I have a blue ten-speed Schwinn" is concrete. A craftsman pins down his **abstractions** with concrete **examples.** A good freshman paper should be 60 percent concrete data. Examples can be worked into the structure of a sentence: "We went to the store" can be changed to "My grandmother and I rode to Safeway on her Honda 450 to get a sixpack." Effective writing is both abstract and concrete, moving back and forth as necessary for communication.

Connotation is any meaning a word might have in addition to its **denotation.** There is cultural connotation as well as personal. The word "pig" has cultural connotations of dirty, messy, generally sloppy. "Piggish" and "pig sty" are common terms for "mess" used by people who have been no closer to a pig than morning bacon. "Pig" may also have personal connotations. It is a common term for police in slum and ghetto parts of our cities. It is just possible that "pig" might have positive emotional tones for some people. (As sweet as a pig?) Boar has a different connotation than "pig," as does "swine." "Hog" has different connotations than any of the other terms, yet it is possible that they all refer to the identical mammal in reality. See **Denotation.**

Context means the surroundings, specifically the words leading up to and coming after a particular word or passage.

Contrast. See **Comparison and contrast.**

Controlling purpose is a more generalized term for **thesis.**

Coordinate point is a useful term given to one of an author's main or *primary supports.* It is called "coordinate" because all points are at the same level of **abstraction.** A coordinate point is, in turn, supported with specific examples, details, or data.

Dead metaphor means a metaphor that was once a striking image but has now become a common noun or phrase. Such ex-vivid images as "mouth of a river" or "hands of a clock," have become standard usage. In contrast, it is the *dying* metaphors that are **trite.**

Deduction or **deductive logic** is formal logic that follows a specific pattern called a *syllogism.* The classic example is:

All men are mortal. (Major premise) all A is B.
Socrates is a man. (Minor premise) c is A.
Socrates is mortal. (Conclusion) c is B.

The syllogism may also be shown graphically by the use of circles.

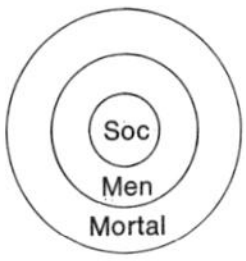

Soc
Men
Mortal

A deductive paragraph or essay would first prove the major premise or idea; it would then offer proof for the minor premise; it would end with the proven conclusion. If the major and the minor are valid and true, the conclusion must be true.

The syllogism may be developed in several other forms.

Universal—Affirmative: All men are mortal.
Universal—Negative: No men are mortal.
Particular—Affirmative: Some men are mortal.
Particular—Negative: Some men are not mortal.

For a complete discussion of logic see one of the books mentioned at the beginning of the Glossary or a standard encyclopedia.

Definition means to set forth the meaning of a word, to describe exactly, to set limits, to explain, or to interpret. It is primarily a request to share experience. If I use the word "witch" and you have known the word before, we will communicate where our experiences overlap.

This is the witch that is communicated. If you have no experience with the term I use, you request definition. There are three basic ways to define: to *SHOW*, to *TELL*, and to *DIRECT*.

To *SHOW*:
1. Point to the thing.
2. Perform the act; do the deed.

To *TELL*:
1. Give a synonym (perhaps an antonym).
2. Use classical definition.
    a. Classify (place term in a class).
    b. Differentiate (tell how it differs).

Example:

To be defined	*Genus*	*differentia*
kitty	furry animal	that purrs
skunk	furry animal	that stinks
man	animal	that reasons
democracy	form of government	where people hold power

Note: a. Be certain to place item in a class.
(*Not*: "Happiness is a warm puppy." There is no class of things called "warmpuppy" of which happiness is a subset.)
b. Do not make the *genus* too large. (*Hippie* is a word.)
c. Make *differentia* as specific as possible.
("*Stoonch* is a game played with a ball" is no help.)
d. Avoid excessive technicality. (A hexagon is a hexiform polygon.) ⬡
e. Do not use the term in its own definition. (Certified mail is mail that is certified.)

To *DIRECT*: Give a set of directions that will lead the questioner to have the same set of experiences. The *directed* definition is the one used in science (experiments) and medicine (prescriptions).

Denotation is the direct, explicit, literal meaning of a word. It may be the dictionary definition without any emotional or subjective overtones. The word "pig," for example denotes a cloven hoofed, bristly haired, short-legged mammal of the family *suidae*. See also **Connotation.**

Description is that form of discourse which presents a picture or information about an object or an event. It usually presents *realistic* (purely factual) information or *impressionistic* (evaluative and subjective) information. It often contains **figurative language.** See Part 2 introduction for a fuller explanation.

Details are the specific examples and the data an author uses to support his **thesis** or his **coordinate points.**

Diction means a writer's choice of words. His **style** is a reflection of his diction. Words are selected with an awareness of both **denotative** and **connotative** meaning. Words should be effective, clear, and purposeful. Depending on his purpose, a writer may call a nearly adult *Homo sapiens* a *youth, teen-ager, kid, youngster, young man,* or *fellow.*

Discourse is any organized communication, oral, written, or electronic, that is put in one of the four forms or modes of discourse: **narration, description, exposition,** or **argumentation.**

Effect. See **Cause and effect.**

Emphasis refers to the deliberate construction of a sentence, a paragraph, or an essay so that one part stands out or is stronger than another. One obvious way to make one idea seem more important than another is to make it bigger, to use more space to tell about it. Another way would be to repeat the idea several times in a given essay. A third method, somewhat more subtle, is to place the most important idea last. For example, compare "While we slumbered the rain came pouring in" with "Even though the rain came pouring in, we slumbered on." In the first, the emphasis is the rain; in the second, we feel the tiredness of the slumberers more. See **Periodic sentence.**

Enumeration is the making of a list in some kind of rational sequence. It is often used as a type of definition. "What are marsupials? Let me enumerate: opossums, kangaroos, koala bears, bandicoots and wombats."

Equivocation. See **Fallacy.**

Essay means, primarily, an attempt. It is a composition in prose on a single topic. It usually expresses the author's personal views. Some essays are formal, and they range to very informal or personal. The type that is less personal and more objective may be called an **article.**

Euphemism is the use of gentler words for harsh events or things. "Passed away" for "died," "mortician" for "embalmer," "sanitary engineer" for "janitor."

Evaluation is a type of criticism that tries to determine the worth or value of a piece of writing. Poetry, prose, fiction and nonfiction all have different methods of evaluation. When a student evaluates a piece of exposition, he finds the **thesis,** determines whether it is validated or not, and decides how worthwhile it is to present. He also considers the author's purpose in writing the essay. A fine shape to follow for evaluation follows.

1. Write the bibliographical data (author, title, other).
2. Write the **thesis statement.**
3. Write the main **coordinate points.**
4. Write a statement telling whether the coordinate points are **valid.**
   a. Do they actually support the thesis?
   b. Are they accurate, true, up to date, logical?
   c. Be sure to tell if they have no relation to the thesis or are hokum.
5. Write a statement telling whether you agree with the thesis *on the basis of the validity of the support*! Do not agree just because of a previous emotional set, knowledge, or evidence.
6. Write a statement telling what the essay was worth and to whom? Did the author fulfill his purpose? Did he say anything new or valuable? Did he phrase an old truth in a new or exciting way?
7. If you feel competent, tell if the essay is well written. Stylistic evaluation is very difficult, so be specific.

Evidence refers to the data, the examples upon which a judgment or conclusion is based. Evidence constitutes the **details** of an essay sought by the reader and used by the writer. There are four main types of valid evidence.

1. Use data, facts, statistics, natural phenomena. A scholar is honest and does not distort his data.
2. Use reliable authorities.
   a. From the proper field. Be wary of sociological advice from a television comedian or medical instruction from an English professor.
   b. Relevant to the audience. An edict on correct behavior by the Khedive would little impress an audience of southern Baptists. Make sure the authority is timely, too.
   c. Well regarded by others in the field of expertise. Be wary of oddballs.
   d. With acceptable motives for making such a statement.
3. Use valid **inferences, deductive** and **inductive generalizations,** and **conclusions** drawn from factual data and authoritative statements.
4. **Define,** define, define. As Plato said, it clarifies the argument.

Naturally, the careful writer and canny reader will be aware of and avoid all **fallacies** and also clever writers using **analogy** and **metaphors** as evidence; these devices should be regarded as clarification, not as evidence.

Examples are the most common method of developing a paragraph. To *exemplify* means to give clear, specific instances to illustrate a general idea. An example is a particular member of a class chosen to represent the whole class. The Derringer might exemplify the whole class of pocket guns; the Mazda R-3 rotary engine exemplifies Japanese mechanical techniques; the events (or an event) in your English class could be an example of higher education in America. Be very careful, though, as you read and as you write, to make sure the examples are valid. In the three instances above, the first is accurate (the Derringer), the second less valid (the rotary engine was invented by Wankel, a German), and the third might not be typical at all colleges elsewhere. Using examples is one kind of **illustration.**

Exposition is one of the main forms of **discourse;** it explains or informs. Eighty-six percent of all college papers are expository in nature. The six main methods of exposition are explained in this Glossary and in the text. They are **analysis** (which includes **cause and effect**), **classification, comparison and contrast, definition, description,** and **illustration** (including use of **example**). For a fuller treatment of exposition see Part 3 introduction.

Fable. See **Narrative.**

Fallacy is incorrect thinking or distortion in the process of thinking. Most fallacies are based on *insufficient evidence, irrelevance* evidence not related to the problem at hand, and *ambiguity* or confusion of meaning. The college student should recognize the more common fallacies in his reading and learn to avoid them in his writing. Fallacies are usually known by their Latin names. An approximate translation follows.

Ad hominem ("attack the man") is the tactic of trying to discredit the individual who makes the statement rather than the statement itself. It is a frequent political fallacy. For example: "Since Oscar Wilde was a homosexual his poetry must be terrible." "How could we believe Candidate Jones when his grandfather was a known atheist?"

Ad verecundiam (Appeal to authority, improper authority) is to cite testimony of someone who is not qualified to be an authority. He may be an authority in another field, but not in the one under discussion. For example: A famous baseball player recommends a headache medicine. A competent general advises everybody to exercise. A glamorous movie star recommends a mechanic.

Equivocation (double meaning) is the use, deliberate or accidental, of a word in a different sense from that intended by the user. This fallacy is possible because most words have more than one meaning. For example: "That was a *bad* movie." ("Immoral, ill-made, out of focus?) "Bring me a bag of *coke.*" (A soft drink, a drug, some charcoal?)

Hasty generalization (unqualified generalization) is a conclusion based on too few bits of evidence. An example might be hearing a few college students using profanity and making the generalization that all college students "talk dirty." Most statements that use the words "all" or "everybody" are unqualified generalizations. For example: "*Everybody* should exercise daily." Not true for cardiac patients, among many others. The bulk of our prejudicial statements are hasty generalizations.

Non sequitur ("does not follow") is the fallacy in which the conclusion does not follow from the data. For example: "She is ugly and stupid; she must have been raised in a slum." "Small children are silent in the presence of their elders, so they must be unable to speak."

Petitio principii ("begging the question" or circular reasoning) is using as proof or evidence the same element that was stated in the proposition. For example: "Faith is universal, for everyone has faith in something." "You will like the food in the cafeteria because it will taste good to you."

Post hoc ergo propter hoc ("after this, therefore because of this"). This fallacy is one that has no common English name so we tend to use the Latin, *post hoc.* This is the fallacy that the first event in time caused the event that followed it. For example: "Every time I wash my car it seems to rain." "A white pigeon flew overhead and I failed the test; white pigeons cause bad luck."

Tu quoque ("you are another") is the answering of a charge with a countercharge. The most common is, "Why call me a cheater? You cheated on that Math test!"

Others: There are some dozens of others: an appeal to pity rather than reason, the use of force, or threats, claiming that "everybody does it." Read Stuart Chase's entertaining book *Guides To Straight Thinking* for a understandable presentation.

Figurative language. See **Figures of speech.**

Figures of speech means the use of language that reaches beyond the literal meaning of words. The primary use of figures of speech is to make language more colorful, more emphatic, more easily understood. There are dozens of figures of speech, a great many used in poetry. The ones listed here are those that have the greatest value to a prose writer.

Allusion is a hinted or *indirect reference* to a known person, place, or object from history or literature. It is used to evoke quickly an atmosphere or an emotion. For example: "If one face launched a thousand ships, why can't I get a date?" The allusion is to both Helen of Troy and to Marlowe's *Faust*.

Hyperbole is the use of exaggeration for rhetorical or dramatic effect. For example: "Tickets to the New Year's game cost an arm and a leg."

Irony can be either verbal irony or dramatic irony; both use a sense of difference. Verbal irony means to say one thing and mean the opposite. Someone drops a bowl of waffle batter into the silverware drawer. Ironic comment: "That was cleverly done." Dramatic irony occurs when the audience knows something that the character does not know—that Oedipus has killed his father and wed his mother—so the character's statements—Oedipus curses the man who killed his father—become ironic.

Metaphor is one of the basic figures of speech in which two unlike items are compared for the purpose of making an idea or an attitude more clear. "He was a tiger on the football field but a pussycat at a party." That tells as much about "his" behavior as would a thousand words of narration. "He is a pig" is a **metaphor** that clarifies the attitude of the speaker towards "him."

Personification is the giving of human feelings or qualities to a nonhuman thing. For example: "The *cruel* desert parched his skin." "The *sad, sad* cypress drooped their *weary* branches to the ground."

Sarcasm is usually classed as a form of irony, but has as its purpose the wounding of the victim. A statement like, "If I had your skill with words, I'd learn to do something clever with my hands," is sarcastic; it is meant to hurt.

Simile is very like a metaphor, but it uses "like" or "as" to compare. A metaphor would state, "The road is a ribbon of moonlight," while a **simile** would phrase it, "The road is *like* a ribbon of moonlight."

Understatement is a form of **irony** (sometimes called *litotes*) that tends to affirm an idea by denying the opposite. For example, "He was not such a bad actor" implies that he was a good actor.

Flashback is a narrative device in which an author starts his story at a given time—say June 3, 1970—and then jumps, or "flashes," backwards to—say June 3, 1950—for dramatic effect. See Part 1 introduction for a fuller treatment.

Functional analysis. See **Analysis as development.**

Generalization is a statement that covers a great many particular cases. It is a conclusion based on inductive logic (see **Induction**) where sufficient specific examples warrant a true general statement. Some, like "Television is bad for the motion picture theaters" and "Mean people are lonely," are generally true. Some generalizations are always true—"All men living today will die sometime."

Hasty generalization. See **Fallacy.**

Hyperbole. See **Figures of speech.**

Idiom is a phrase or expression that is peculiar to one language; a word for word translation would make no sense in any other language. For example: "Look me up." "That's swell!" or "Knock it off!" They are agreed upon deviations from the standard grammar and may be found at all **levels of usage.**

Illustration is one of the most common methods used in expository writing to explain an idea. The proper use of illustration requires specific or concrete instances, occurrence, facts, conditions (see **Example**). The writer makes a general statement, "The American Indians were badly treated by the United States' government." Then he offers some evidence—"the massacre at Wounded Knee." He may use one excellent illustration (called **example**) or several. A writer may also use **anecdotes** as support for the thesis.

Imagery is an attempt to create an emotion or a sense impression through the use of language. There can be visual images; auditory images; touch, taste, smell images. The image is evoked in the mind of the reader mainly by the use of **figures of speech.**

Impressionistic description. See **Description.**

Induction or **inductive reasoning** is the formation of a general statement after an adequate number of instances have been observed. There are four rules to observe to insure validity of the conclusion.

1. An adequate number of cases must be observed.
2. All of the cases must be typical.
3. Any atypical cases must be explained (not ignored).

4. The conclusion must account for all cases.

When instigated by a hypothesis or a question and carried out by experimentation, induction becomes the scientific method.

Inference is the process of making predictions about the unknown based upon the known. An inference is an educated guess, a statement about the future from present data. We see a house with the grass uncut, paint peeling, dirty windows, newspapers piled up on the porch. We then make **inferences**:

1. The house is empty or abandoned.
2. The people are away on a vacation.
3. The residents are rude, crude, and uncouth.

The effectiveness with which we meet reality is directly proportional to our ability to **infer.** (Do not confuse *infer* with *imply* —see a dictionary.)

Introductions are written deliberately to introduce the topic, to catch the reader's interest, or to limit the subject. Introductions are often written after the body has been finished. Common *ineffective* introductions may: (a) refer to the title, "This topic is an interesting one"; (b) start, "I am going to tell about . . ."; (c) apologize. Here are nine *effective* introductory devices.

1. Open with a striking statistic or **example.**
2. Use a quotation from a famous person.
3. Explain the subject.
4. Open with a brief **narrative.**
5. **Define** strange or special terms.
6. Ask a leading question.
7. Use **comparison.**
8. Use **contrast.**
9. Use a topical reference (to something in the news or an especially catchy song, commercial, film).

Introductions are tailored for the specific subject and the intended audience; they just do not happen.

Irony. See **Figures of speech.**

Jargon generally is used to mean "unintelligible language," but it also has a more precise meaning: it is the specialized vocabulary of a trade, profession, or special group of people. An astronaut might say, "Sequence A-OK, negative abort." A surfer "hangs ten in the curl before he wipes out." A teacher reports to a parent that "Sonny reacts negatively to possession patterns displayed by peers by attempting to encourage multiple ownership" when the kid steals somebody's ball. We use jargon for specific needs, like "mockup," or to show our expertise.

Key words are the main or most important words in a sentence. When they occur in a topic sentence they are often repeated again in the paragraph as a device to gain **coherence.** For example, "Pollution can surely be controlled" has two key words (or terms), "pollution" and "controlled." These words or variants like "polluted," "pollute" or "control, controlling" will be used to hold the paragraph together, to give it **unity.**

Legend. See **Narrative.**

Levels of usage refers to the distinction between non-standard diction and usage and Uniform Standard American. We are gradually developing in this country, like it or not, a Uniform Standard American dialect, which we shall call Standard. It has three levels: *formal, written informal,* and *spoken informal* (see **Colloquial**). In college written English the proper level is *written informal;* very rarely will formal English be used by the student. Avoid words labeled "informal" or "colloquial" when writing. There is another level called *nonstandard* or *illiterate,* which includes most slang, obscenities, vulgarisms, and localisms. These levels overlap! There is no clear division, unhappily; one term may be accepted in one part of the country and not in another. Some words, like *up tight* may soon move from slang to colloquial to Standard as did *banter* and *boycott* (once slang, now accepted.)

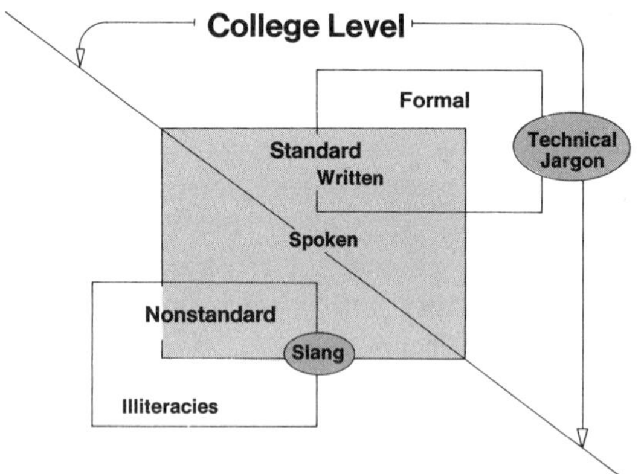

Litotes. See **Understatement.**

Logic means using correct reasoning to find truth. There are two main patterns of reasoning, **induction** and **deduction.** A logical statement shows a valid conclusion from the available data: "An eclipse of the sun indicates something has come between the earth and the sun." An illogical statement draws another conclusion from the same data or draws an incorrect conclusion from no data: "An eclipse means a dragon is devouring the sun god."

or

"The sun is going out because man has been evil."

Loose sentences are sentences that have the meaning, the main idea, or the emphasis placed at the beginning rather than at the end. "The lad died from an excess of raw fish."

Metaphor. See **Figures of speech.**

Mixed metaphor is the joining of two or more **metaphors** usually with a comical effect that was not meant. "While Chaucer had one foot in the Middle Ages, with the other he hailed a new day in English Literature." "The Communist octopus has sung its swan song."

Mood is the dominant emotional effect of a piece of writing.

Myth. See **Narration.**

Narration, or the **narrative,** is one of the four main modes of rhetoric. It is primarily the telling of a story or the relation of a sequence of events. For a fuller discussion and some narrative devices see Part 1 introduction. A narrative may be either factual or fictional; the fictional narratives form the larger part of the body of literature such as narrative poetry, novels, short stories, and the various forms of drama. The factual narrative is often used to illustrate, set mood, exemplify, or offer proof. Some specialized types of narration may be useful to know.

Allegory is a narration that is primarily an extended metaphor; it is a tale in which the characters represent abstractions or qualities. The characters may even be named Everyman, Goodlife, or Death. Generally, it is the purpose of allegory to teach a lesson.

Fable is also a didactic narrative, but the characters are usually animals or inanimate objects that speak and act.

Legend is a tale, developed from an actual person or event, that has grown and changed through time. The basis is factual, but the details are invented.

Myth is a kind of narrative that has developed for a people to explain history or a cultural habit or the unknown.

Parable is similar to fable, for both strive for a moral lesson. The purpose of a parable is to explain a lesson by analogy.

Non sequitur. See **Fallacy.**

Objective and **subjective** writing differ in that the former is impersonal; it is a report; the writer's emotions are not obvious. The emphasis is on the object being discussed. **Subjective** writing is highly personal and impressionistic; the writer's emotions are plainly seen. The emphasis is upon the writer's reaction to the topic.

Organization refers to the deliberate effort to give shape and pattern to written work. The methods will vary with the rhetorical mode used. For more information see the introductions to each section in the text and **Paragraph development** in this Glossary.

Parable. See **Narration.**

Paradox is a statement that seemingly contradicts itself but may still be true. For example: "It is man's humanity that makes him inhuman," or "Cowards die many times before their deaths," or ". . . each man kills the thing he loves."

Paragraph is a distinct portion of a written work, usually marked by an indentation. The word is derived from the Greek *para* ("beside") and graph ("written mark"), for the Greeks placed a check beside each paragraph. The paragraph is a very sophisticated method of organizing thoughts. There are no paragraphs in speech or in primitive writing. Children indent faithfully every four and one-half inches. The paragraph has four specific characteristics that make it a strong, mature aid to communication.

1. The content is limited to one generalization (see **Unity**).
2. The ideas are arranged for a specific emphasis (see **Emphasis**).
3. All concepts fit together and fit with the main generalization (see **Coherence**).
4. The generalization, or **topic sentence,** is explained or developed as completely as possible.

The paragraph is composed of sentences; it is a planned, rhetorical unit, not a grammatical one. There is a difference, not usually noted by novice writers, between a paragraph and a group of related sentences. The sentences in a paragraph can best be classified by their level of abstraction.

Generalizations:

Very abstract: **Topic sentence** (usually first)
Elaboration of topic sentence

Less abstract: **Coordinate Point.**

Specifics or ***Details***:

Concrete: Minor support, data, facts, specific examples.

Perhaps these levels of abstraction can be made clear by an example.

The Ugly Bug

The ugly bug or Volkswagen may not be the safest car on the road as Ralph Nader states, but it is the ideal car for college students. (1) It is inexpensive to buy and to run, for one thing. (2) A used 1967 VW will cost about $700.00 to a careful shopper. (3) It will get 26 miles per gallon, use little oil, no antifreeze, and repairs are correspondingly inexpensive. (4) It is convenient, too. (5) It will turn in a 17-foot radius, will park almost anywhere, will go through snow or sand without chains. (6) Perhaps unsafe, clearly economical and convenient, the Ugly Bug is the car for students. (7)

(1) States main idea (topic sentence).
(2) Coordinate point or major support.
(3) Detail
(4) Detail.
(5) Coordinate point two.
(6) Detail.
(7) Conclusion.

This student paragraph shows clearly the levels of abstraction used in developing a paragraph. Note that the second part of sentence (4), "and repairs are correspondingly inexpensive," is not as convincing as the first part, which presents checkable facts. The *topic sentence* is the most general statement. It is supported by two *coordinate points,* each of which has two or more *details* as *evidence.* The *introduction*—the reference to Ralph Nader—is made part of the topic sentence, and the *conclusion* is a summary or restatement.

Paragraph development refers to the eight standard methods of developing the idea that is presented in the **topic sentence.** Each of these methods is given a separate entry in this Glossary for more useful information.

1. **Analysis**
   a. Causal
   b. Process
   c. Functional
   d. Technical
2. **Cause and effect**
3. **Comparison and contrast**
   a. Analogy
   b. Known with unknown
4. **Definition**
   a. Classification
   b. Operational definition (direct)
   c. Extended definition
5. **Description**
   a. Spatial order

b. Chronological order
c. Realistic
d. Impressionistic
6. **Evidence**
a. Data and inference
b. Logical presentation
7. **Illustration**
a. Anecdote
b. Example
8. A combination of any of the above.

Parallel structure is a rhetorical technique using similar grammatical patterns for similar thought patterns. "The sky was grey; the sun was hot; the sea was calm; but I was not." "I came; I saw; I conquered."

Pathetic fallacy is the excessive use of **personification.**

Periodic sentence is a sentence constructed so that the main idea, meaning, or emphasis is placed at the end. "After eating one dozen raw fish, the lad died."

Personification. See **Figures of speech.**

Plagiarism is mental theft, the stealing of the ideas or writings of another and passing them off as your own. It is also considered plagiarism to use another's sequence of ideas and his research, even if you paraphrase them. Give credit!

Point of view is the author's vantage point. In **description,** it is primarily his physical position, but it may also include his mental ability. For example does the description stop at a closed door or can the author "see" through the door and describe further? In **narration,** point of view is the person telling the tale. For example, "*I* was walking home," or, "*He* was striding down the road." Does the author limit himself to describing, or can he tell the character's thoughts? In **exposition** the point of view is the grammatical person used: first person, *I*; second person, *you*; third person, *he* or *she* (see also: Stance).

Polar thinking is believing that everybody is on either one side or another, good/bad, for us/against us. It omits all middle ground or alternatives. It is classed by some as a fallacy, by some as propaganda, by some as a semantic error (Law of the Excluded Middle).

Premise is an assumption to be argued or one of the three main elements of a syllogism used in **deduction.**

Rhetoric is, basically, the art of using language effectively. It was developed by early Greek speakers and has been studied and taught ever since. *Rhetorical techniques* are the techniques that fuse an idea, logic, and an individual style into effective prose. See the Introduction to the text for a more complete discussion of rhetoric and its four main parts. The study of language can be classified into three parts.

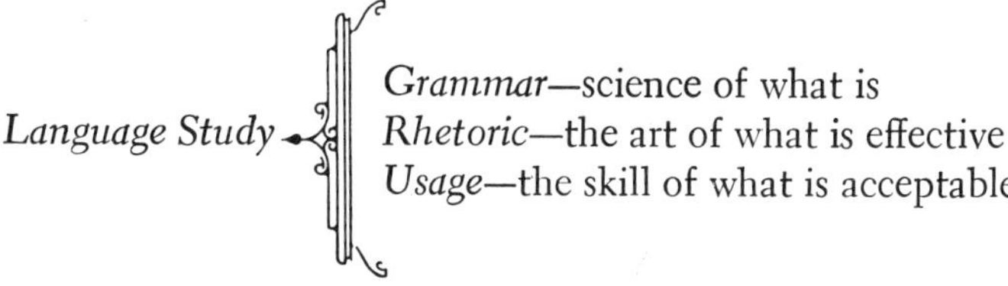

Rhetorical question is a question asked to encourage thought rather than to seek information. It may also be asked to make a comment or prove a point: "Is that what Washington and Jefferson would have done?" No answer is expected to a rhetorical question.

Rhetorical outline. See **Analyzing essays.**

Sarcasm. See **Figures of speech.**

Satire is criticism usually of human folly; its goal is reform; its method is humor. The humor may be gentle laughter or biting **irony** or sarcasm.

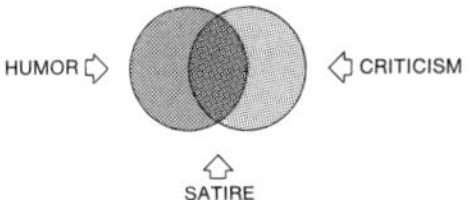

Satirists often employ **hyperbole** or **understatement** to point up man's folly.

Simile. See **Figures of speech.**

Slang consists of words and phrases that have not yet been used widely enough to be classified as standard. Some slang enters the standard vocabulary and some dies. "O.K." is understood around the world, but "Twenty-three Skidoo" is defunct. Slang may develop from **jargon,** from local dialects, from youth groups, and from the underworld.

Stance is the position a writer takes when he writes; it means his attitude toward the subject and the audience. For example, a writer describing the shape, color, size, and texture of the moon shining over a lake would have different style, vocabulary, tone, mood—in short, different stances if he were writing to

1. His beloved, inducing her to join him.

2. His mother, describing a placid scene.
3. His neighbor, admiring the fishing possibilities.
4. A possible purchaser of the property, showing the idyllic nature of the scene.
5. An astronomer, pointing out a feature of the lunar landscape.

Style is an expression of the author's personality through his choice of words (**diction**), imagery, **figures of speech**, sentence patterns, rhythm, **tone**, and rhetorical mode and devices. Style is *the way* he writes, not *what* he says. Although many authors have a distinguishable style (Hemmingway, Joyce, Faulkner, Poe, Mencken) that can even be parodied, and although it is possible to mimic the style of the Bible, *Time* magazine, or Shakespeare, style is an extension of the individual, his background, his education, and his attitude toward the subject.

Subjective. See **Objective and subjective.**

Subordination is the technique of using grammatically subordinate (less important) constructions for ideas that are subordinate to the main idea in a sentence. Such writing emphasizes the main idea. The most commonly used constructions are adverb and adjective clauses.

Although he was short, Joshua was a mighty warrior.

subordinate *main idea*

The walls came tumbling down when he blew his horn.

main idea *subordinate*

Syllogism is the formal argument in deductive logic (see **Deduction**).

Symbol is what we call an item or a word that is used to represent something else. It may have reality and meaning of its own, but when used *symbolically*, it suggests something more. There are natural symbols like the sun, fog, clouds; there are arbitrary symbols like the olive branch, the cross, flags; and there are personal symbols (some poets use very private, personal symbolism).

Some standard **symbols;** what do they mean?

Syntax is a combination of grammar, arrangements, and rhetoric to achieve effective, coherent, balanced sentences. It is a very abstract term. If there were a tax on sin it would probably be called something else.

Technical analysis. See **Analysis.**

Theme is the main subject of a story or other piece of writing. It is the general topic the author writes about. Most essays do not have themes; most narratives do. The **theme** of "The Cyclone" is "battling a storm." The **thesis** is, "Powerful emotion is a recollection, not an experience." Sometimes a written assignment or short essay is loosely called a theme.

Thesis is the **premise** or statement of a proposition or a generalization that an author attempts to prove by argument, maintain by illustration, or prove by logic. A thesis may be an assumption or generalization about life that the author has perceived, or it may be a principle of thought or action that he believes to be fundamental. It need not be profound or earth-shattering; it may be quite simple. A written requirement for a degree is also called a *thesis.*

Thesis statement is a single declarative sentence that tells the author's **thesis** clearly and compactly. A carefully written thesis statement, carefully supported by **coordinate points,** serves to give unity to an essay. A thesis statement, to be effective, follows certain criteria.

1. It is a single declarative statement (not a question).
2. It clearly limits the topic of the essay.
3. It usually sets the tone of the essay.
4. It contains no **figurative language.**

The careful student writer will develop the thesis for his own essay and phrase it in a clearly understood thesis statement before he begins to write the paper.

Tone of a work is the emotional or affective element. Tone is usually determined by the use of language; some types of tone are *ironic, serious, humorous, cynical,* and *condescending.* There are, of course, as many more as there are emotional attitudes.

Topic sentence is the sentence in a paragraph that summarizes or generalizes the main purpose of the paragraph. It is identical in function to a thesis in a longer work. Although it may be implied, it is usually stated near the beginning of the paragraph.

Transitions might best be called bridges from one idea to another.

Transition word or phrase

Idea one Similar idea Two

Transitions may be classified by the kinds of relationships they show between two or more ideas.

and, and then, besides, also, in addition, next, finally.	To combine ideas.
likewise, similarly, too, in the same way	To compare ideas.
since, because, therefore hence, consequently, thus	To show result.
here, there, beyond, nearby then, while, at once, later	To show [space / time] relation.
but, yet, however, nevertheless, still, on the other hand	To contrast ideas.

There are, of course, many, many more transitions.

Trite. See **Cliché.**

Truth is sometimes defined as the result of induction that has been empirically verified. A scientific definition might be "truth is an invariant under a transformation of axes." A careful rhetorician will distinguish between poetic truth and scientific truth.

Tu quoque. See **Fallacy.**

Understatement. See **Figures of speech.**

Unity means the singleness of content that marks a competent **paragraph** or **essay.** In the case of the former, the **topic sentence** is supported by every other sentence in the paragraph. There is nothing in the paragraph that is not covered by the topic sentence (and vice versa). The same concept holds true with the **thesis statement** and an essay.

Unqualified generalization. See **Fallacy, hasty generalization.**

Usage refers to the level of language. Good usage is the skill of using acceptable word choice, grammar, **level of usage** for the specific time, place, and company.

Valid means that a **conclusion** has been logically derived from the **premises.** *To validate* a **thesis** would be to offer evidence.

Verisimilitude means "has the appearance of truth or real." It is used to describe a character, setting, or situation created by an author if there is the appearance of reality. Sherlock Holmes would be a character that has verisimilitude; Superman would not.